FOOD AND POPULATION: PRIORITIES IN DECISION MAKING

The country case studies of Kenya, India, Republic of Korea and Indonesia are revised and condensed versions of papers presented at the IAAE/FAO/UNFPA Seminar in Rome in December 1975, which have been published in their original versions in "Food Enough or Starvation for Millions" by D. Ensminger, published by Tata McGraw-Hill. They, are published here with the kind permission of the Food and Agriculture Organization of the United Nations, the copyright holder."

Food and Population: Priorities in Decision Making

Report of a Meeting
of the International
Conference of Agricultural
Economists, Nairobi, August 1976.

EDITED BY
T. DAMS
the late K.E. HUNT
G.J. TYLER

SAXON HOUSE

© The International Association of Agricultural Economists, 1978

All rights reserved. No part of this publication may be reproduced, stored in a retrieval system, or transmitted in any form or by any means, electronic, mechanical, photocopying, recording or otherwise without the prior permission of Teakfield Limited.

Published by Saxon House
Teakfield Limited, Westmead, Farnborough,
Hants, England.

 British Library Cataloguing in Publication Data

```
International Conference of Agricultural Economists,
16th, Nairobi 1976
Food and population.
1. Food supply - Congresses  2. Population policy -
Congresses
I. Dams, T  II. Hunt, Kenneth Edward  III. Tyler, G
338.1'9        HD9000.5

ISBN 0-566-00250-7
```

Printed in Great Britain by Biddles Limited, Guildford, Surrey.
Typeset by Supreme Litho Typesetting, Ilford, Essex.

Contents

Foreword   vii

PLENARY SESSION – ACHIEVING A BALANCE BETWEEN
POPULATION AND FOOD: PRIORITIES IN DECISION MAKING   1

   The Main Problems Identified and Approaches to Solutions   3
      S. Krasovec and T. Singh

   Reflections on Aspects of Population and Agricultural Development
   in Selected Countries   24
      J.P. Bhattacharjee

   Can We Feed the World? – an Optimistic Note   37
      K. Campbell

   The Prospects of the Food Situation in the World: from the
   Pessimistic Standpoint   43
      J. Klatzmann

   Discussion on papers by S. Krasovec and T. Singh and
   by J.P. Bhattacharjee   49
      A. Valdés

   Discussion on papers by Campbell and by Klatzmann   53
      I.I. May-Parker

   Summary of discussion from floor   55

   J.P. Bhattacharjee in reply   60

SPECIAL SESSION I – ACHIEVING A BALANCE BETWEEN
POPULATION AND FOOD: AFRICA   63

   Food, Population and Rural Development in Kenya: Progress,
   Policies, Problems and Prospects   65
      L.P. Mureithi and J.O. Otieno

Achieving Food and Population Balance in Nigeria:
Priorities in Decision Making 103
   S.M. Essang

Discussion on papers by Mureithi and Otieno and by Essang 114
   O.A. Hakim

SPECIAL SESSION II – ACHIEVING A BALANCE BETWEEN
POPULATION AND FOOD: ASIA 117

Achieving a Balance Between Population and Food:
The Indian Case 119
   V.M. Dandekar

Population and Food Production in Indonesia 130
   S. Baharsjah

Achieving a Balance Between Population and Food:
The Korean Case 140
   S.H. Kim

Discussion on papers by Dandekar, Baharsjah and Kim 165
   W.G. Farmer

SPECIAL SESSION III – INCREASING AGRICULTURAL
PRODUCTION ON THE SMALL FARM AND MOTIVATING
FOR FAMILY PLANNING 167

Increasing Agricultural Production on the Small Farm and
Motivating for Family Planning 169
   F.C. Sturrock

Discussion on paper by Sturrock 177
   N. Amerasinghe

SPECIAL SESSION IV – POLICIES AND PROGRAMMES FOR
AGRICULTURAL DEVELOPMENT 179

Policies and Programmes for Agricultural Development: The Role
of Economic-Social Science Analysis and of Research Agencies
in Seeking Solutions 181
   A.R. Teixera Filho

Discussion on paper by Teixera Filho 191
   B.B. Quraishi

Foreword

This publication contains the papers, with their discussion, presented at a group of meetings on population and food which formed a part of the XVIth International Conference of Agricultural Economists, held in Nairobi, in August 1976.

The subject falls within the general area of *Decision-Making and Agriculture* which formed the theme of the conference and the title of the Conference Proceedings volume published jointly by Nebraska University Press and the International Association of Agricultural Economists. However, because the group of sessions on population and food formed a coherent and substantial body of material with its own particular interest, it is being published separately here.

The first part of this book contains papers which review the food and population situation in the light of available general evidence and the results of case studies of particular countries. It also contains papers which demonstrate, and attempt to identify the causes for, the diversity of views on this subject.

The second part of this book consists mainly of the country case studies, most of which were developed from those presented at a seminar held in Rome in December 1975 under the joint sponsorship of the International Association of Agricultural Economists (IAAE), the Food and Agriculture Organisation (FAO) and the United Nations Fund for Population Activities (UNFPA).

The programme of the conference, including that for the group of sessions concerned with Food and Population was organised by Professor T. Dams, University of Freiburg. The preparation for publication of the papers and of the report of the discussion was begun by the late Mr K.E. Hunt, former Director of the Agricultural Economics Institute, Oxford University and completed by Dr. G.J. Tyler of the same Institute.

Denis K. Britton,
President, IAAE

PLENARY SESSION

Achieving a Balance Between Population and Food: Priorities in Decision Making

The main problems identified and approaches to solutions

Stane Krasovec and Tarlok Singh

The primary purpose of the seminar on Population and Food and Agricultural Development convened in December 1975 in Rome by the IAAE, in co-operation with FAO and UNFPA, was to examine key issues which arose at the present time in the relationship between food production and population. Profiting from the global assessments and the recommendations made by the World Population Conference in Bucharest in August 1974, and the World Food Conference in Rome in November 1974, the seminar sought to underline the basic issues and the priority areas of study with a view to assisting agricultural economists to make a fuller contribution towards the solution of the world population and food crisis. Beside the proposals of the two world conferences, the seminar had before it six country studies (Brazil, Yugoslavia, the Republic of Korea, Indonesia, India and Kenya) and twenty-seven papers by individual authors. These studies and papers have been since edited by the Chairman of the IAAE Committee on Population and Food, Dr Douglas Ensminger, in a volume entitled *Food Enough or Starvation for Millions*. An official report on the seminar has been already presented by the FAO Secretariat. In supplementing this report, the present paper draws attention selectively to the critical problems identified and approaches to solutions suggested in the course of discussions in the Rome seminar.

World conferences on population and food

While acknowledging the diversity of conditions within and among countries, the World Population Plan of Action, accepted at Bucharest, emphasised that population and development were interrelated, population variables influencing and being influenced by development variables and that population policies gained their greatest force and significance as constituent elements of comprehensive socio-economic policies. Therefore, the capacities of countries to deal effectively with their population problems had to be deepened and expanded. At the same time, in keeping with the growing interdependence among nations, there must be increasing international action towards the solution of development and population problems. Giving its main attention to the broader aspects of population policy, the World Population Conference was seized of the fact that the solution of the problem of population growth depended largely on a balance between the size of the world's population and the world's production of foodstuffs and volume of available resources. It realised too that grain stocks were now at lower levels than in earlier years, so that the risks of malnutrition and possible starvation had increased. Therefore, all countries were urged to give higher priority to food production and fertiliser production, to devise ways of overcoming shortages and replenishing stocks, to expand food and agricultural output and to raise the volume of employment in rural areas. As part of a policy of intensive social and economic development, the World Population Conference stressed the role of rural development, including diversified agriculture, agrarian change, social welfare programmes and services for rural areas, rural industries, rural settlement schemes to relieve population pressure and the fullest participation of women in educational, economic, social and political life, on an equal basis with men.

The World Food Conference met under the shadow of the global food crisis which began with the widespread droughts of 1972 and was accentuated by the poor harvests of 1973 and 1974. The crisis has both short-term and long-term features, the latter being aggravated by the rate of population growth in the less developed countries compared to rising demand for food and modest rates of increase in food production. The relevant facts and analysis were presented by FAO in two earlier studies, namely, *Population, Food Supply and Agricultural Development* [1] and *Assessment of the World Food Situation – Present and Future* [2]. Being immediately concerned with practical steps which national governments and the international community could initiate for the management of the crisis which already loomed large, the World Food Conference addressed itself specially to the medium-term period of the next ten years or so, during which the rate of population growth was more or less predetermined. In particular, it urged improved planning of food aid, including provision of at least ten million tons of grain as food aid every year, an International Undertaking on World Food Security, involving a co-ordinated system of national food reserves and an improved Global Information and Early Warning System on Food and Agriculture. However, there were also many points of common emphasis between the two world conferences and these had particular interest for agricultural economists.

For the World Food Conference, the essential gravity of the food crisis lay in the fact that two-thirds of the world's population living in the developing countries produced about one-third of the world's food. Most of the world's hungry and ill-nourished lived in the developing countries and the present imbalance was likely to increase over the next decade. The means by which the Universal Declaration on the Eradication of Hunger and Malnutrition, drawn up by the World Food Conference, and the improvement of levels of living and the quality of life of the people, set as the principal goal by the World Population Conference, were to be realised over a period, formed the common theme of several of the resolutions of the two conferences. Thus they included in relation to the developing countries:

— achieving a desirable balance between population and food supply;
— highest priority to policies and programmes for increasing food production and improving food utilisation;
— striving, in accordance with each country's potentials, for the maximum

possible degree of self-sufficiency in basic foods;
- expanding and improving the productivity base of agriculture;
- reducing rural unemployment by enhancing the capacity of the rural community to expand, intensify, and diversify its activities;
- pursuing the concept of integrated rural development as appropriate to the conditions of each country;
- bringing about progressive agrarian reforms appropriate to the circumstances of each country;
- implementing policies and programmes to improve nutrition;
- involving women fully in all aspects of a total development strategy, including food production, nutrition policies, medical and social services, provision for education and training and promotion of equal rights and responsibilities for men and women.

The papers presented to the Rome seminar covered a wide ground. Several issues were viewed from different standpoints in more than one paper. For the present review, we have found it convenient to look at different contributions as throwing light primarily on one or the other of the following themes of concern to agricultural economists. The various contributions, referred to by numbers in paranthesis represent chapters in Douglas Ensminger (ed.), *Food Enough or Starvation for Millions* (Tata McGraw-Hill, New Delhi, India, 1976), are listed at the end of this paper.

1. The global perspective;
2. Demographic elements in agricultural and rural development;
3. Removing the production constraints of the small farmer;
4. Strategies for rural development and the organisation of agriculture;
5. Research in demographic aspects of agricultural development;
6. International action.

The global perspective

The 'emerging equation between population and food supply', as bearing on two main groups of countries, the developed and the developing, was elaborated in three different ways: firstly, in relation to population and agricultural labour force projections; secondly, in relation to food production and demand for food; and thirdly, in terms of alternative futures for the less developed world.

The United Nations paper on the world population situation (7) provided for eight major geographic areas and twenty-four regions, analysis of trends for the period 1960–1975 and projections up to the year 2000. At the centre of the population perspective was the contrast in rates of population growth between the more and the less developed regions. In 1975, the latter formed 71.5 per cent of the total world population compared to 67.3 per cent in 1960. Over the period

1960–1975, the less developed regions grew in population at 2.3 per cent per annum, while the annual rate of population growth in the more developed regions fell from 1.2 per cent in the early sixties to 0.9 per cent in the early seventies. The social, economic and demographic consequences of such disparities in rates of population growth are well known. The United Nations paper examined the demographic aspects in some detail, especially fertility, mortality, life expectation, sex and age structure and growth of urban population. According to the 'medium' variant of the United Nations projections, the world population may grow from 3,967 million in 1975 to 6,253 million in 2000, about 90 per cent of the increase occurring in the less developed regions. The paper proceeded to describe the implications of these projections in terms of birth and death rates and gross reproduction between rural and urban population. For agricultural economists, aside from overall contrasts between probable trends in the more and the less developed regions and differences among the latter, a specially significant field of study is the marked decline in birth rates which is believed to have occurred in the Asian centrally planned economies, especially China and the social and economic policies to which this decline may be causally related.

In a paper which gave particular attention to questions of methodology, Naiken and Schulte (9) presented projections up to 1985 for total population, total labour force, agricultural labour force and agricultural population separately for developed market economies, developing market economies and centrally planned economies. As a proportion of the total labour force, the labour force in agriculture in the developing market economies is expected to form 53.3 per cent in 1985 compared to 61.5 per cent in 1975, the corresponding proportions for developed market economies being respectively 7.5 and 11.5 per cent. The authors drew attention to the need for projections of labour force demand to which projections of agricultural labour force could be compared. They also pointed to the essential distinction between 'agricultural' and 'rural' population or labour force.

The food supply and demand aspects of the population and food problem were discussed by Bhattacharjee in the background of the two FAO studies mentioned earlier as well as FAO's Provisional Indicative World Plan for Agricultural Development (18). Although both developed and developing countries increased their food production at 3.1 per cent per year in the fifties and at about 2.8 per cent in the sixties, for the less developed countries the gains were largely offset by growth of population at 2.4 per cent in the fifties, around 2.6 per cent in the sixties, and 2.7 per cent in the early seventies. Bhattacharjee drew attention to differences in the situation of different regions and especially of Africa where population and food supply increased about equally until the early seventies when moreover, the effects of drought were much more severe than elsewhere.

The growing dependence of developing countries on food imports, as seen from the rise in the annual level of imports (excluding China) from 12.4 million tons during 1949–1951 to 45.5 million tons in 1973–1974, is regarded as posing the biggest problem for the future. As Perkins also pointed out (8), in developing countries increases in population up to 1985 account for 70 per cent of the projected growth of demand. It is already apparent that, in 1985, the net cereals deficit may be of the order of 85 million tons. In keeping with trends in the growth of demand, food production in the developing countries should increase at an average of not less than 3.6 per cent per annum, varying from 3.4 per cent for Asia to 4 per cent for the Near East. FAO's studies indicate that the necessary potential for increasing cereal production is available in Asia and Latin America but Africa poses the major problem in the short and the medium-term. As Bhattacharjee pointed out, population growth in the developing countries has so aggravated the incidence of hunger and malnutrition as to raise sharply the issue of comprehensive development strategy and structural change, embracing the whole field of production, consumption, investment, employment and distribution within countries. This is now as important as the necessity of international action and bilateral co-operation in trade, aid and development. In the last analysis, population problems must be looked at, not only in relation to food supply but in the total context of patterns of agricultural and rural development in so far as they determine and are, in turn, determined by the human factors that population represents.

The problems highlighted in the perspectives sketched by Bhattacharjee and the United Nations projections were presented in a different form in the US Department of Agriculture study described by Rojko and O'Brien (19). Through an econometric study, they investigated the prospects of the less developed countries under three sets of conditions or scenarios. In the first of these, between 1970 and 2000, against an annual increase in population in the developed countries of 0.7 per cent per annum, the less developed countries grow at 2.6 per cent per annum. In the second scenario, the population of the less developed countries rises at 1.9 per cent per annum. In the third scenario, which is considered the most realistic, the population of these countries grows at 2.2 per cent per annum. Corresponding to the three scenarios, three alternative futures are projected. In Future I, the cereal import gap could increase to as much as 105 million tons, with but little improvement in *per capita* consumption of cereals. In Future II, net imports of cereals could be close to the level of the early 1970s, that is, about 28 million tons. In Future III, cereal imports are projected at 62 million tons. From this prognosis, Rojko and O'Brien went on to study the implications in terms of alternative farming systems. As they observed, the successful reorganisation of agriculture depends on injections of improved inputs and upgraded technology so that the developing countries can replace a relatively closed energy system, with low returns to man, with a more open system yielding appreciably higher returns. A high-return tropical agriculture can be organised but only on the basis of substantially higher energy inputs in the form of water control, fertilisers, pesticides, improved varieties, mechanisation and multiple cropping.

From the discussions in the Rome seminar on population growth and its consequences for food supply and agricultural development, two main sets of challenges emerged, those deriving directly from demographic factors and those relating to the removal of existing constraints on the volume and pattern of agricultural production. These questions are considered in the following sections in the light of contributions by various participants.

Demographic elements in agricultural and rural development

The rural condition in most of the less developed countries is marked by a number of familiar features: high rates of fertility, high rates of infant mortality, widespread malnutrition and undernutrition, especially among the very young and women, large-scale underemployment and unemployment accompanied by migration from rural to urban areas and mounting urban unemployment, the impelling necessity to hold the increasing rural surplus within agriculture and failure to bring about a fundamental change in the quality of life of the lowest 40 per cent or more of the rural population. All these are aspects of a state of poverty which is directly, though by no means exclusively, related to the rate of growth of population and specially of the growth of the agricultural population and the agricultural labour force. The theme was considered from different angles at the Rome seminar in contributions from Wajihuddin Ahmed (10), Jean McNaughton (12), K.C. Abercrombie (11), Keith Compbell (25), H.R. Kötter (21) and R. Sinha and H.R. Kötter (13). Eva Mueller (31) turned the theme around and enquired into the possible channels or processes through which economic development and, in particular, rural development, might have direct and indirect repercussions on demographic events, especially on fertility. The questions raised inevitably revealed gaps in data and knowledge and suggested problems for further study. These have been brought together in a later section of this paper.

Any attempt to probe into demographic factors in agricultural and rural development brings us to the core of the problem of rural poverty. Ahmed (10) emphasised this to explain high birth rates among the rural poor. As he put it, a poor peasant's child is also his working capital and a source of profit. Children bred in poverty seem to cost too little. The poor beget more children than they want since they must reckon with the uncertainty of survival. Eva Mueller (31) also constructed an important part of her analysis around the notion of *perceived* costs and benefits of children for rural parents. Acknowledging the unsatisfactory data base, she suggested, nevertheless, that while the economic cost of children might exceed their economic value, non-economic satisfactions and security motives seemed to contribute significantly to pronatalist attitudes.

High rates of population growth in low-income countries and regions were considered a major factor in the prevailing malnutrition, underemployment, unemployment and rural–urban migration. However, they do not operate alone. They combine with other factors, notably inequitable distribution, an inadequate resource base in agriculture, lack of non-agricultural employment opportunities in rural areas and failure to bring about structural and institutional changes. In assessing each of the consequences, various contributors demonstrated their multiple

8

causation and, in turn, pointed to remedial measures which are also multiple in nature, calling for nothing short of a systems approach.

Jean McNaughton (12) reviewed population and nutrition interrelationships both at the micro level, as affecting households and individuals and at the macro level, the latter being but a summation derived, very approximately, from the former. She cited FAO data showing that energy supplies do not exceed 105 per cent of estimated requirements in any of the developing regions and in three of them are less than 100 per cent. Considering the unequal distribution of food supplies among different socio-economic groups, the conclusion is inescapable that a severe energy deficit must exist among several segments of the population. On a cautious reckoning, over 400 million individuals in the developing countries may have insufficient food intakes. The numbers may well be considerably larger.

Abercrombie (11), Kötter (32) and Sinha and Kötter (13) covered much common ground and were basically agreed on fundamentals. The essential point is that population and the agricultural resource base have to be brought into a state of dynamic balance. That is to say, on the one hand conditions have to be created for rapid agricultural development and increase in food production; on the other, there must be increasing (productive) absorption of the labour force in the agricultural sector until, at a future date, the non-agricultural sector can siphon off the surplus labour. Any imbalance between population growth and resource use often tends to perpetuate the deprivation of the poor and it is no accident that, under present conditions, substantial numbers would not be able to share equitably in the product of economic growth nor contribute significantly to socio-economic development. The principal element in the opportunity to participate and contribute is employment, whether on one's own account or for wages, a subject investigated in some depth by Abercrombie (11). Defining the agricultural labour force as comprising those born in the agricultural sector who cannot find jobs outside it, Abercrombie examined the factors at work both on the supply side and the demand side. The rate of growth of population determines the supply of agricultural labour. According to present projections, while the situation will vary from country to country, for the less developed world as a whole the turning point may only be reached by the second decade of the next century. In other words, the present agricultural employment problems of the developing countries are certain to last for a long time to come. The issue, therefore, resolves itself into action, firstly, to slow down the growth of the agricultural labour force by appropriate population policies and, secondly, to achieve a faster expansion of non-agricultural employment. On the demand side, the principal influences bearing on agricultural labour are the level and pattern of agricultural production, technology and the organisation of agriculture. As we shall see, Abercrombie (11), Kötter (32) and Sinha and Kötter (13) advanced similar propositions on the subject of organisation and their views on a selective approach to technological change, with due attention to the need to use the present human resource base as effectively as possible, are widely shared.

The agricultural labour force and the rural scene cannot be viewed in isolation from the rates of urbanisation prevailing currently. Keith Campbell (25) examined the ways in which growth of cities affects the structure of, and income distribution in, the rural hinterland. As he put it, it is primarily through labour transfer that the process of urbanisation affects the agricultural sector. On the other hand, particularly in more developed countries or some of them, through this exodus, in many areas, rural homes are deprived of the most vigorous and the most vital groups of labour, intellectually more able, while land is left over to aging groups which in themselves are more conservative and not open to any technological and economic improvement. The phenomenon of rural—urban migration implies in fact the transfer of unemployment and poverty from the rural areas to the cities. While urbanisation undoubtedly influences the allocation of available investible resources, its most direct rural impact is upon the effective demand for food. Measures to slow down migration to the cities through rural development and labour-intensive industries are certainly relevant. However, on any longer term view, population control policies are seen as a vital ingredient in dealing with urbanisation and associated employment problems.

How demographic and development variables influence one another is a theme remaining to be probed in depth and there is need to go beyond assumptions derived from historical experience to analysis of causal elements and processes. Eva Mueller advanced some hypotheses in pursuance of such an analysis (31). In her conceptual scheme, as rural development occurs farm income, agricultural and other economic factors and community characteristics undergo large changes, so as to transform the farm household's economic environment. The consequential impact on fertility is largely indirect. The precise mechanisms involved are still a matter for surmise and Eva Mueller postulated several 'intervening variables', such as group norms, values and tastes, familial institutions, 'economic attitudes' (perceived costs and benefits of raising children) and changes in aspirations. The processes may differ in their operation between societies and between groups and individuals. It is important to mark, however, that any rural development strategy will have positive effects along with negative ones and there will be lags in the response of familial norms and values to economic change. In other words, the need for effective family planning programmes remains. Rural development programmes and family planning programmes should complement one another and much is to be gained from some degree of integration between them.

Two general observations may be added. The authors of this paper share the view that natural resources are limited and while a smaller or larger increase of the exploitation of many of them or their substitution is theoretically possible, this increase in practice requires a certain time lag with various economic implications (financing, trade, labour). It remains questionable whether and for how long this increase can practically proceed in step with the ever increasing rate of growth of population. The energy crisis and the emerging environmental difficulties provoke doubts about that. This topic is to be dealt with more closely later, so we just mention it here. Secondly, savings are also limited and one cannot use the same savings both for demographic and for economic investments. After all, children are not born with new tools and new plots of land; additional new workers cannot currently produce more goods and income unless they are supplied with sufficient means of production or find new jobs available.

Removing the production constraints of the small farmer

The handicaps under which the small farmer labours and ways to reduce them formed the keynote of several contributions at the Rome seminar, notably those by D.W. Norman and M.S. Krishnaswamy (24), Douglas Ensminger (27) and Stanley Andrews (33). A paper by Robert W. Herdt and Randolph Barker examining the implications of proven farm production practices (23), prepared subsequent to the seminar, has also for its main interest the economics of the small farmer. This is also true of the contribution by B.A. Stout and Charles M. Downing (26) examining the concept of 'selective' or 'appropriate' mechanisation of agriculture. Three other questions, which bear in an overall sense on levels of agricultural production, namely, the influence of changes in weather conditions, statistics of food-energy balance and the role of price incentives, were considered in contributions by James D. McQuigg (17), Harold F. Breimyer (16) and R. Thamarajakshi (21). As these latter papers stand somewhat on their own, to be followed up apart from the main theme of the Rome seminar, it is convenient to refer first to the principal propositions presented in them.

It is not uncommon for national development plans and ministries of agriculture to advance projections of future levels of output of foodgrains and other agricultural commodities on the assumption of 'normal weather'. On the basis of extensive work done in the US, McQuigg (17) explained the pitfalls in all such propositions. He argued that statements concerning future yield trends can be more usefully made in terms of estimates of future variability of yields based on an adequate sample of climatic data. Moreover, in this form, in view of historical and real-time meteorological information that is now available on a global scale, policy and programmes vital to the world economy and population can be based on more realistic knowledge than was possible in the past.

The 'green revolution', involving the spread of modern technology and greater use of industrial inputs, has spread thus far only to a segment of the potential area. Even so, it has already raised the question of availability and cost of energy obtained from fossil fuels. Breimyer (16), therefore, insisted that statistics of food-energy balance should now be added to the two familiar productivity ratios in agriculture, namely, production per unit of land area and production per man. However, he went on to suggest that it is necessary to recognise not a single food-energy balance but two. The first relates to the conversion of the energy of the sun into foodstuffs. This is truly the basic balance. The second pertains to use of fossil fuel energy. There is need, on the one hand, to develop cultural practices that reduce the quantity of fossil fuel energy required and, on the other, to search for new strains or even new species of plants that will convert the sun's energy efficiently at less cost in fertiliser and other materials that come from fossil fuel. From a global aspect, Breimyer also made the point that the richer countries, accustomed to eating the food products of animal agriculture, can achieve substantial saving of fossil fuels by increasing the consumption of cereal foods directly instead of converting them via livestock and poultry. Finally, in view of the high cost of fossil fuel and limited availability, Breimyer stressed the imperative need to protect the resource of the soil more assiduously than in the past.

The 'green revolution' has made it necessary to re-examine public policies in several directions, including technology, employment, credit and marketing and not the least of the areas thus opened up is that of agricultural price policy. In this context, R. Thamarajakshi (21) reviewed the Indian experience since the early fifties and traced the movement in favour of a production oriented price policy for agriculture. She cautioned, however, that a positive price policy is a necessary but not a sufficient condition. The prime mover is technological advance, not only directly but also in facilitating a better response from agriculture to economic stimuli. In this connection she emphasised the significance of well developed market organisations for economic stimuli to reach growers fully, without being lost or diluted at intermediate points.

The considerations urged by McQuigg, Breimyer and Thamarajakshi bear on agriculture as a whole but are of no less concern to small farmers. However, in the present day agriculture in the less developed world, in numbers and area, the small farmer is, as it were, the representative farmer and the progress of agriculture along modern, scientific lines may be measured by the advance achieved by the great body of small farmers. Changes in the organisation of agriculture, however radical and however urgent, will take time, so that the small farmer and the means by which his capacity and productivity may be enhanced form the core of national agricultural policy. Ensminger (27) is not alone in thinking that the small farmer has lived for too long outside institutions serving agriculture. Whether the failure comes from administrative or political and social causes may be a matter of opinion but there is no question that a new institutional structure to which the small farmer can relate needs to be created and this entails new obligations for research institutions, for institutions delivering the recommended inputs, for the marketing system and for government policies in general.

The crux of the problem, as Norman and Krishnaswamy (24) argued, is that for a variety of reasons beyond his control, despite his farming system being well adapted to the environment, the small farmer is caught in a characteristic 'low productivity trap'. Small farmers need types of technology that will be relevant to their specific needs, that is to say technology that is highly divisible (e.g. seeds, fertilisers and herbicides), which is comparatively simple to adopt, will be dependable in return and will require a fairly low level of improved inputs. Correspondingly, there must be an adequate infrastructural support system which can create conditions conducive to the adoption of improved technology. The small farmer must be convinced of the value of the technology; he must be ensured the necessary financial resources for its adoption; and the necessary inputs must be available to him at the right place and at the right time. The role of the extension agent and of effective communication can be scarcely underestimated. Since the various elements are closely interrelated, the issue of co-ordination has critical importance. The circumstances of the small farmer and the numbers involved inevitably demand decentralised administration of agricultural development programmes. In this context, Norman and Krishnaswamy urged that the ideal administrative strategy is one which treats the village as the basic unit of development or, at any rate, groups of contiguous and more or less homogeneous villages might be treated as units of development. The prime need is for government to create viable institutions at the grass roots level. It is not denied that the task of building up the right kind of institutions and services in support of the small farmer is rendered difficult by the existence of inequalities among farm community members. This very fact calls, in turn, for additional developmental strategies.

The dividing line between the small farmer and the agricultural labourer is often thin. Both are dependent on available opportunity for wage employment either wholly or as an indispensable supplement. Hence the plea advanced by Abercrombie (11) for intelligent use of technology keeping in view the prevailing social conditions and the more specific case made out by Stout and Downing (26) in favour of 'selective mechanisation', defined as mechanisation that will not decrease the demand for labour per unit of land. Stout and Downing recognise and indeed emphasise the positive role of agricultural mechanisation. Rightly, they take mechanisation to encompass the use of hand and animal operated tools and implements, equally with motorised equipment, the common purpose being to reduce human effort, improve quality, perform operations that cannot be done by other means and improve the timeliness of various farm operations. Too frequently, mechanisation systems fail on account of faulty planning and execution rather than the concept itself. Therefore, judicious selection and application of existing machines or their modification requires first a thorough analysis of the production processes on the farm. Only with such an analysis is it possible to ensure rational selection, proper operation, organisation and management, such as may be compatible with local agricultural, economic and social needs. From this aspect, it becomes singularly important to strengthen agricultural mechanisation research, including the effects of various levels and types of mechanisation on employment at the micro and macro level.

Strategies for rural development and the organisation of agriculture

The proposal of the two world conferences on Population and Food represented substantial continuity with earlier deliberations connected with the United Nations Strategy for the Second Development Decade. A common feature of much of the discussion in recent years, both national and international, has been the growing concern with the conditions and opportunities of the poorer groups within the rural community and the necessity of adopting an integrated approach to problems of rural development. Integration involves, at the same time, a cohesive view of regional or area problems and resources, a unified view of the entire population and special measures and policies on behalf of those segments of the rural community who have in the past remained at subsistence levels. It is natural that the approach of rural development should throw up a wide range of questions, beginning with the concept and its underlying economic and social assumptions and extending to the agencies available, the content of development, the manner in which agriculture as the primary industry is to be organised and the purposes for which the human and natural resources available in society are to be organised and developed. These issues were reflected at the Rome seminar in several discussions and, in particular, formed the theme of contributions by Uma Lele (28), E.R. Krystall (30), John Higgs (29), Elinor K. Kennedy (22) and Tarlok Singh (20). Aspects of the subject of rural development and approaches to it were examined also in papers reviewed earlier by Abercrombie (11), Bhattacharjee (18) and R. Sinha and H.R. Kötter (13). Although, on a theme of such range and comprehension the discussions at the Rome seminar were necessarily selective, they posed several basic questions.

Uma Lele's contribution (28) provided the broad economic background to the consideration of problems of integrated rural development. Her definition of rural development as improving living standards of the mass of the low income population residing in rural areas and making the process of their development self-sustaining provides a useful starting point for considering how rural development programmes may be designed and implemented. As she emphasised, if the objectives of rural development are to be realised, both productive and social services have to be provided simultaneously. But there has to be a 'desirable' balance over time between welfare and productivity as relating to the low income population. This necessitates certain priorities in mobilising and allocating resources. If the low income population are to benefit fairly from rural development programmes, it is necessary that (a) resources should be allocated to less developed regions and classes on a priority basis and (b) the productive and social services must actually reach the 'target groups'. Further, for the rural development process to become self-sustaining, available resources should be used effectively first to augment the productivity of the low income rural groups. Without a major thrust towards increasing their productivity, health, education, nutrition and other services may often fail to produce the desired results.

For the process of rural development to become viable in relation to low income groups and to secure the necessary mass participation, Uma Lele suggested that rural development strategy should be viewed as part of a continuous, dynamic process, thus bypassing choices such as 'extensive' versus 'intensive' or 'integrated' versus 'minimum' effort. In planning and implementing a rural development strategy, the approach should be 'sequential', that is to say, there should be carefully considered time-phasing and clear priorities. The sequential approach places particular emphasis on manpower and institutional development from the early stages of implementation, so that the scope can be enlarged and modified progressively. Finally, Uma Lele makes the important point, which is implicit in all discussions on rural development, that there must be a national and, in the best sense, 'political' commitment to translate the rural development programmes into appropriate policies and institutions and into the necessary investment priorities.

Before turning to the major issue of pattern of rural development and the organisation of agriculture as an industry, a few of the propositions advanced by Higgs (29), Krystall (30) and Elinor Kennedy (22) should be briefly mentioned at this point. Higgs (29) advanced the view that, though the technical ability to solve the problems of poverty, food and population already exists, the main reason for the relative lack of success of so many rural development schemes lies probably in their failure to involve the people concerned. He went on to examine the factors which inhibit the development of effective democratic farmers' groups and identified these as being (a) the marginality of the majority of peasants, (b) 'distance' between the educated elites and the peasantry and (c) lack of confidence between government and farmers and a certain underrating of the contribution rural people can make to development. The communications gap, which frequently exists between government and the people, has to be overcome but extension services often seem to work *for* rather than *with* the community. Peasant motivation has to be enhanced by providing educational opportunity of a kind that encourages individuals and groups to participate willingly and with understanding in all the processes of development. The problems of very small farmers invariably call for some form of group or co-operative action. However, co-operatives as institutions frequently tend to limit the scope and possibilities of co-operation itself. They do so when they are obliged, under governmental rules and guidance, to restrict their activities to such specific aspects as credit or marketing rather than seek the broader framework of earning and living within the community. Therefore, Higgs urged the need to foster groups with a wider than agricultural objective. Broad-based group action, based on community responsibility, could do much to hasten the acceptance of rural population programmes. He noted with approval the criteria for rural development programmes established by the FAO Freedom from Hunger/Action for Development Programme. These emphasise especially that institutions at the grass roots level should be strengthened and, further, that the essential resources being those of the community, the function of external resources should be primarily supplementary or enabling.

Whatever the scheme of rural development and agricultural change, Higgs' main propositions will hold good. This is equally true of the several constructive suggestions put forward by Elinor Kennedy on the role of women in food production and family planning (22). These suggestions, being derived from wide ranging observation in the Pacific island societies, in Thailand, in Malaysia, in the Philippines and elsewhere, have indeed a general validity and unquestionable importance for the success of integrated rural development strategies.

Krystall's contribution (30) on rural communications systems for agricultural and family improvement fits in well with the suggestions made by Higgs and Elinor

Kennedy. He focussed attention on the need for an effective communications system which can introduce ideas and practices to families with little or no formal education. Such action calls equally for the education of rural families and of all levels of personnel, both governmental and non-governmental. At the same time, all available channels of communication with rural families must be harnessed, including formal and non-formal educational activities, women's groups, cooperatives, the mass media, etc. Krystall spelt out some of the implications of this approach for the training, organisation and functioning of rural extension services. He noted, in particular, that various activities and services should be channelled to rural families to meet their felt needs, not in a fragmented way but in a way which deals with the total problem. This involves teamwork on the part of extension workers accompanied by a shift from individual to group extension. Above all, equally with Higgs, Krystall assigned a central role to the educational aspects of rural development programmes, for families that have learnt the lessons of development in one area of activity will remain open to further messages and will help accelerate the pace of development.

Which pattern of rural development and agricultural organisation to choose for the future, having regard especially to population factors, is a question that faces most of the less developed countries. While in a small number of countries social patterns can now be taken to have been set definitely (as in China, USSR, Eastern Europe and Israel), in the less developed world as a whole, agrarian systems are still in transition and, at best, the fundamentals of future social and economic organisation may be said to be in the process of being established. Rural societies in this situation may be better able to plan their own transition, in keeping with their social, economic and cultural environment, in the light of experience gained in countries with similar conditions, as well as with collectives, communes, Kibbutz, moshav and the *ujamaa* villages. A comparative, but necessarily summary, presentation of these various forms of agricultural organisation and of the problems faced by agrarian systems in transition, is offered by Tarlok Singh in his paper on alternative forms of agricultural organisation in relation to population factors (20).

In view of developmental efforts of the past two or three decades, the expression 'form of agricultural organisation' has come to have a wider meaning than in the past. It comprehends, at the same time, (a) the state of ownership and operation of the typical farm unit or units, (b) the changing distribution of land and of rights and obligations which form the core of the man—land relationship in the economy, (c) levels of techniques employed, (d) institutional services pertaining to agricultural input like fertiliser, seed, water and energy and the extension network and (e) arrangements for marketing and processing agricultural produce. A comparative study of different systems of agricultural organisation suggests that there are strong similarities between the institutional facilities required by farmers in different countries. However, changes in the structure and operation of farm units constitute a critical point in all rural transformation. Examining various factors which bear on the productivity of land and labour, Tarlok Singh came to the conclusion, hinted at already by Abercrombie, Kötter and others, that a progressive changeover from traditional systems of farm organisation to a system, adapted to the circumstances of each given society, in which all or most of the farm units are able to profit from new technological and economic possibilities, can be expected to raise the productivity of both land and labour. Reconstruction at the farm unit level provides an important means for absorbing and accelerating other changes and for greatly enlarging the gains from development reaching out specifically to those among the rural population who have remained at the margins of subsistence for lack of the minimum security and employment.

Two principal streams of organisational development in agriculture can be distinguished according to whether land is held by individuals or by a collective entity, which may be the community or the state or an agency functioning on behalf of the state. Where land is held by individuals, farm units can be modified or enlarged mainly through some form of consent or co-operation. Careful study of experience with socialist forms of agriculture shows that, if well managed and if individual and group incentives are fairly harmonised, they can be adapted to different stages in agricultural and economic development. They can be modelled to deal with conditions of rapid population growth and pressure on resources as well as those of rapid rural-urban migration and decline in rural population.

In densely populated low income countries with transitional agrarian systems, in which land is distributed highly inequitably, small and marginal cultivators and landless labourers constitute the mass of the rural poor. It is among them that demographic pressures are felt most harshly and immediately. The growth of population and subdivision of holdings (invariably also accompanied by fragmentation) have the effect of increasing the numbers of rural poor. Their poverty is deepened by lack of work opportunities outside agriculture. As several speakers at the seminar pointed out, in these circumstances, work and livelihood for the bulk of the growing rural population can only be found within agriculture and the rural economy. On one side, as Abercrombie pointed out, 'It is certain that the present level of underemployment is much higher than is inevitable' and on the other hand, the economic and social advantages of creation of non-agricultural rural jobs should not be neglected (savings in housing and all kind of infrastructure) and the same is true of the advantages of combined agricultural and non-agricultural activities, as far as it is feasible. The papers presented by Abercrombie (11), Bhattacharjee (18), Campbell (25), Singh (20), Kötter (32), Sinha and Kötter (13) enter more closely into this matter.

In connection with these alternatives and choices, the law of economies of scale should not be conceived too mechanically. In the same way as large agricultural holdings were not under any circumstances, either in ancient or in modern times, the most efficient form of organisation, there is much experience and evidence also today that the success of the one or the other type is not merely a question of technology and economic organisation but also of human relations, of social and political organisation and spirit. The success depends on a remuneration which does satisfy the producer socially, economically and psychologically, with appropriate sharing of income, services and social security (Singh (20) and Kötter (32)).

How, then, could the rural economy be so reorganised and strengthened that there would be both steady growth in agricultural output and increasingly intensive utilisation of available labour resources? In answer to this question, to many students co-operation in farm production, including progressive pooling of land and crop planning, supported by expanding co-operative and state services, has seemed to be an indispensable part of any adequate approach. On the available evidence, it appeared most unlikely to Tarlok Singh that, without transforming agriculture along co-operative lines in a manner suited to the demographic and social conditions of each region, it would be possible to raise adequately or quickly enough the productivity of much of the land and of vast numbers in the present and future labour force. In densely populated countries, as in South Asia, even under favourable circumstances of supply of capital and technology, it was difficult to conceive of the problems of mass poverty and mass employment being resolved without fundamental changes in the agrarian system.

Research in demographic aspects of agricultural development

Discussions in the Rome seminar touched on several questions on which the understanding presently available was felt to be inadequate. The theme could not receive sufficiently close attention and the underlying feeling remained that, perhaps at a future date, more specific treatment of research in demographic problems pertaining to agricultural and rural development might become possible. A general scheme for this purpose was already available in a contribution by S.R. Sen (14). Sen pointed out that, while demographic and agricultural trends could co-exist in a variety of combinations and some quite significant correlations between stages of socio-economic development and demographic trends could be observed, the causes and the effects were not easy to identify. At best, certain broad hypotheses could be formulated about the relative role of social factors, of natural endowments, of science and technology and of economic factors. It was apparent that our understanding, for instance, about which social factors helped acceptance of which particular innovations and at what stages in development, was very inadequate. The situation indeed varied from area to area. A scheme outlined by Sen for classifying areas by rate of population growth, rate of agricultural (or economic) growth, population status, agricultural status and other economic consideration, might be of help in the interpretation of available research into demographic–agricultural relationships and in planning new area studies.

Sen's plea for composite study of demographic and agricultural factors was further reinforced by Eva Mueller (31) who stressed the need for sample surveys of individual farm households, providing agricultural and demographic information for the same families. This suggestion forms part of a broader view in favour of surveys combining agricultural and demographic enquiries. Eva Mueller also noted other important gaps in research presently available, for instance in respect of employment data for women and children, information on children's work (hours, time use, wages etc.), data on the frequency of intra-family transfer (old age support, migrant remittances, etc.) and data on the economic contribution of children and their economic costs. With Sen, Eva Mueller recognised that economic–demographic relations might differ between economic settings and cultures and that the influence of areal characteristics had to be explored through carefully designed surveys.

The relationship between population and employment, especially rural employment, was not known clearly enough for purposes of planning and policy formulation. There were also conflicts between the several objectives with which social and economic development was undertaken. Abercrombie (11) noted that almost all the studies so far made on possible 'trade-offs' between different objectives were theoretical and hypothetical. Yet this was an area in which empirical studies were badly needed, for some of the supposed trade-offs might turn out to be small or temporary or even illusory. Two other questions calling for closer study, mentioned in Abercrombie's paper as well as in other contributions, concern (a) the assessment of the nature and magnitude of underemployment and (b) the experience of China, where demographic and socio-economic measures appear to have converged so as to bring an appreciable decline in the birth rate and improvement in health conditions and in expectation of life at birth.

One important area in which more needs to be known about demographic aspects is that of nutrition, both at the micro and at the macro level. In this connection, Jean McNaughton (12) noted the great need for documented evidence of cause and effect. The subject of malnutrition is now widely discussed but, she asked, how much do we know about the numbers who are malnourished, their location and the reasons for their malnutrition. Clearly, there is need for applied research in several related areas so that there may be a better base for food and nutrition planning. Among priority areas for research which relate population and nutrition, Jean McNaughton drew particular attention to:—

(a) methods for measuring a limited number of characteristics that will define the nutritional status of a population or of individuals;
(b) methods for collecting disaggregated data on food consumption and population;
(c) consequences of various substandard intakes of energy on different population groups (agricultural workers, pregnant and lactating women, etc.);
(d) indicators to identify population groups at nutritional risk;
(e) among socio-economic and cultural factors affecting nutrition, effects of migration from rural to urban areas and reverse influence of urban–rural movement in terms of effects on rural consumption behaviour;
(f) nutritional implications of government policy on population, agriculture, health, education, etc.;
(g) possibility of access to benefits of nutrition and health programmes by socio-economic groups most in need of these.

In dealing with population as an integral part of socio-economic development policies, the concept of research has itself to be broadened to include action-research and planned experimentation. Thus, as pointed out in the paper on alternative forms of agricultural organisation (20), solutions would be rendered easier if the transitions in the application of social and technological innovations were based on some degree of testing and conscious experiment. Unless technical and organisational problems are resolved satisfactorily on the ground, patterns of development which may seem feasible in theory cannot be given practical shape on any scale. This is true, for instance, of issues such as dovetailing planning of the use of natural resources with planning for the use of human resources, co-ordinated physical planning of the use of land, water and other resources, methods of allocating and rewarding work, provision of individual and group incentives and methods of integrated planning at the farm unit level and village and area plans. Answers to such questions have to be found through planned experimentation within the social, economic and cultural milieu of each country and region.

International action

Since the early seventies, step by step through the concerns increasingly felt by member-countries of the United Nations there has been a continuing effort to erect a structure for international co-operation and for transfer of resources and technology. The aspirations behind these endeavours have been but partially fulfilled. Even so, the series of international strategies which have been drawn up in the recent past are beacons for the future and landmarks in their own right. Mention need only be made in this context of the International Development Strategy for the Second Development Decade, United Nations World Plan of Action for the Application of Science and Technology to Development, Programme of Action on a New International Economic Order, World Population Plan of Action, World Plan of Action on Integration of Women in Development, the Universal Declaration on the Eradication of Hunger and Malnutrition and the International Undertaking on World Food Security. These and other declarations seek, on the one hand, to give more positive and purposeful direction to international co-operation and, on the other, to enlarge the scope and substance of international action. Thus, Bhattacharjee (18) drew attention to the measures for international action stressed by the World Food Conference and cited FAO's estimate that, over the period 1975–1980, there was need to bring about a fourfold increase in external development assistance to agriculture.

At the Rome seminar, the theme of co-ordination of international assistance for population and rural development was developed, especially from the perspective of the United Nations Fund for Population Activities by H. Gille (15). He recalled the main assumptions which increasingly guided international action in the area of population. These were:

1. promoting population activities within the framework of economic and social development;
2. promoting programmes in support of underprivileged population groups and combating poverty;
3. improving the delivery of assistance at the global and regional levels through greater co-operation and co-ordination between UNFPA and other agencies of the United Nations as well as improved internal co-ordination and planning within national systems;
4. giving primacy to the needs of the poorest countries and building up self reliance within developing countries;
5. seeking integrated action in the area of population through funding population activities increasingly in conjunction with activities in health, education, rural development, community development and other programmes of economic and social development; and
6. determining high and low priority areas for assistance on the part of UNFPA so as to facilitate greater co-ordination and more unified impact between population and other development programmes and, at the same time, to strengthen the population policy and programme infrastructures within each country.

Problems arising from the growth of population and their consequences for agriculture and rural development and the effects of economic and agricultural development on the pattern of population growth reach out to all aspects of national economic and social policy. Therefore, at the Rome seminar, it was realised that adequate policy and action within countries was of the highest importance. At the same time, everything possible had to be done to bring the resources and knowledge of the international community to the support of efforts at the national level.

Notes

[1] Published initially as Chapter 3 of FAO, *The State of Food and Agriculture 1974*, Rome, 1974.
[2] Presented to the United Nations World Food Conference, Rome, November 1974.
[3] D. Ensminger (ed.), *Food Enough or Starvation for Millions* (Tata McGraw-Hill, New Delhi, 1977).

Annexure

Papers contributed to the seminar on Food, Population and Agricultural Development*, Rome, 1–5 December 1975.

Chapter	Author(s)	Topic
7	Robert Agile (United Nations Population Division)	World Population Situation.
8	R.J. Perkins	Demographic Aspects of Long-term Demand Projections.
9	L. Naiken and W. Schulte	Projections of Agricultural Population and Agricultural Labour Force in relation to Agricultural Planning.
10	Wajihuddin Ahmed	More Food Means Fewer Babies.
11	K.C. Abercrombie	Population and Rural Employment.
12	Jean McNaughton	Population and Nutrition.
13	R. Sinha and H.R. Kötter	Population Aspects of Integrated Rural Development.
14	S.R. Sen	Research in Demographic Aspects of Agricultural Development.
15	H. Gille	Co-ordination of International Assistance for Population and Rural Development.
16	H. Breimyer	The Food–Energy Balance.
17	James D. McQuigg	Effective Use of Weather Information in Projections of Global Grain Production.
18	J.P. Bhattacharjee	Population, Food and Agricultural Development: A Medium Term View.
19	Anthony S. Rojko and Patrick M. O'Brien	Organising Agriculture for the Year 2000.
20	Tarlok Singh	Alternative Forms of Agricultural Organisation in relation to Population Factors.
21	R. Thamarajakshi	Role of Price Incentives in Stimulating Agricultural Production in a Developing Economy.
22	Elinor K. Kennedy	The Role of Women in Food Production and Family Planning.

* Chapter references are to Douglas Ensminger (ed.), *Food Enough or Starvation for Millions*.

Chapter	Author(s)	Topic
23	Robert W. Herdt and Randolph Barker	Intensification of Proven Farm Production Practices.
24	D.W. Norman	Communicating Improved and New Technology.
25	Keith Campbell	The Effects of Rapid Urbanisation on Agriculture.
26	B.A. Stout and Charles M. Downing	Increasing Productivity of Human, Animal and Engine Power.
27	Douglas Ensminger	Social and Cultural Constraints to World Food Production.
28	Uma Lele	Integrated Rural Development.
29	John Higgs	Farmers' Organisations and People's Participation in Rural Development.
30	E.R. Krystall	Rural Communication System for Agricultural and Family Improvement.
31	Eva Mueller	Effects of Different Patterns of Rural Development on Demographic Change.
32	H.R. Kötter	Population Aspects of Rural Development: 21 Theses.
33	Stanley Andrews	The Forgotten and the Neglected.

Reflections on aspects of population and agricultural development in selected countries

J.P. Bhattacharjee [1]

In the necessarily abstract and aggregated presentation of the problems of population and food and agricultural development in the developing world, it is easy to slur over the diversity of situations and experiences that the countries individually have faced. The perception of the problems and the approach to tackling them through policies and programmes reveal different patterns and are best understood against the background of political, social and economic policies in each country. This appreciation of the need for in-depth country studies was the reason for commissioning case studies on six different countries (Brazil, India, Indonesia, Kenya, the Republic of Korea and Yugoslavia) for discussion at the Rome seminar on Population and Food and Agricultural Development [2]. The studies were carried out by well known scholars on the basis of professional analysis. Most of them have adopted a comprehensive framework, but concentrated on selected problems that they consider important. The conclusions drawn and the views expressed are their own and do not reflect those of the government concerned. A similar interpretation should be attached to the reflections presented in this paper.

It is not my intention to write a critique of these studies. Nor it is the purpose of this paper to summarise, even in a cross sectional way, these separate studies. In general, the authors have analysed the experiences in these countries over the last two to three decades in respect of population changes, increase in the demand and supply of food and agricultural products and development of the agricultural sector within the framework of the economy. They also have given a broad synoptic picture of the medium and long term scenario in the problem areas focussed by them. Within this general outline, the authors have concentrated on different problems and the policy approaches to tackling them. It is on a few of these problem areas that I shall offer some reflections in an attempt to draw some broader conclusions. I hope the authors will correct me if I am wrong in my deductions.

The problems analysed in these studies can be conveniently grouped into four areas, namely, population and food, migration and employment, farming structure and adjustments, and family planning and welfare. Such a grouping permits consideration of the interactions between the demographic factors and a number of aspects of socio-economic development and provides the framework of this paper, the objective of which is to reflect the light thrown by the case studies on the pertinent policy issues in these areas. There are, of course, many other studies of these countries covering one or more of these areas. But it is beyond the scope of this paper to bring those into our discussion.

Food and population

All the case studies have analysed the relationship between the growth of population and of food production at each country level along with some regional breakdown. Some of them have gone further and discussed changes in the composition of the food demand and their implications for production and supply. A picture has also been given in a few studies of the availability for consumption of foodstuffs and its nutritional implications. It is against the background of analysis of country experiences over the last two to three decades and a brief indication of the medium term scenario that the authors have discussed relevant policies and programmes.

The setting shows interesting differences among these countries, almost as in a spectrum. Brazil, India, Indonesia and Kenya had experienced acceleration in the growth rate of their populations in the three decades from the 1940s and by the end of the 1960s were having annual growth rates varying from around 2.2 per cent (India) to about 3.3 per cent (Kenya). There is an indication in the paper on India of a likely decline in that country's population growth rate during the seventies. the Republic of Korea had also gone through this phase of accelerated population growth, but has experienced its reversal since 1966, the annual rate having declined from 2.9 per cent to 1.6 per cent. Yugoslavia started the post-War era with a comparatively smaller population growth rate, about 1.5 per cent, which has now come down to 1 per cent and is projected to decline to 0.6 per cent. Yugoslavia appears to have completed its process of demographic transition.

The growth of food demand shows a wider variation and in the poorer of these countries has been determined largely by the population growth factor — changes in the number and age composition of the people. The effect of increase in consumer income has also been significant, particularly in the high growth countries of Brazil, the Republic of Korea and Yugoslavia and also in Kenya. Since the development strategy in these countries has been instrumental in accelerating the rate of urbanisation, it is on the latter that the authors have focussed their analysis and in the process have taken into account a part of the effect of changes in income distribution. As a result of the play of all these forces, food demand has grown at different rates, ranging from over 3 per cent per year in India to 4.9 per cent in Brazil and 5.1 per cent in Yugoslavia. The commodity composition of demand has undergone a change in pattern, with high elasticity commodities (milk, meat, fruits, sugar, etc.) showing proportionately much larger increases. Further, the influence of the urban consumption pattern has manifested itself, particularly in Kenya and Brazil, in the substitution of root crops and other traditional staples with cereals which are not locally grown in significant quantities and have had to be largely imported.

The response of food and agricultural production to the challenge of population and demand increase in these countries has been assessed by the authors; and I am relying on their conclusions. On Brazil, Alves, Teixeira Filho and Tollini felt that 'The rate of population growth, despite the fact that it is high, does not seem to be a major problem'; 'the agricultural sector of Brazil has played its role quite satisfactorily' ... and 'as long as the solution of Brazil's food problem depends on quantities produced, the agricultural sector will solve it'. Dandekar's quantitative assessment of the Indian situation was that 'the rate of growth of output of foodgrains in India has had a small margin over the rate of growth of population, leading to some improvement in the *per capita* output of foodgrains (at an annual rate of about 0.349 per cent)', but unless performances improve 'the output of foodgrains in 1981 may be shorter (than the target) by about 20 million tons'. Regarding Indonesia, Baharsjah stated that 'practically the whole effort to increase food production was devoted to rice', 'even though current performance would bring about near self sufficiency by 1978, it might not be maintained unless family planning programmes lowered the population growth rate significantly'. Mureithi and Otieno stated that the situation in Kenya is 'an uneasy balance between agricultural production and population growth', 'the hybrid maize revolution and improvements in crop husbandry have recently tended to reverse the bleak picture of the food situation'. Kim and Kim assessed the Korean situation in the following terms: 'From 1965–1974 total foodgrain production increased by only 4.3 per cent, whereas foodgrain consumption jumped by almost 29.3 per cent'; however, 'Korean agriculture can, for a sustained period of time, feed more than her population with self-supplied grains by fully exploiting her hidden resources'. As for Yugoslavia, Tomic and Breznik wrote that 'the total demand for agricultural products has been growing at an average annual rate of 5.1 per cent, while the final agricultural production has increased at 3.3 per cent'; 'in the forthcoming period, in one or two decades, one expects the balancing of the supply and demand for food to be achieved'.

It is to be expected that this overall synoptic picture does not bring out the variations among the regions in each country. The case studies on Brazil, Kenya and India have analysed them within their respective frameworks and those on Yugoslavia and Indonesia have recognised their importance. Variations in factor endowment resulting from ecological differences and differential demographic forces emerge from these analyses, as the conditions underlying the disparities. These regional imbalances have significant implications for development policy, programme priorities, resource allocation and transfer, institutional organisation and development of human resources. However, it should also be recognized that the disparities have their roots in social and political history and that while 'balanced regional development' is a recognised policy goal, the design and implementation of policies and programmes to achieve it present formidable difficulties.

In the last analysis, the interaction between population growth and food production needs to be judged by its impact on the nutritional situation of the population at risk. This is recognised in all the studies and discussed at some length in the ones on Brazil, Kenya and the Republic of Korea. National food balance sheets do not throw light on the incidence and distribution of malnutrition; and household data are difficult to come by. The Brazil study provided data on daily *per capita* intake of calories and proteins by region, sector, source and income class, based on household surveys. These survey results help to identify the sections of population in different regions suffering from calorie-protein deficiency. The poorer income groups, particularly in urban areas and the poorer regions, are the main loci of these deficiencies. The survey concluded that 'the North East is the region with highest nutritional deficits. In all the regions of the country the urban sector also shows higher deficiencies', in relation to the requirements. Similar findings are also mentioned in the study of the Republic of Korea which additionally provided data on intake of minerals and vitamins. The analysis of the nutrition situation has not however been carried forward to a discussion of its implications for policies and programmes, perhaps because an integrated, inter-sector nutrition policy has not been formulated or adopted in these countries. Mureithi and Otieno candidly stated that 'Kenya does not have as yet a clearly worked out nutrition policy, although in the current development plan it was hoped that national nutritional policy regarding the marketing, production and distribution of foodstuffs, food technology, improvement of nutritive quality, nutrition education and research would be formulated and that a national food and nutrition council would be formed to implement that policy'.

The policies and programmes discussed in the case studies, besides being country-specific, are too numerous to be considered in detail. The best I can do is to offer some observations on some of the broader aspects of the strategies adopted in the countries. The authors have rightly discussed aspects of these strategies in their medium and longer term perspectives. The analysis of the past performance in food and agricultural development establishes beyond doubt that the recent trends give cause for concern. The growth of food production in all the countries, except Brazil, has not matched the growth of demand; it has only run slightly ahead of the population growth. The nutrition situation can be assumed to have worsened in the low income countries. However, the evidence on adoption of an integrated nutrition policy is lacking.

The one factor that has brought about a change in the inertia of complacence is the global food crisis of the mid-1970s. It has precipitated a sense of alarm and forced governments and international organisations to have a fresh look at trends and reconsider their policies. The task of achieving considerably accelerated rates of growth of food production and equitable distribution is no longer a talking point but is seen as a challenge to be faced. That the meeting of this challenge is physically possible and economically feasible is not in doubt and none of the authors have raised questions on this score. What is, therefore, at issue is the political will for taking the difficult decisions on the priorities, design and implementation of integrated policies and programmes for agricultural and rural development with an undiluted commitment to the pursuit of the objective of growth balanced with equity among different economic (income) and geographical (region) units. Agricultural economists can help in this political process if they depart from their adherence to value-neutral positivism and incorporate into their analysis considerations of political feasibility of different policy options and their consequences.

The overall development strategy has been, to use some recent terminology, 'uni-modal' in some countries and 'bi-modal' in others. The high-level growth strategy based on industrialisation in Brazil, the Republic of Korea and Yugoslavia, had apparently brought about structural transformations in these economies without any perceptible problems in food supply, as long as the world food situation was stable and international food prices relatively low. However, in the present situation, even these countries appear to be emphasising policies of food self-sufficiency and import-substitution. Other countries have traditionally been following this policy and now realise even more strongly the importance of stepping up achievements in food and agricultural production. Further, Brazil and Yugoslavia had developed an export oriented strategy, even in agriculture and the recent swings in international trade in food products have introduced an element of uncertainty in their production strategy. On the whole, the different strategies have made different claims on the agricultural sector in respect of the commodity demands to be satisfied and these have not been easy to meet.

Within the agricultural sector, the production priority appears to have been placed on cereals in India, Indonesia, Kenya and the Republic of Korea, with only recent recognition of the importance of the livestock sub-sector. In Brazil and Yugoslavia, however, the production priorities have combined crops and livestock and, in the latter the priority was perhaps higher on livestock. Food self sufficiency and import substitution appear to have played an overriding role in decisions on these strategies, especially in India. However, since the labour intensity in the production of crops and livestock differs, it would be interesting to consider in the context of all the countries what crop and livestock mixes should be included and at what stages in the production evolution, if a labour-intensive strategy of growth was to be adopted. This is an area that deserves further policy analysis and attention [3].

The authors of the Kenya and Yugoslavia case studies made pointed references to the importance of changes in the socio-economic structure and income distribution. There appears to be a dearth of analysis of policy options in this area, although its importance is generally recognised. There is the known view that structural changes, including land reform and other programmes, tend to impede the growth of agricultural production in the transition period which is of unknown duration. To what extent this is true and what programmes of domestic and external assistance can be designed to help smooth over this transition are issues that deserve further consideration. The Yugoslav study indicated that the problems of the small farmers have not been satisfactorily resolved after more than two decades.

The production development programme in the different countries raise a number of interesting issues of approach and content, to one or two of which I shall briefly refer. It appears that the strategy for production development in all these countries, except Brazil, has been predominantly oriented to intensification, in the sense of vertical expansion. In Brazil, the approach has historically been horizontal expansion through extension of cultivation. However, according to the authors of the case study, even in Brazil — which has the world's largest potential of unused land area — intensification of agriculture through policies and programmes for increasing yields has now been recognised in official policy. In Indonesia, where there are sparsely populated islands, the author stated that in the present transmigration programmes 'demographic objectives, though still important, are no longer regarded as the main goals'. Transmigration programmes are becoming more and more regarded as part of the integral effort to develop the backward regions of the country. Such experiences give a jolt to the wishful thought of wide, empty spaces where populations can be transferred and demographic pressures in the densely settled areas can be eased.

Various aspects of resource development and other programmes have been mentioned in the papers. These have tended to be country-specific. Out of these, one particular problem area has been emphasised in every study, namely the need for development of improved technology for crop and livestock production. Priority attention deserves to be given particularly to the technology for rain fed and deep water paddy (rice), pulses, sorghum, millets, root crops and tropical pastures. To correct the imbalances in the past approach, greater attention needs to be given to the farming system while developing technology for individual crops. Research for the development of such technology clearly requires both national and international effort.

Migration and employment

The population dependent on agriculture for employment or occupation has undergone a decline both in absolute numbers and in proportion in Brazil, the Republic of Korea and Yugoslavia, the ratio falling from around two-thirds in the early postwar period to well below 50 per cent now [4]. This decline has been associated with a very high rate of urbanisation through rural—urban migration. There is also another migration to which the Yugoslav study refers, namely migration out of agriculture into non-agricultural occupations without a geographical move into urban areas. Migration out of agriculture is thus larger than the exodus from rural areas. These movements have aggravated the problems of urban development, employment and labour supply in agriculture. Since the urban problems were beyond the scope of the case studies, the authors analysed the employment implications of the migration patterns for the agricultural and rural sectors. However, the Brazilian study also examined the interactions between the urban and the agricultural labour markets.

The authors of the Brazil study tried first to analyse the 'push and pull' factors behind the tremendous inter-regional migration in that country in terms of income at the place of origin, expected income in their new location, inequality of income, education, urbanisation in the neighbourhood and the density of population at the original place of residence. The broad findings of the analysis is that out-migration is negatively correlated with income levels and urbanisation at the original place of residence and positively correlated with most of the other variables. The data also tend to support that 'as more people get educated, out-migration increases'. The authors then go on to analyse intraregional migration which is the smaller part of the total movement. Here they find that the levels of *per capita* income in the rural sector as well as in the urban sector are positively correlated with migration as well as income distribution in the rural sector. Perhaps of greater interest is the conclusion derived from their smaller model, namely that the higher the ratio of urban to rural incomes the more will people migrate and that people tend to migrate from places where the income distribution is uneven in the hope of having a higher income level at their destination. These findings were supported by the Kenya study. While mentioning dearth of employment and shortage of land as the immediate reasons for migration, the authors pointed out that the main factors underlying migration are differentials in earning power, social amenities and employment between different regions.

The case study of the Republic of Korea threw a different light, namely, no conclusive evidence that differences between urban expected income and rural expected income were solely responsible for pulling rural people into urban sectors, nor that migrants were being pushed out of rural areas by low rural income expectations. Thus we find two contrary findings on the hypothesis elaborated in the work of M. Todaro [5]. The explanation of the migration flow in the Republic of Korea was given in terms of the stream of recent migration which has sequentially determined its future growth and the motivation is found in the desire and expectation of parents to provide their children with better education and greater opportunities for a better life in urban areas.

However, all the studies agreed on two points, namely the importance of the education factor in the motivation for migration and the poorer assessment of the opportunities for a better life in agriculture and rural areas. Both have implications for policies on education and nutrition and programmes designed to provide 'basic minimum services' in rural areas. They also suggest the need for appropriate policies on minimum wages in agriculture and on pricing of capital goods.

The rural—urban migration has affected agricultural labour supply vis-à-vis employment in different ways. The Korean case study gave particular attention to the effect of the heavy out-migration of farm labour on labour availability during the peak periods of demand in agriculture. It was estimated that the shortage during the peak seasons in June and October 1970 was as much as 19.7 and 16.3 per cent. These shortages have led to a doubling of agricultural wage rates in the course of five years and have given an impetus to mechanisation. Looking to the future, the study came to the conclusion that under any situation the shortage of labour on farms will increase while the capital formation required for mechanisation is unlikely to be provided for. The recommendation is therefore for a policy of decentralisation to rural areas, of the location of non-agricultural employment creation. Interestingly, this is also a policy mentioned in the Yugoslavia case study. The authors of the Kenya study, however, suggested policies to increase employment in agriculture by the development of small farms and labour-intensive cropping pattern. Their main objective is to improve the distribution of incomes as well as to increase productivity per unit of land, which is recognised to be high in terms of area yields on small farms.

The diverse findings of these studies generally point to the need for an intersectoral approach for tackling problems of migration and employment in agriculture and in the rural areas. The present thinking in this direction favours the so called integrated rural development approach encompassing agricultural productivity growth, appropriate technology, promotion of small labour intensive industries in rural areas, provision of social services and amenities with a view to providing more employment and income to the rural people and a better standard of living. In short, there is a strong case for a new approach to development planning incorporating disaggregation to different levels and focussing on target regions and populations.

Farming structure and adjustments

The farm sector in all these countries has faced difficult and sometimes unresolved problems in responding to the claims made on it by the demand for food and other products of an increasing population with changing age structure and rapidly growing urban component. Further, it has had to adjust to labour supply as affected by out-migration. All these adjustments have been taking place within the constraints imposed by the farm structure, resource availability, technology and development policies and priorities of the governments. The case studies stressed that the farming system and structure will have to make even greater adjustments in the next ten to fifteen years and will face uncertain or unknown parameters.

Size and organisation of farms constitute a critical area of adjustment and the directions do not appear clearly in some of the studies. For example, the authors of the case study of the Republic of Korea emphasised the critical importance of appropriate farm mechanisation in the future scenarios which point to further shortages of labour at least in peak seasons. But this prescription does not answer the question as to whether a mechanisation policy should be formulated without one on the size and organisational structure of farms. In Brazil, where labour and not land is the constraining factor, the authors strongly recommended a policy for sustained increases in land productivity. Normally, this would require increases in labour intensity in farming which would, in turn, have implications for farm size and structure.

In the Kenya and Yugoslavia studies, on the other hand, there were recommendations about the farm size policy. For Kenya, considerations of employment and productivity led the authors to make a case 'for the promotion of small-scale land tenure rather than large-scale farm units'. This would mean a reversal of the past trend of a decline in the labour force employed in agriculture. In India and Indonesia, where the opposite trend has been in force, there is presumably a stronger case for a policy of small farmer development. The contrasting picture is in Yugoslavia where the long term development goal of agriculture is in the direction of large-scale socially organised production in vertically integrated agro-industrial units with which the individual farmers – their numbers diminishing – will co-operate on a 'self management' basis. In this connection, the authors pointed to the need for studies of the problems of formation and development of the agro-industrial complexes.

An interesting development in Yugoslavia has been the emergence of 'mixed households' or part time farmers. This phenomenon along with the aging of the operators on private farms (on account of migration of young people) has catalysed 'the process of penetration of modern technical-technological processes on individual agricultural holdings'. The authors of the Korea and Kenya studies favoured such a development as a means of increasing employment and earnings of the farm family [6] and preventing urban drift and accordingly recommend a decentralised industrial location policy. Such a policy is compatible with the strategy of integrated rural development and should also be relevant to the high density countries.

Major adjustments will be needed in farm enterprises and operations, farm business and living. These will have implications for policies in many fields ranging from education to irrigation and land development. The major instruments for bringing about these adjustments are prices, credit and investment and extension and training. Among these, credit and price policies have been covered more extensively in the case studies. Nearly all the case studies emphasised the need for much larger flows of investment on farms, the financing of which will require considerable expansion in short and medium-term credit. Within this general expansion, the access of small farmers and tenants to credit will need to increase proportionately much more, if the objectives, earlier stated, are to be achieved. Whether this would be possible within the framework of the existing credit institutions and policies is an issue of crucial importance, on which two of the studies cast doubts. Institutional innovations as well as new departures in credit policy in respect of coverage of risks, administrative costs, subsidies and interest rates are badly needed in this field.

Extension and training cover another important area of policy and programme which deserves serious attention. Since the case studies (except Brazil) have not discussed it, I will not go into it and quickly pass on to price policy. A number of the case studies have emphasised the need for major changes in the present or erstwhile price policies in the countries. The weaknesses in the price policies, as pointed out, are the familiar ones: depressed food prices (the Republic of Korea) in the interests of urban consumers and wage labourers, adverse terms of trade for agricultural products as an instrument to serve the growth of the secondary and tertiary sectors (Yugoslavia), inequitable gains by large scale farmers through price manipulation (Kenya) and instability in prices (Brazil).

Agricultural price policy in each country has been shaped historically by the play of political forces (pressure groups) within the accepted development strategy and is thus not easy to change. However, the present food crisis has led to considerable rethinking in the countries studied. The direction of change appears to be towards minimum or support pricing at levels 'remunerative to producers and fair to consumers'. Obviously, both output and input pricing should be consistently formulated in such a policy, which should seek to bring about a dynamic balance between the production and the consumption patterns within a clearly spelt out goal of the extent of self sufficiency. It is a familiar and favourite area of study for agricultural economists; and the question we should address ourselves is how far we have been able to reconcile the interests of farmers, the consumers and the governments and of the agricultural sector and the overall economy in a consistent framework for agricultural price policy.

Family planning and welfare

The authors of the case studies of India, Kenya, the Republic of Korea and Indonesia stressed the urgency of the need for effective policies and programmes for bringing down the population growth rate. Since Yugoslavia may be said to have completed the demographic transition, its population policy is likely to have meaningful lessons for the other countries. Curiously enough, the authors stated that 'The Yugoslav society's goals in the sphere of population reproduction are not sufficiently defined. However, policies relating to economic, educational, social, health and other spheres more and more affect the population trends and demographic structures'. The decline in the birth rate and family size is thus sought to be explained in terms of complex interacting relationships involving economic, social and cultural factors. Evidence of this is found in the wide differential in the demographic variables between the advanced and the less advanced regions and this has led to a population policy which can perhaps be defined in terms of 'a rapid lessening of regional differences'.

A different finding was presented in the Indian case study on the basis of a correlation analysis of the inter-state differences. In the author's words, 'at best only a weak relationship may exist between the rate of growth of the population and food-cum-agricultural development' and an 'even weaker relationship' between the growth rates of food production and the proportion of women protected by family planning measures. The author argued that 'an inter-relationship (between food and agricultural development and population growth) even if discovered, would be only of academic interest with little operational implications ... One would not, presumably, want to advocate agricultural development as a measure of population control'. The author rightly concluded that the programmes for food and agricultural development and for family planning do not compete for the same real resources and, though not directly interrelated, will mutually strengthen each other.

The need for pursuing both sets of programmes 'simultaneously and vigorously' was also stressed by the authors of the Kenya and Korea studies. It would have been useful if the authors had shed light on how this can be done and, in particular, how the family planning programme can be made more effective. While there is evidence of the emphasis placed on this programme by the governments, the case studies also pointed out serious slippages and shortfalls. Since the practice of family planning is essentially a matter of individual choice in the family setting and compulsion has to be ruled out, even a vigorously stepped up programme can only provide for 'cafeteria services'. In the last analysis it is, therefore, the motivation of the individual and the family which will determine the progress of family planning. Indeed, there is widespread recognition of this among demographers and social scientists.

At the level of the family, there is evidence of a decline in fertility associated with improvements in education, income and nutrition status, decline in infant mortality, and other factors which determine the quality of life. While it may be difficult to translate these micro-level choice factors into a macro-level policy, it has also to be recognised that no population policy can be formulated only in terms of a family planning programme. It must embrace all the pertinent elements of felt needs and measures for their satisfaction that determine the quality of life and the welfare of the family. It must also envisage improvement in the status and role of women, with its implications for the family structure. In emphasising what may be considered an obvious point, I am not minimising the difficulty of translating such a policy into operational instruments. The concept of 'basic minimum needs for each family' provides an initial operational approach. Some attempts have been made in India and a few other countries to incorporate this approach in planning and programme formulation; however the field is still relatively little explored.

Concluding observations

This paper has offered some reflections on the policy implications that the authors of the six case studies drew from their analyses of the population and food and agricultural development problems in these countries. I have resisted the temptation to critically examine the methodological aspects of their analyses, as this would not fit into the structure and length of the paper. It is difficult to sum up the different strands of thought, even if I were to confine myself to the main thrust of the policies discussed. After all, a summary of a paper which summarises and comments on six elaborate studies faces the danger of rarefaction to the point of losing substance. Instead, I will conclude with some observations of a general nature on what appears to me to be the present state of developing country policies on food and agricultural development.

The period 1972–1975 appears in retrospect to have marked a qualitative change in most developing countries in their perception of the nature and importance of the problems of food and agricultural development. The global crisis in food, fertilisers, fossil fuels and in exchange rates and balance of payments have undoubtedly precipitated a serious anxiety and concern in these countries on their future development prospects. Their agricultural policies and programmes have undergone re-examination; and there is evidence of a high priority being attached to the achievement of food self sufficiency. Much larger efforts are being made to step up production programmes, embracing development of land and water resources, application of improved technology and expansion of the supply and distribution of production inputs. In this phase of reorientation, investment, credit, prices, research, extension and other instruments appear to be accorded greater political importance than before. There is also an apparent acceptance of the importance of the equity goals and their implications for the social and economic structures. However, the latter have still to be crystallised in the design and implementation of appropriate reforms in land tenure and tenancy and in adjustment of the farming structures and systems.

Equally, there is evidence of much greater concern in the developing countries in regard to the worsening employment situation. While much of it relates, for obvious reasons, to the visible unemployment situation in the urban areas, there is also recognition of its basic roots in the process of rural—urban migration. Available policy options in this field cannot but unavoidably point to the need for re-examination and re-formulation of a large number of policy issues such as mechanisation, small farmer productivity, labour intensive technology, and rural industrialisation. The further one proceeds in this direction, the more one notices the inter-sectoral overlap in any meaningful approach to rural development in the future. The concept of integrated rural development does provide an inter-sectoral framework and appears to be widely accepted. However, it appears to me to be still a talking point and at best a programme in its pilot phase. We, as sectoral economists, cannot but avoid our share of the blame for not developing ahead of time inter-sectoral (and also disaggregated) approaches to planning and programme formulation for rural development.

In the light of these remarks, the question I would like to pose is whether the overall development strategy in the developing countries is undergoing any major shifts that would have beneficial implications for the course and speed of food and agricultural development in the future. While there are hopeful signs here and there, I am not yet convinced that a serious re-evaluation of the overall strategy has yet taken place in any significant number of countries. As evidence I will mention the lack of any well formulated and consistent policy on nutrition in most developing countries. Satisfaction of the other basic human needs constitutes further aspects of the development goals that have yet to be integrated into development strategies and programmes in many countries. Indeed, it is only when these goals and strategies have been politically accepted that attempts at land reform and other structural changes would have their full impact. This can be said even more strongly as far as population policy is concerned. Integrated rural development thus faces an uncertain situation; and as long as it lasts, one cannot be too sure in stating that the mid-seventies have been a period of watershed in the development of the developing countries. Only history will tell.

Notes

[1] The views expressed in this paper are those of the author and do not necessarily represent the views of FAO.
[2] The six case studies are:
E.R. Alves, A.R. Teixeira Filho and M. Tollini – 'Country Case Study – Brazil'.
L.P. Mureithi and J.O. Otieno – 'Food, Population and Rural Development in Kenya: Progress, Policies, Problems and Prospects'.
S.H. Kim and D.M. Kim – 'Facts and Analyses of Population, Food and Agricultural Development in the Republic of Korea'.
V.M. Dandekar – 'Population and Food In India'.
S. Baharsjah – 'The Interrelationship between Population and Food and Agricultural Development in Indonesia'.
D. Tomic and D. Breznik – 'The Interrelationship between Population and Food and Agricultural Development: Country Case Study of Yugoslavia'.
These are published in *Food Enough or Starvation for Millions* – D. Ensminger (ed.) Chs. 1–6.
[3] cf. Ch. 7 of J.W. Mellor, *The New Economics of Growth*, Cornell University Press, 1976.
[4] The Kenya case study appears to imply that such a change has taken place also in that country. The data quoted in the study to show the steady decline in farm employment apparently relate to wage labour on commercial farms. In the absence of relevant information for small-holders and subsistence farmers, it cannot be said that the above pattern of change has been established in Kenya.
[5] M. Todaro, 'A model of labour migration and urban employment in less developed countries', *American Economic Review*, vol. 59, no. 1, 1969.
[6] It is worth emphasising in this connection that the anatomy of so called 'part-time farming' is not the same in different countries, which makes a generalised policy prescription rather unrealistic.

Can we feed the world?
— an optimistic note

Keith O. Campbell

> 'Where there is no hope, there can be no endeavour.'
> Samuel Johnson

In spite of the grim forebodings of the doomsday men and the depressing defeatism of some agricultural scientists and economists, I remain sanguine about man's capacity to feed himself in the years to come. The fact that I am optimistic does not, however, mean I am complacent. The overwhelming impression I brought away from the Rome seminar in December 1975 was that, despite the multiplicity of problems of food production and distribution it laid bare, the problems can be overcome if governments are more fully informed, better motivated and act more rationally. But act they must and act more purposefully on agricultural matters than they have done in the past.

Prolegomena

Before outlining some of the grounds for my position, three preliminary points need to be made. First, my comments are not made against a presumed background of unlimited, much less exponential, population growth. Recent UN demographic projections suggest that the world population will reach a peak somewhere between 11 and 15 billion about a century from now [1]. Some demographers would question their ability to make confident estimates beyond the next 15 to 25 years but I believe it is useful to have some idea of the relevant orders of magnitude. In crude terms, then, we have to think in terms of feeding fifty per cent more people by the year 2000 and three times our present numbers in a hundred years' time. I believe this assignment to be well within man's capability.

Second, I am not concerned with a time scale which stretches to the ultimate exhaustion of the planet. It has become fashionable recently for some writers who wish to deprecate the power of science and technology to raise living standards to find philosophical justification for their pessimism in the second law of thermodynamics [2]. Whatever the implications of the law of entropy for the ultimate fate of future generations, it ill becomes agricultural economists from affluent countries to deny less advantaged sections of mankind (at least by implication), the benefits which agricultural science can bring for the relief of human conditions [3].

Regard, of course, has to be paid to possible ecological consequences of particular kinds of technology. But, contrary to the absolutist views of the more strident conservationists, the necessity for trade-offs between environmental costs and other costs should be recognised. It is neither rational nor sensible to pursue public policies on a 'no risk' basis — in accordance with the view that a particular technique or substance should be outlawed if the possibility of its damaging human life is even infinitesimal. It should further be accepted that the relevant trade-offs may vary substantially between affluent and developing nations. The affluent can afford the luxury of restraints on the use of powerful agents for the improvement of human welfare. The developing countries, on the other hand, rightly accord more importance to the well-being of their human population than their country's bird life. Restrictions on the use of DDT and other insecticides in the United States are cases in point.

The resource situation

Turning to the determinants of food production, I see no physical resource restraints within the time horizon posited earlier. The world currently uses less than half the land area potentially suitable to grow food crops and raise livestock [4]. Moreover there is little reason to expect any reversal of the trend towards substituting other inputs for land. It may not even be necessary to have resort to the two major needed technical breakthroughs set out by Pawley in 1971 [5], namely techniques for continuous cultivation in the humid tropics and reduction of desalination costs to permit the use of erstwhile saline water for irrigation. It would be wrong, I believe, to make too much of recent short term difficulties regarding petroleum and fertiliser supplies in considering long term possibilities. Despite the burgeoning literature on energy in relation to the rural industries, world agriculture is a relatively small user of fossil fuel.

Institutional restraints

The ways in which agricultural production is organised and in particular the systems of land tenure in use, clearly have implications for agricultural productivity. The slow rate of expansion of food production is sometimes attributed to the failure of developing countries to proceed faster with land reform.

My own predilection is to discount the immediate need for, and potential benefit from, institutional change. Many countries are still searching for more satisfactory forms of agrarian structure. In these and others the initial impact of hasty reform could prove so disruptive as to do more harm than good in the short term, however great may be the long term benefits [6]. Since the time and effort necessary to effect changes in tenure and other rural institutions are inevitably great, it would seem more fruitful for developing countries to direct their efforts in the immediate future to remedying deficiencies in their input and their product market systems.

Agricultural research

As regards research, I have confidence in the ability of agricultural and other scientists to effect substantial improvements in the food-producing capacity of the world, if they are given the necessary resources. Even in the more advanced agricultural countries there is only spasmodic reference to, and little hard evidence of, the likelihood of the physiological limits to plant and animal improvement being approached [7]. In any case, past experience suggests that new genotypes will be found or new sources of improvement will come to light. For example, the advent of the Mexican 'miracle'wheats changed expectations about yield improvements in a number of countries overnight.

There is reason to be concerned however about the trivial proportion of the world's scientific resources being devoted to world food production problems and the geographical distribution of such research activities. Evenson and Kislev have estimated that total world expenditure on government agricultural research was $(US) 1.1 billion in 1965 [8]. This might be compared with Barbara Ward's recent estimate of $(US) 250 billion a year for the world's likely expenditure on armaments over the next ten years [9]. If this were a true reflection of man's priorities, there would surely be reason to ask whether there is, in fact, any world food problem. Perhaps, there will be some reassessment of research priorities in agriculture's favour if the situation deteriorates, but clearly much could be accomplished if the scientists of the world were to apply themselves to rural problems in a serious way.

The Evenson-Kislev study also indicates that 89 per cent of the world rural research budget and 83 per cent of the scientists working in publicly financed agricultural research centres were supported by the high income countries. Two points should be made about this situation. First, much of the applied agricultural research is specific to particular regions. The international transfer of new wheat and rice varieties associated with the 'green revolution' was the exception rather than the rule. On the other hand, many of the innovations of the high income countries which do potentially have wider application (particularly agricultural chemicals) do not reach the less developed countries either because of the latter's protectionist trade policies or because of local pricing policies.

The second point is that agricultural research allocations in advanced countries tend inevitably to be influenced by their domestic food situation, often one of surplus or, at least, one dominated by problems of market access. This, combined with the relative decline of the agricultural sector of such countries over time, encourages contraction rather than expansion of subventions for rural research. Thus only limited contributions to food production problems in less developed countries can be expected as a byproduct of research work in affluent countries.

Technical aid programmes, of course, should not be dismissed but they are small in comparison with the magnitude of the problem and they tend to involve applied rather than fundamental research. The development of international research centres (such as CIMMYT and IRRI) by the private foundations also help but they are excessively expensive in anybody's language. It is hard to believe that these are the only, or the most appropriate, way to achieve technological improvements in the agriculture of the developing countries.

The priority given to agricultural improvement by low income countries themselves and the standard of excellence expected leave much to be desired. Preoccupation with industrialisation and with problems arising from abnormally high rates of urbanisation has led to the neglect of their agricultural industries [10].

The braking effect of national agricultural policies

The lack of public concern for the agricultural sector of the low income countries is manifest in other ways than in the neglect of agricultural research. Many policy measures are tantamount to disincentives to food production, even though there is now abundant evidence that farmers in developing countries will respond in an economically rational way to production incentives if they are provided. Many such countries have resorted to controls over food prices in the interests of the urban consumer. Acceptance of external food aid has been allowed to discourage the expansion of domestic food production. Costs of inputs such as fertilisers have been set too high because of import restrictions. Marketing boards have been allowed to divert receipts from international trade and as a consequence producers' prices have been depressed.

The agricultural policies pursued by the high income countries have had equally counter productive effects on world food output and, more seriously, have impeded the efforts of the developing countries to increase their agricultural potential. The negative consequences of the high degree of protection of agricultural products in the EEC, for instance, have been amply demonstrated many times [11]. The insulation of the price structures of countries, the one from the other, not only reduces incentives directly but also discourages production through the enhancement of price instability.

Efforts to resolve this unsatisfactory state of affairs through international negotiation, whether in the forums of FAO, GATT or UNCTAD, have been singularly disappointing due to the attitude of member governments.

A question of priorities and organisation

It would appear then that neither land resources, agricultural technology nor farm people stand in the way of expansion of food production. Such restraints on agricultural advancement as exist are principally of man's own making, taking the form mainly of sins of omission and commission on the part of national governments.

When inter-governmental conferences and the international agencies which are their servants issue pronouncements on world food problems, they usually shy away from, and are silent on, the obvious facts about the economic mismanagement of member governments in relation to their agricultural industries. Considerations of national sovereignty together with narrow self interest generally stand in the way of the acceptance by individual countries of external criticism or advice, unless manifested as technical aid. It is a pity that the example which the OECD has set in producing more incisive and more challenging criticisms of member countries' policies, is not more widely followed by international agencies. Incidentally, one advantage of the IAAE's association with the FAO in the seminar in December 1975 was that it enabled the latter organisation to throw off some of its customary shackles.

If the foregoing diagnosis be correct, the major problem of world food production is to devise ways of inspiring and influencing leaders and governments, particularly those of the developing countries, to upgrade the standard of their performance with respect to the agricultural sector. One thing is plain. Appropriate motivation is unlikely to be forthcoming as a result of periodic false alarms about imminent disasters. These only serve to encourage the old 'fire! fire!' syndrome. Adverse seasons and other natural disasters seem to do little to encourage positive action as they tend to be dismissed as 'acts of God'.

In most of the developing countries, farmers, despite the relative superiority of their numbers, are usually ineffective in influencing government action. Indeed, in some countries, (in Latin America for instance), governments have even taken steps to repress farmers' organisations because they recognise them as a potential challenge to their authority [12]. In advanced countries, such organisations as well as agriculturally based political parties are losing their basis of power because of dwindling farmer numbers. An early resolution to the problem is therefore unlikely to come through farmer pressure.

Conclusion

To sum up, it is clear that even now there is a wealth of knowledge about methods of achieving agricultural development. What is lacking is knowledge of ways of getting the appropriate action implemented. This is basically a problem in human organisation, not a problem of resources, of technology or of economics.

Notes

[1] United Nations, Department of Social and Economic Affairs, *Concise Report on the World Population Situation in 1970–75 and its Long-Range*

Implications, Population Studies No. 56, New York, 1974, pp. 37–70.
[2] See, for example, N. Georgescu-Roegen, 'Energy and Economic Myths', *Southern Economic Journal*, vol. 41, no. 3, January 1975, pp. 347–381.
[3] I refer, in particular, to Randall's recent derogatory remarks concerning the observations of Schultz and Ruttan elaborated at the previous conference of the IAAE. See Alan Randall, 'Growth, Resources and Environment: Some Conceptual Issues', *American Journal of Agricultural Economics*, vol. 57, no. 5, December 1975, p. 804.
[4] United States Department of Agriculture, Economic Research Service, *The World Food Situation and Prospects to 1985*, Foreign Agricultural Economic Report no. 98, p. 59.
[5] W.H. Pawley, 'In the year 2070', *Ceres*, vol. 4, no. 4, July-August 1971, pp. 22–27.
[6] A.S. Rojko and P.M. O'Brien, 'Organizing Agriculture for the Year 2000', in Douglas Ensminger (ed.), *Food Enough or Starvation for Millions*, Tata McGraw-Hill, New Delhi, 1977, p. 347.
[7] Cf. US National Academy of Sciences, *Agricultural Production Efficiency*, Washington, 1975, pp. 132–149.
[8] R.E. Evenson and Y. Kislev, *Agricultural Research and Productivity*, Yale University Press, New Haven, 1975, p. 16.
[9] *Sydney Morning Herald*, 31 May, 1976.
[10] Keith O. Campbell, 'The Effects of Urbanization on Agriculture', in Douglas Ensminger (ed.), *op. cit.*, pp. 441 and 446.
[11] For example, see D. Gale Johnson, *World Agriculture in Disarray*, Macmillan, London, 1973.
[12] J.W.Y. Higgs, 'Farmers' Organization and People's Participation in Rural Development', in Douglas Ensminger (ed.), *op. cit.*, pp. 507–8 .

The prospects of the food situation in the world: from the pessimistic standpoint

Joseph Klatzmann

It may seem rather paradoxical that I was asked to speak on the world food problem from the pessimistic standpoint, when various people consider me to be of the optimistic group. In fact, there is no contradiction. I am optimistic as far as natural resources and the possibilities of techniques are concerned. I am pessimistic as far as human behaviour is concerned.

Before going any further, one wonders about the real extent of the food problem in the world. Opinions vary in this respect. Certain experts accuse the FAO of voluntarily worsening the situation. I have recently read an article published in a very serious American review in which the author states that only seventy million people in the world are suffering from lack of food. We must not be too surprised to find such contradictory opinions. In fact, to appreciate the food situation of a country or of a certain group of people one has to compare consumptions which are not well known to needs which are no better known. The FAO evaluations often vary as well for the needs as for the appreciation of the food situation of some countries.

The problem stated

This is the reason why, disregarding the notion of needs, I have defined what I call the 'satisfactory' nutrition level — that which is abundant and varied enough to fulfil man's wants without affecting his health. I am not concerned if experts 'prove' that we can live very well with 1,600 calories daily. The important thing for me is that an individual who has got only 1,600 calories effectively suffers from hunger. On this basis, it can be considered that billions of people suffer from insufficient nutrition, hundreds of millions are hungry, while some hundreds of millions of people affect their health by an excess of nutrition.

Whatever some people say, the food problem in the world is just there. I want to remind you that the food is so unevenly distributed that the problem could really be dealt with by a better allocation. After all, the food production in the world at present corresponds closely to 2,400 calories per person daily, with an amount of protein which meets people's needs to a large extent and with twenty grams of animal protein. This production increases slightly faster than the population. It can even be noted that twenty million tons of cereals (less than two per cent of world production) are needed to increase the calories of the most underfed people from 1,500 to 2,000 per person daily, thus making the problem of hunger disappear. To obtain these twenty million tons of cereals, those people who affect their health by an excessive consumption of animal fats must be prepared to reduce by a few kilos per person annually their consumption of meat which would still be excessive after this reduction. Everybody, the wealthiest as well as the poorest, will then benefit from better health.

But all these considerations regarding a better distribution are not practical. The only way of resolving the world food problem is, in fact, to increase production. I have calculated that, to make sure that the whole population in the world is provided with what I call satisfactory nutrition, the actual food resources should be increased by more than fifty per cent. I believe neither in a massive production of foods which are originally non-agricultural (including sea foods), nor in a significant extension of cultivated land. I have, however, come to the conclusion that it would be possible to increase food production by at least four times and this would allow a population of more than ten billion to have a satisfactory amount of food. With some precautions, this performance could be achieved without hazarding the future at the expense of pollution and destruction of natural resources.

Lastly, I hold today a point of view which I have already expressed several times: there is no obstacle which cannot be overcome technically to getting the agricultural potential of the world started; even the most traditional small scale agriculture can undergo evolution, if necessary means are used (such as extension services, financial assistance, etc.). Certainly progress cannot occur overnight everywhere. But a growth rate of four or five per cent per annum is certainly not impossible to achieve in countries where application of the techniques which are already known would enable the output per unit surface area to increase by twice or even three times.

However, despite these possibilities, the situation does not improve at all. During the development decade between 1960 and 1970, the production of food *per capita* has scarcely changed at all in the countries of the Third World, whether in Africa, Asia or Latin America. And if this is so for the average for an entire continent, it necessarily implies that the food resources per head in many countries have decreased, sometimes to a very large degree. Even if we take into account the unfavourable weather conditions of certain years, the analysis of the course of events ever since 1970 is not encouraging at all. There is no indication of improvement whatsoever. It is not worthwhile to mention again here figures which are already very well known.

Necessary conditions for solving the problem

If the agricultural potential of the world is so badly utilised, there must be some reason. Certain conditions ought to be fulfilled, and they are not. It is these conditions which I am going to mention now. And the conclusion will follow naturally thereafter. I will undoubtedly be blamed for not giving examples in my exposé. But when what I am saying is applicable to twenty, sixty or hundred countries, why should I mention one rather than the other, why should I point out this one rather than the other one? I will also be told that I just restate things that everyone knows. But this reminder is necessary to justify my conclusion.

No agricultural progress can occur without important investments and consequently without financial and technical help from rich countries to poor countries. Undoubtedly, for a certain period of time, a huge sum of money would have to be spent yearly in order to be able to solve the food problem in the world fast enough. But this sum is relatively insignificant compared to military expenditure which amounts to hundreds of billions of dollars. One wonders if there are grounds these days to hope for a reduction of military expenditure in the world.

For sure, public opinion in rich countries is today aware of the food problem. But not to the extent of being prepared to pay the costs involved to solve this problem. What are the election chances of a political party which included in its programme a high increase of taxes to assist poor countries? Today's reality is rather a reduction in assistance, in terms of percentage of Net National Product. On the other hand, assistance from the rich countries can be accepted by the poor countries only if it is not involved with political pressures. A multilateral aid, granted by an international organisation, is in this case a necessary but unfortunately insufficient condition. But it would be entirely unrealistic to dare to hope that the rich, whoever they are, and the owners of raw materials will be prepared to grant disinterested aid. All the international meetings throw light on the national selfishness and the dependence of poor countries upon the few big powers. And this dependence can lead the poor countries to refuse, because of its origin, technical assistance which could have been useful to them.

Among the kinds of assistance which rich countries grant to the poor, the supply of food products can play an essential role. In the very short run, only this can withstand crisis situations. At the intermediate stage, it may help to achieve necessary investments. But I wonder if we can hope that the conditions will be realised which will make this assistance effective. Do the countries which receive food aid have the necessary equipment to keep the products without waste and to transport them quickly to where they are most needed? Do they have the indispensable administrative organisation so that the assistance can be utilised effectively? For their rich consumers should not derive benefits from low priced sale. The food aid should not restrain the growth of local production and it should not benefit speculators. When we think of the difficulties of distributing aid in the best equipped countries, in terms of both administration and infrastructure, one can imagine how the situation could be in most less favoured countries.

In many countries, it is the system of ownership which constitutes the main obstacle to agricultural development. Certainly, many agrarian reforms have already been realised. But how many of these reforms were successful and without secondary negative effects?

In agriculturally advanced countries, which must increase (or rather which ought to increase) their agricultural production in order to increase their food aid to the poor countries, it is possible to define the types of agriculture which would limit the risks of pollution and exhaustion of natural resources. In particular, the farmers of these countries ought to give up specialisation and come back to a mixed agricultural system, combining plant and animal production. But who will find the economic incentives which will stimulate the farmers to take into consideration the long term interests against their immediate interests? And who will find the economic incentives to realise economies of energy which are possible in the agribusiness system? Certainly, it is not the ideas which are lacking in this realm. But which countries have been successful in taking effective measures, against the coalition of pressure groups?

The political will

I have already mentioned many conditions. But I have not yet reached the essential one, the condition which involves all the others — and this is the will. This one can produce wonders, provided that it is possessed at the same time by those who help and those who receive assistance. Thanks to this double will, we have seen some countries of the Third World succeed, in a few years, in building modern and effective armies. Would there still be insurmountable obstacles if this same will was applied to agricultural development?

But what does 'want' mean? Is there only one political leader of a country of the Third World who will say that he does not want to solve the food problem in his country? But if one really wants to do something, this means that he has made up his mind to carry out whatever is necessary to have his intentions fulfilled. As far as the food problem is concerned, this implies giving an effective priority to agriculture. There is no hope as long as the leaders of a country remain convinced that the secret of development lies in industrialisation — and more particularly in the creation of heavy industry. In such a context, it is not only regarding the distribution of investments that agriculture is in an unfavourable position. Being considered as an activity of secondary importance for the future of the country, it bears a not too high social status. The consequences of such a situation are more serious than one thinks.

In fact, there cannot be a true agricultural development without progress of the large mass of small and traditional farmers. It is not by just creating a modern sector that the problem can be solved in the long term. To make traditional agriculture undergo progress, the indispensable financial aid must be coupled with a considerable effort. Past experience shows that intensive extension service can achieve wonders, provided that the people involved are numerous, competent and dedicated. The basic extension worker who works directly with the peasants must possess numerous qualities. He does not have the right to make mistakes on the technical plan because any mistake that he makes would lead to a loss of faith in progress which is still fragile on the part of small farmers. Moreover, he must be a good psychologist, else his action might undergo the risk of being entirely inefficient. How does one find such men who would dedicate themselves to agriculture, if their rewards and social status are much inferior to those of their friends who work in the central administration of the capital of the country? Certainly, a few good souls will be found, but there will never be enough good souls, in any country, to make the big mass of traditional agriculture progress.

I would be told that the declarations concerning the essential role of agriculture are not lacking in the countries of the Third World. But it is not the declarations which are involved. It is the efficient ways of handling matters on the part of those in charge which will show the essential role that agriculture plays in the economic future and independence of the country and which must convince the people involved that agriculture actually bears a high social status. In how many countries is it so, today, in the world? To believe that this place will be yielded to agriculture, in spirit and in the hearts, is to dream, is to believe in Utopia. But I am now going to reach the peak of Utopia: the existence of a world organisation which will be in charge of the resources in the world – an organisation which would be independent of all political pressure and which would have at its disposition all the means to apply its decisions.

In fact, various actions cannot be executed at the level of the countries themselves. Can we allow a country alone to make the decision of carrying out a big operation which involves ecological threats to the world at large? And how does one determine the priorities among large investments, which cannot be fulfilled all at the same time? By what means and where does one start? How does one best distribute the means of production which for some reason exist in insufficient quantities for certain periods of time? Contrary to what some people think, I am not suggesting the creation of a new world organisation, for it would be a 'caricature' of what I consider as desirable. I can only say that in the absence of such an organisation, the world resources will be misused.

If agricultural progress is not fast enough, can we hope to solve the world food problem by a decreased population growth in the poor countries? The fact is that unforeseen changes occur sometimes. Who had foreseen the high drop in birth rate in most wealthy countries? Who consequently is able to foresee what is likely to happen in the poor countries? In 1976, nobody knows for sure what the world population will be at the end of the century, the margin of error is equal to some hundred millions. However, we must not believe that a slow down of the population growth will allow us to solve the world food problem in the next decades. Most of the adults of the year 2000 have already been born. A high decrease in birth rates, towards the end of the century, would change the age pyramids but this would have a limited impact upon the world needs for food, the needs of young children for energy being much lower than those of adults. As regards a very important and very rapid decrease in birth rates, it does not seem possible and is especially not something to wish for. In fact, the rapid transition of a growth rate of three per cent, for instance, to a growth rate of zero, would completely transform the structure of the age pyramid, with unfavourable consequences which would still be very acute after half a century, if not a century. Thus, even if we wish for a certain slow down of demographic growth in the countries of the Third World, the only way in which the world food problem can be solved is to increase resources of food and hence of agricultural production.

But if the military expenses do not decrease in the world, if the wealthy countries keep on cutting down their assistance to the poor, instead of increasing it, if there is absolutely no hope that food aid will be highly increased and utilised much more efficiently, if a sufficient priority is not granted to agriculture in the poor countries, if the desire of creating modern armies overrides that of improving agriculture, if the utilisation of resources is directed to meet the interests of the powerful and not towards a neutral end, how can we be optimistic? Of course, I am not now talking about the year 2050. I am convinced that, in the long run, humanity will eventually be able to solve the problem prior to a specific disaster. For the next decades alas, nothing allows us to hope for a significant improvement of the food situation in the world. Billions of people will still suffer from malnutrition and hundreds of millions from hunger. I can only wish for one thing, and that is that reality defies these pessimistic outlooks. I wish it will but I dare not hope for it.

Discussion on papers by Krasovec and Singh and by Bhattacharjee

Alberto Valdés

Messrs Singh and Krasovec and Bhattacharjee have presented us with a comprehensive and perceptive synopsis of the Rome seminar. They have been remarkably successful in extracting the common views from such a vast array of economic and socio-political situations. My congratulations to these authors.

In this opportunity it is not possible for me to examine the very specific aspects of their interpretation of the papers presented in Rome. To do so would require me to have had the forty-one papers at hand and time to have ready them. Three days while simultaneously attending the conference precludes this.

At the Rome seminar, in addition to discussion of the relationship between food production and population at a global level, emphasis was given to the interactions between demographic and socio-economic factors in rural development in the setting of the six country studies. I understand that the authors of the country studies are to be present today; they, as authors, are more qualified than I to judge the paper by Bhattacharjee. Therefore, assuming that they will contribute to the general discussion on the subject, I will not refer to any particular country study. Instead, most of my comments will be addressed to (a) aspects related to the discussion on the global food demand and supply gap, and (b) some issues related to economic policies in general.

On the first aspect, Krasovec and Singh are right when they argue that the growing dependence on LDCs (Less Developed Countries) on food imports from DCs (Developed Countries) is seen as posing the biggest problem for the future. Food imports refer to cereals (wheat, rice, coarse grains and millets), which dominate the issue of food supply in LDCs. In fact, very recent projections for the next decade found in a recent study — and my apologies for not referring to the year 2000, but it exceeds my comprehension — conclude that 'unless the trend in production in LDCs (developing market economies only) improves, the production of cereals will fall short of meeting food demand in food deficit countries by approximately 100 million tons in 1985/86. This compares with shortfalls of 45 million tons during the food crisis years (1974/75) and an average of 28 million tons in the relatively good production years 1969/71' [1].

This relatively short time interval (until 1985/86) precludes the possibility of significantly altering the population factor. This implies that, during the next decade, the food demand and supply balance depends, to a large extent, on increasing the supply of food. In addition, what makes the problem even more difficult within the LDCs is the fact that the core of the food deficit problem exists in the low income countries (i.e. with *per capita* incomes of less than $200 per year). The same study concludes that 'to finance imports of such magnitude would appear to be beyond any prospects of these countries having the foreign exchange to do so.' These conclusions project a dramatic, arduous situation for the next decade.

However, as useful as they are, the discussions concerning global projections fail to present the problem in a manner which lends itself to practical analysis and action. In discussing the food situation, assuming that grain exporters will have the capacity to meet the growing world demand at reasonable prices, a critical issue which I believe did not receive adequate attention at the Rome seminar is that of linking explicitly the food deficit to the foreign exchange position. We usually assume, implicitly, a positive correlation between food deficit and foreign exchange deficit countries. Is this so?

Of the six countries reported in J.P. Bhattacharjee's paper on the issue of food and population, only one of them, India, is a serious food deficit country. This, in spite of the fact that these six were chosen as representative of the different LDCs position in the food/population equation. What we urgently need, in my opinion, is to develop a country typology which would help us define the various situations in which a country might find itself. One of the criteria would be to classify countries according to their position − over time − in terms of degree of self sufficiency, foreign exchange constraints and major food supply policies. This classification would allow us to distinguish, for example, in which countries the food problem is soluble by increased imports (e.g. OPEC countries), those countries having no serious payments or aggregate food problems (Argentina, Brazil, Thailand, Colombia), those countries in which the food problem is aggravated by trade problems (probably the case of India, Bangladesh and some in the Sub-Sahara region), those countries which exhibit possible category change (Indonesia, if the 1967/74 trend prevails) etc. Such categorisation among countries would help to isolate the different policy choices and the needs and forms of international action for each country situation.

In the two papers in question, mention is made of the differentiation between effective demand and 'target' demand, considering food distribution and nutrition within a country. However, I believe we are still a long way from successfully presenting an analysis conducive to practical solutions in the area of food distribution oriented towards target population groups. This problem area is under-researched.

There are some contrasts between the studies reported by Krasovec and Singh on the general issues and the country studies reported by Bhattacharjee, which, I believe, reflect the difficulty of discussions at the global level. Two that draw my attention are related to the areas of (a) resource development (including public investment in research and physical infrastructure) and (b) price and trade policies, broadly defined.

The country studies reported by Bhattacharjee give emphasis to these aspects. In contrast, the papers reported in Krasovec and Singh practically omit these topics altogether. Is this by design, or is it inherent in a global discussion with reference to no particular country?

When we speak about removing the constraints which affect the performance of the small farmer — the representative farmer in LDCs — both at the Rome seminar and at this meeting in Nairobi I sense a growing amount of agreement around the belief that the most serious constraint is not the farmer's behaviour *per se*. A growing body of evidence shows that the most serious constraints to the farmer are environmental; moreover, many of these constraints are state-imposed. Others are the result of input and output market imperfections. Thus, as it was argued yesterday by a participant from Pakistan, the scope for increasing resource productivity by action at the broad policy level is relatively greater than that at the farmer's level.

As argued in general terms by Krasovec and Singh, 'a new institutional structure to which the farmer can relate needs to be created', and this entails new obligations for research, infrastructure and input and output market policies.

However, as Professor Schultz has said, and rightly so in my opinion, although economics is sufficiently robust to examine alternative policie, we agricultural economists, with few exceptions, have been rather unable to challenge the politicians on their economic and institutional policies for agriculture. But perhaps this can only be discussed in the setting of a particular country. The resulting, perhaps inevitable, generality that occurs whenever we discuss issues which belong to the area of domestic policies is one of the difficulties I find in global overviews as in the papers reported by Krasovec and Singh.

Firstly, in the area of resource development, there is no need to defend the claim that in the long run, in most regions of the world, the prime mover of agricultural production has been technological change. And in most cases, technological change has been the result of government investment in research and infrastructure. A clear exception, however, can be seen in the exportable non-food agricultural raw materials, whose promotion and research have been predominantly in the hands of the private sector. In contrast, studies such as those by Evenson and Kislev [2] show us how little most of the LDCs are investing, relative to DCs, in agricultural research. We, as agricultural economists, aside from our rhetoric regarding the need for development of improved technology for crops and livestock production, have been of questionable efficacy in helping the biologist in the design of technology and in assisting the policy maker in the allocation of public funds for technological development. The lack of attention to these issues in the reports themselves is indicative of the inadequate awareness within the profession. With the exception of EMBRAPA in Brazil and the efforts of a couple of non-Latin Americans, Latin America could be cited as an example of this unfortunate situation. In the field of international action, it was unfortunate that at the Rome seminar we missed the opportunity of learning about the past achievements and expected contributions, in terms of productivity change, from the nine international agricultural research network centres, located in Asia, Africa and Latin America.

Secondly, on the issue of price policies, J.P. Bhattacharjee points out that according to the country reports, the weaknesses of these countries' policies are the familiar ones. My concern and difficulty with these reports is that I somehow feel that we are failing to represent adequately the policy options, considering the interests of producers, consumers and the government. Self sufficiency, as an objective, appears in nearly every case. But we agree, I believe, that effective government strategies with respect to food supplies must necessarily involve more than one, in fact, a mix of objectives, such as:

— minimising the social cost of food, perhaps at the expense of some increased variability;
— increasing the degree of self sufficiency, and what is not necessarily the same,
— increasing food security;
— relating the effect of the above to income distribution between urban consumers and agricultural producers.

It is difficult to see how governments can thoroughly examine issues such as pricing of domestic supplies or determine the 'required' degree of intervention in domestic markets and in trade, etc., without some explicit recognition of a possible trade-off between these objectives. Could Dr Bhattacharjee expand his comments explaining the kind of conceptual framework behind the food supply strategies pursued by the countries studied? What can we learn about the actual policy options and trade-offs of these policies?

Finally, I expect a lively debate from the audience in this plenary session around Dr Singh's conclusion — which I believe is his own rather than the paper's — in which he argues that, without transforming agriculture along co-operative lines, it is most unlikely that land and labour productivity will be raised 'adequately'. I presume he means social production entities and not simply co-operatives for the supply of certain input and/or marketing of production.

Notes

[1] IFPRI — 'Meeting Food Needs in the Developing World: The Location and Magnitude of the Task in the Next Decade', Research Report Number 1, February 1976, Washington, D.C.
[2] R. Evenson and Y. Kislev, *Agricultural Research and Productivity*, Yale University Press, New Haven, Connecticut, 1975.

Discussion on papers by Campbell and Klatzmann

I.I. May-Parker

I think that both speakers have looked at the same coin but from opposite sides and have come to almost the same conclusions. Before making a few points which have been insufficiently stressed there are two items I would like to make clear:
1. It is clear from the two major papers that when we are discussing increased food production and population control we are usually referring to the developing economies.
2. Agriculture in these economies should not be looked upon solely as a profession but also as a way of life for the majority of the people.

The variables required for increasing production which I feel have not been adequately stressed include the available techniques and institutions.

Both Campbell and Klatzmann seemed to have assumed that the available techniques for increasing production in developing countries already exist. Klatzmann says 'a growth rate of four to five per cent per annum is certainly not impossible to achieve in countries where application of the techniques which are already known would enable the output per unit surface area to increase by twice or even three times.' I do not agree with this. The techniques which are already available are not easily applicable in developing agricultures. The required techniques in most cases have not yet been developed. Often when known techniques have been applied they have failed. Why have farmers not taken up new techniques as fast as we expect? Do we recognise that techniques often call for other inputs which the farmers generally cannot afford and call for new methods of farming which might change the farmers' way of life? In order to increase production as envisaged by most optimists about developing agriculture we need to develop techniques which are suited to the large number of small farmers who make up much of the industry in the developing world.

Both Campbell and Klatzmann mentioned the part which institutions could play in creating grounds for optimism — or pessimism. In most developing economies farmers are still in the subsistence state or are just moving out of it. The institutions available to them do tend to be those which are suited to subsistence agriculture. Further, most of the new institutions that have been developed are replicas of those of the old colonial mother countries and not applicable in the developing countries, or are institutions set up to meet the needs of the mother countries. Any change in agricultural practice to promote food production should also lead to changes in the institutional pattern. I therefore disagree with Campbell when he says 'we should discount the immediate need for, and potential benefits from, institutional structure that could cater for the small farmers.'

Among institutional variables which are not suited to the developing agriculture are the market delivery system for both inputs and outputs, particularly for food crops. This is very poor or is non-existent in traditional agriculture — farmers hardly purchase any inputs and most of their output is sold at the farmgate.

Summary of discussion from the floor

Perhaps the aspects of the whole food and population situation which seemed to attract most discussion were those of political will and political skill in implementing policy, the choice of appropriate policy, the effectiveness of customary approaches to population control, institutions, and aspects of education, technological and general.

The discussion of policy, though occupying more time than that on most other issues, was not wholly coherent. There seemed to be a feeling that policies had not been rigorously enough developed. For example, it was argued that long term contracts for food such as those between the US and Japan and USSR were, as effected, as much of a disincentive to developing countries' agricultural output as was food aid. They mean that surpluses which might be available from LDCs would not find a worthwhile market and thus these countries would be forced to a policy geared purely to satisfy their own internal needs. Policies should in fact be keyed to the resource/population pattern of the countries concerned. Much too little attention had been given to handling the problems of regional policies for agriculture in developing countries where, often, regional disparities in situation were very considerable. In relation to the resources used to feed those sectors of the world's population eating at very high levels it was commented that criticism of the situation was frequently met but it was not developed to the point of a policy proposal. One might be (though the implications of this were not developed) a policy of taxation of meat. Bearing in mind that many countries had experienced massive migration from rural areas to towns the importance of distinguishing in policy matters between marketed food supplies and total food supplies was stressed. What governments needed was usually supplies which could flow to where they were needed. There was some feeling that the really important decisions might still remain to be made and the responsibility of the economist in choosing his research areas and disseminating the results of his researches in order to make for more effective policy was stressed. There was not, however, any extended discussion of the problems of relating the central policy decision maker to the researcher.

In respect of population, although the general problems created by pressing numbers of people were recognised, there were various hints of greater complexities in the population story than had been tabled in the main paper. For example, evidence was referred to that showed that the level of fertility varied between countries and regions and that certain economic variables affected the birth rate. Again, evidence from South East Asia was referred to suggesting that where the asset level of the family (mainly land) was low the desire for children was greater — perhaps to be seen as an investment in security. However, this pattern was subject to variation with the likely opportunity for labour earnings. Where, for example, the labour market for a particular caste was saturated the birth rate was high, whereas if it were work for another caste then the birth rate was lower. This suggested that a good deal more research on motivation as regards desired family size was needed. There was also reference to a question whether family planning as an attack on population problems was likely to be effective where tribalism was still an emphatic feature of the scene. Family planning might need, in such situations, to be deferred until the pattern of tribal emphais had been modified.

The lack of human will for development and the factors affecting it was a subject of varied comment. Some felt that the operations of large enterprises, dominant in rich countries and exploiting poor countries by a variety of activities, were important. Poor countries needed to put themselves, if they could, into good strong positions for negotiation — as OPEC had done over oil — if they were to be able to take the road to a better situation. More attention needed to be given to an inventory of ways of improving the joint operation of developing countries and much more attention needed to be given to this. Others saw the kind of capital intensive approaches interlocking with 'the green revolution', as by their nature almost designed to disrupt the will to achieve better things of the body of the population of developing countries.

Institutional changes were also a subject of a diversity of contribution. The idea that they led to a fall in output was contested, Chilean data being quoted to show a rise in output per unit and per head following land reform measures. Though the importance of the institutional element in the whole picture clearly got general support, the discussion did not help greatly in deciding whether the pessimists were justified in their view that necessary institutional changes were unlikely to occur rapidly.

The special problems of small part-time farmers were discussed at some length. There were obviously doubts as to whether extension services were in fact effectively helping the small farmer to develop or indeed whether thoroughly perceptive research into the economic behaviour of small farmers had been undertaken on the scale required. The reference to part time farming attracted a question about where such farmers were going to operate — were they on the fringes of towns only? If so, did this have any particular relevance to the great mass of agricultural activity in the country?

Although the subject did not always arise directly there were numerous references to the importance of marketing in furthering agricultural economic development. Considerable need was discerned for further studies identifying the local problems of marketing and distribution, particularly for the needs of countries' internal markets and for developing appropriate processing and marketing organisation. Finally a very forceful emphasis was given to the importance of developing general education as a fundamental requirement if many of the changes spoken of under specific headings were to be feasible. This was linked to the importance of effective extension services, information services, international flows of situation appraisal information and the like.

The importance of improved inter-human and international relationships came up from a number of original contributions. The nationalistic behaviour of many countries was seen as, in effect, a form of 'apartheid' and there was some feeling that all kinds of 'apartheid' were severely detrimental to human development and that there might be benefit from recognising that most countries behave indefensively.

The general discussion followed a series of somewhat disparate lines of thought. Fairly general agreement was expressed on the importance of 'integrated rural development', but it was emphasised that trying to do everything at once would bring disaster. Priorities were essential. Some saw 'unimodal' strategies for agricultural development which would promote increases in productivity and income amongst a large and growing fraction of households as high on the list, as it becomes recognised as a strategy which makes feasible both employment and livelihood for a growing farm population. It was seen, too, as possibly providing a favourable environment for the spread of family planning. An important associated development was seen to be an integrated programme for the delivery of nutrition, health and family planning services in a way that would achieve very wide coverage of the rural population. In turn this was seen as involving active participation of local communities and provision for using local resources in eliminating under-nutrition. Some of the speakers believed that there were ample resources at the grass roots level to achieve this but unless there was the will effectively applied at the village level there was no hope of getting change simply through promotion at the national level.

The technical possibilities for expansion were referred to at various levels. For instance, the importance of increased supplies of inputs (e.g. fertilisers) in India in recent years in creating an output level which was not previously expected for another 5 years held the hope that, with still further increases in technical inputs, advances in production could be looked for at a very attractive rate. However, even though a 'doomsday' outlook did not figure largely in the discussion it was stressed that a number of resources were likely to become more costly as less accessible and less convenient sources had to be drawn on. There was also some discussion of the factors which in practice would govern the carbon producing capacity of the world and the possible interaction of the systems leading to food production and the live systems in the natural — or more or less natural — environment. This line of thought suggested that we may be being unduly complacent when we think of agriculture as requiring only a small part of the energy used in any industrialised country. We may need to consider the energy demands of the industrial sector on a very wide scale if we are to assess the prospective situation realistically.

Various contributors to the discussion agreed with Klatzmann's pessimism in saying that economic assistance by rich countries could not solve the food problems of the poor countries. It was noted, incidentally, that apart from a few minor countries and the OPEC group, developing countries are exporters of food. We distort the picture when we think in terms of cereals alone. However the next stage in this argument did not attract a similar consensus. While it might be agreed that a solution to the world food problem should be sought primarily in mobilisation of the internal resources of particular countries, there was a difference of view about the role of industrialisation. Some doubted the extent of its role in providing a basis for the development of agriculture in poor countries. Others regarded it as the key to solving these problems. They were not thinking in terms of heavy industry necessarily, though in some countries it did in fact provide the foundations for the development of agriculture. Some stressed the importance of a balanced industrial investment, which in poor countries might be largely orientated towards providing foundations for agricultural development based on direct deliveries of the domestic means of production of industrial origin and by financing imports of those means.

Some forceful sections of the discussion were concerned with the fact that the total supply of foodstuff relative to the total needs was not an effective indicator of the state of wellbeing of the food situation. Depending on the operation of the socio-political institutions and programmes, increased production could simply result in the rich eating better and the poor still starving. Distribution of income is man-determined. Those stressing this aspect did not think that the papers presented provided a concept of the problem in terms which contributed effectively to its solution. The core of the problem was the rapid growth of the numbers of people who were without adequate means of subsistence — without land and without sufficiently productive employment. Typically, such people have no political voice. We cannot expect that extra food supplies will be produced for those who cannot afford to pay for them and mere increase in food supplies will not prevent a growth of numbers of the people unable to get access to them. It was quite possible to picture science and technology itself precipitating a crisis — for example if new technologies permitted rapid increase in crop yields with reduction in the labour requirements. In principle such innovations could be beneficial but, in practice, with our present operational arrangements they probably would not be. We should, in these discussions, see food supply and income distribution as interdependent problems to be handled together. Put another way, the central problem is how both to absorb non-subsistence labour productively and to increase total production. If we are to progress on the critically important question of whose incomes, whose output and whose employment have to be improved we have to make fundamental changes in agricultural planning techniques.

Though strategies for increasing labour intensive technologies spreading the range of people benefiting under policy measures might be useful they would not make enough impact on the problem in many countries — the agricultural population was too big a proportion of the total. Application will have to be selective. Such approaches demanded a degree of political will with which we are not customarily familiar. It also needed the means to steer the economy more closely than we are accustomed to. Agricultural economists would need to play their part in identifying the target groups and means of reaching them. We confused the picture when we asked 'Will humanity avoid disaster?'; it is tolerating massive chronic and growing disaster all the time. The question is when will it be recognised as a disaster?

Much of the discussion related to governments, marketing and farmers but participants were urged to pay much more attention to the behaviour of the housewife and its importance in this picture. Housewives in low income farm households could respond to better opportunities much as could farmers. There was scope for better food storage, better household equipment and generally cheaper consumer durables. The prices of the latter are often very high because of inefficient manufacture or import substitution. We know that the human life span in low income countries has increased by forty per cent in the last twenty-five years but we fail to see the profound implications of this gain for productive labour and for the fewer births which would be needed — and, no doubt, desired — when adjustment to the longer life span is perceived.

Innovations generally were seen by some participants in the discussion as very closely linked with credit. Some aspects of this cross linked with discussions under other headings of the input picture; more credit means that a farmer has more productive energy under his control generally. However, we ought to give rather special emphasis to aspects of grass root involvement in the credit story. On the one hand, it was critically important to get farmers themselves involved with the operation of loan boards so that there would be widespread participation in the knowledge of the realities of credit. Further, working with this level should tap sources of funds which would free farmers from such heavy dependence on central government sources and would leave their destiny very much in their own hands.

Participants in the discussion included: M.K. Alhigazi, *Pakistan*; G. Ancey, *France*; P.C. Bansil, *Zambia*; H.F. Breimyer, *USA*; J. Brossier, *France*; W. Herer, *Poland*; B.F. Johnston, *USA*; L. Joy, *UK*; S. Kakli, *Pakistan*; D.H. Kim, *Korea*; J.F.S. Levi, *UK*; H.C. Love, *Canada*; M.E. Mlambiti, *Tanzania*; M.A.M. Maro, *Tanzania*; J.T. van Riemsdijk, *Netherlands*; R. Saran, *India*; T. Schultz, *USA*; R.G.F. Spitze, *USA*; J. Strasma, *USA*; D. Tomic, *Yugoslavia*; P. de la Vaissiere, *France*; A. Weber, *Federal Republic of Germany*.

J.P. Bhattacharjee in reply

I must express surprise at the lack of intervention in this discussion by the authors of the case studies. The main conclusions of these studies have not been challenged except in one case, but they will, I hope, be discussed in detail and critically in the Special Sessions.

Ram Saran, citing the record level of food grain production attained in 1975–76 in India, has rightly questioned, indeed challenged, the validity of Dandekar's rather gloomy projection about the likelihood of shortfall below the 1981 target. In support of his argument, Saran has mentioned the improved availability of critical inputs. I agree with his optimistic note as far as the supply and prices of fertilisers are concerned. It is also true that the 1975–76 performance has placed the growth of food grain production back on the trend of the sixties, and this has happened not only in India but also in the developing regions except Africa. It is too early to say whether this improvement will be sustained and whether the second half of this decade will be like the late sixties. However, there is evidence of a likely improvement in the cereals situation as compared to the 1972–74 period. How far the weather will co-operate is, of course, a critical question, especially in view of its unpredictable vagaries in this decade.

Valdés has made the point, which is widely recognised, that the assessment of the food problem, to be meaningful, should take into account the balance of payments situation of the countries, apart from their food deficit. Attempts to develop a typology for this purpose and classify countries are being made by WFC (the World Food Council) and FAO. In fact, WFC at the last meeting agreed in principle to the concept of 'Food Priority Countries' and recommended that the criteria for classifying such countries be further developed. Judging from the criteria and classification presented by the WFC secretariat, it is clear that the number of such countries will be large, the tentative number being forty-three out of more than a hundred developing countries. We should also keep in mind that the balance of payments deficit plagues all non-oil producing developing countries and there is arbitrariness in categorising its gravity.

The need for fundamental changes in government policies on mechanisation, research, prices and credit has been emphasised by a number of speakers and I have stressed these in my paper. I fully agree with Valdés about the desirability of a balanced approach to the analysis and formulation of price policy for output and input and of clearly spelling out options for decision makers. This is fully in line with my view about the inadequacy and inappropriateness of a limited, partial analysis of price policy and about the need for a systems approach, using simulation and other techniques to indicate the implications of different policies.

Schultz's point about the importance of better opportunities and higher level of living for farm households in contributing to family planning corresponds fully with the findings of the case studies. I would, in particular, emphasise the role and status of women and their integration in the programmes for farm and commodity development.

Joy's plea for a disaggregated, target group approach in the interests of effective nutrition planning is shared by me and has been covered in my observations on this point in the paper. However, one should keep one's balance and recognise that the food problem has a global dimension and a national dimension.

Johnston has sounded a very timely note of warning about the difficult choices involved in setting priorities among policies and design options for rural development. Indeed, unless choices are faced and decision-making proceeds quickly to the programme level, integrated rural development will face the danger of remaining merely as a slogan.

SPECIAL SESSION I

Achieving a Balance Between
Population and Food:

AFRICA

Food, population and rural development in Kenya: progress, policies, problems and prospects[*]

Leopold P. Mureithi and James O. Otieno

Introduction

Kenya's economic set-up

Kenya, by African standards, is a medium sized country covering an area of 582,646 square kilometres. Out of this, land area measures 569,250 square kilometres and the rest is water.

According to the 1962 population census 93 per cent of Kenya's population lived in rural areas. That proportion had declined to 90 per cent in 1969 so that urban population rose from 7 per cent in 1962 to 10 per cent of the total population in 1969. Between the two years rural population rose from 8.1 million to 9.9 million while urban population rose from 0.6 million to 1.1 million. These facts underline two things. The first is that, given the overall rate of population growth (3.3 per cent per annum), the urban areas could have gained in numbers largely due to movement of people from rural to urban areas. This is the familiar phenomenon of rural to urban migration which raises complex issues of population mobility and unemployment. The second is that rural development is synonymous with taking economic benefits where the majority of the people are. This has resource allocation and income distribution implications.

Some of the most interesting characteristics of Kenya's population include the fact that 51 per cent of the total population are children and dependants and only 49 per cent of the population could be considered active labour [1]. If the rate of population growth stays the same, total population will double every 22 years; there will be 15.9 million people in 1980 and about 34.0 million people by the year 2000. By that year urban population which grows at 8 per cent per year will have reached the 3.0 million mark.

GDP (Gross Domestic Product) in 1973 was valued at K£731.1 million in current prices, which is K£586.56 million in constant (1964) prices [2]. This GDP level was in fact 12.1 per cent higher than 1972. Over the ten year period since independence, the rate of growth of GDP at current prices has been in the order of 6.7 per cent per year. This high growth rate has been contributed to by the growth

---

[*] This is a revised version of a paper originally presented at the IAAE/UNFPA/FAO Seminar on Population and Food and Agricultural Development in Rome, Italy, in December 1975. The authors would like to thank J.P. Bhattacharjee, Martin David, Judith Heyer and R.P. Sinha for offering constructive comments, and the Food and Agriculture Organisation of the United Nations for financial assistance. Views express herein are those of the authors and should not be interpreted as reflecting the views of any institutions with which they may be associated.

of the industrial and service sectors whose average growth have been 8.1 per cent over the period. The agricultural sector on the other hand has grown at the rate of 6.5 per cent per year.

The contribution of agriculture (monetary) to GDP rose from K£53.1 million in 1964 to K£89.5 million in 1973 in real terms. There has been a relative decline of the agricultural sector contribution to the economy from 23.8 per cent in 1964 to 19.1 per cent in 1974. Apart from the important fact that the agricultural sector claims 90 per cent of the population it is also important to the economy in two other aspects; namely that it provides almost all the food requirements of the country, and that it is a very important foreign exchange earner. In 1973, for instance, agriculture contributed K£87.6 million to export earnings, which is 54 per cent of the national total. Leading agricultural exports include coffee (29.2 per cent), pyrethrum (3.0 per cent) and meat products (3.1 per cent) [3].

Kenya is primarily an agricultural country and 'rural areas comprise well over 98 per cent of the land area of Kenya' [4]; hence the predominance of agriculture in generating domestic income, creating employment, earning foreign exchange, etc., and the necessity to gear economic development to agriculture and agriculturally based activities.

Policy goals in agriculture

While the 1964—70 Development Plan focused upon rapid growth and the 1970—74 plan attempted to shift the locale of growth to the rural areas, in the 1974—78 Development Plan 'policies which have as their objectives agricultural and rural modernisation and income redistribution appear in every chapter and affect every sector of the economy' [5].

In the field of agriculture, the Kenya government intends, amongst other things, to improve the distribution of rural income by obtaining a significant increase in the proportion of farmers who obtain a cash income from their land; to devise methods of developing the less favoured areas and to promote a more even development among different areas of the country; to increase the opportunities for employment in the agricultural sector; and to improve standards of nutrition in the rural areas [6]. In a nutshell, the economic objectives in the rural areas encompass rural transformation and regional balance, nutritional improvement, employment generation and income distribution.

The primary objective of rural development is the enrichment of the material and social welfare of the rural population. To accomplish this, it may prove necessary to institute comprehensive regional and subregional planning covering all functional sectors. Rural development is a multisectoral activity which includes agricultural development, rural industry, the establishment or improvement of social overhead facilities or infrastructure (schools, clinics, roads, rural electrification, improvement in quality of rural housing, communications, water supply), and welfare services or programmes (e.g. disease control, improved nutrition, adult literacy, family planning).

Some of these factors will be examined in this paper.

Agricultural production and population growth

Recent past experience

In this section we examine the historical experience of Kenya with respect to population change and agricultural output. A count of immigrant (non-African) population in Kenya was undertaken as early as 1911. This was repeated in 1921, 1926 and 1931. In 1946 and 1947 an estimate of African population was made. Total population in those two years was 5.2 million and 5.3 million, respectively. The first reasonably comprehensive census of population in Kenya was undertaken in 1948. Another census was carried out in 1962 and 1969. Estimates for intercensal years are regularly published. Table 1 gives Kenya's population estimates for the period 1946 to 1973 and annual rates of growth implicit in these totals.

Between 1946 and 1973 there has been differing degrees of coverage. Estimates for non-censal years are based on the previous census plus annual adjustments for migration and natural increase. The latter takes into account assumed trends in fertility and mortality. There has been gradual public awareness of the advantage of registration and government extension of the areas of compulsory registration. In this regard, it should be noted that in the years 1968 and 1969 there was a doubling of compulsory registration areas from seven in 1967 to fourteen in 1969. This may have been responsible for the overshooting of the annual rate of population change in 1968. For reasons explained in this paragraph, the estimates for 1958 and 1959 might have been underestimates.

The contribution of agriculture to GDP is given in Table 2. Here too, are included time series of the economy's output of livestock and food crops in both monetary and nonmonetary sectors. These figures are subject to the usual statistical, enumeration and valuation problems inherent in national income estimation in developing countries, in particular, the figures for the nonmonetary sector are imputed educated guesses. But they give a picture of the total foodstuffs available in the economy.

A notion of how the two magnitudes — food and population — have been faring is given by a comparison of their respective rates of growth. The difference between the rate of growth of agricultural production and that of population gives the rate of growth of agricultural production *per capita*. If that gap is negative this is an indication of a lean year. This suggests that the years 1956—58 were years of agricultural prosperity. The years 1960—61 were lean years; in fact there was widespread drought in 1960 and devastating floods in 1961—62. Between 1966 and 1968 agricultural output per head declined markedly. There are indications that the year 1973—74 was a disappointing year for agriculture [7]. The frequency of the incidence of famine and drought in Kenya has been clarified by T.R. Masaya who found that, in a decade, one would expect 3.6 bumper maize harvests and 2

Table 1
Annual population estimates, 1946–1973

Year	Population	Annual rate of change (%)
1946	5,152,000	2.35
1947	5,273,000	2.52
1948	5,405,966	2.26
1949	5,528,000	2.37
1950	5,659,000	2.35
1951	5,792,000	2.33
1952	5,927,000	2.31
1953	6,064,000	2.36
1954	6,207,000	2.40
1955	6,356,000	2.41
1956	6,509,000	2.41
1957	6,666,000	2.27
1958	6,817,000	1.56
1959	7,880,000	1.71
1960	8,115,000	2.92
1961	8,352,000	3.40
1962	8,636,263	2.44
1963	8,847,000	2.90
1964	9,104,000	2.87
1965	9,365,000	2.97
1966	9,643,000	2.96
1967	9,928,000	2.83
1968	10,209,000	7.19
1969	10,942,705	2.58
1970	11,225,000	3.97
1971	11,671,000	3.39
1972	12,067,000	3.44
1973	12,483,000	

Source: Statistical Abstract, various years.

moderate harvests with about 6.4 food shortages [8]. Maize shortage is synonymous with food shortage because of maize's importance as a staple food for many Kenyans. Besides, maize shortage is likely to be ushered in by rainfall shortage so that other crops, e.g. vegetables, etc., are also likely to be short.

What we see is an uneasy balance between agricultural production and population growth. The problem can be solved either from the demand side by reducing increases in consumers (population policy) or from the supply side by augmenting

Table 2
Value of agricultural output in Kenya

Year	Total agricultural product (K£ million)	Annual rate of change (%)	Food crops and livestock (K£ million)	Annual rate of change (%)
1955	69.80	12.2		
1956	78.29	1.3	19.16	2.1
1957	79.27	1.1	20.55	25.1
1958	80.11	1.5	25.71	1.1
1959	81.41	4.5	26.00	7.9
1960	85.04	−4.1	28.06	−26.1
1961	81.52	−16.4	20.75	0.3
1962	68.21	49.4	20.82	5.6
1963	101.95	14.1	21.98	−2.9
1964	126.29	−11.8	21.35	27.2
1965	111.44	25.5	27.15	13.6
1966	139.89	0.8	30.85	18.8
1967	141.03	1.9	36.65	11.9
1968	143.72	0.2	41.01	1.5
1969	144.02	15.3	41.64	3.6
1970	165.99	3.9	43.15	12.7
1971	172.52	17.3	48.65	15.9
1972	202.35	10.9	56.39	
1973	222.49			

Sources: *Statistical Abstract*, various years; *Economic Survey*, 1975.

agricultural production. In the past, deficits in food supply have been made good by importation of maize principally from the United States of America. Progressively, storage facilities of maize and other food crops have been and are being improved so that strategic stocks can be carried over from bumper to lean years. Besides, the hybrid maize revolution and improvements in crop husbandry have recently tended to reverse the bleak picture of the food situation in Kenya.

At the macro level, the picture of food availability is fairly good. But at the micro level, we still have to contend with distributional and accessibility problems so that the quantity of food intake is adequate for each member of the population. Besides, even if the quantity is adequate it does not automatically follow that the quality of food intake is adequate in terms of nutritional characteristics.

'*Per capita* food intake is of special importance because of (a) its direct effect on human welfare and happiness, (b) its indirect effect on output through influence on the capability of a man to perform work and the attitude of man toward work, and (c) its indirect effect on *per capita* income through influence on death rates and hence on population growth. In low income countries, agricultural productivity and incomes are such that both the quantity and quality of food consumed is low ... large numbers of people have a diet which is lacking in important qualitative features, such as certain amino acids and vitamins. As a result, health is impaired, resistance to disease is lowered and capacity to work is reduced.' [9]

Knowledge of the state of human nutrition in such countries as Kenya comes largely from three major types of studies: food balance sheets, dietary surveys and medical and clinical studies.

The most obvious constraint towards making these studies is lack of statistical data. Dietary and clinical surveys of the nutritional status in Kenya have been done but these have been of limited coverage and are of limited usefulness [10]. The most recent attempt to construct a food balance sheet was made by Lawrence Smith in 1973 [11] and was subsequently improved upon by the World Bank Mission of 1973 [12].

The World Bank's, as well as Smith's, analysis of the food situation involved two essential steps. First, an assessment of *per capita* consumption of each food commodity was made. This was done through food balance sheets with apparent consumption levels obtained by substracting net exports and non-food utilisation from domestic availabilities (i.e. production and carryover stock). Household expenditure data were also used for this purpose. The second step was to project *per capita* consumption and population growth rates to derive total future consumption requirements. Indicative estimates for the 1972 position with regard to important food items such as maize, wheat, rice, sorghum, pulses, sugar, edible oils, fats, milk and milk products are given (see Table 3). Also included are data for meat, starchy roots and fish.

Comparing total consumption requirements with production projections, we see clearly that we will not be self sufficient in wheat, rice, and sugar, even if weather conditions are favourable. Kenya may meet her own demand for maize, sorghum, millets, pulses, milk, eggs and meat products. However, the levels of actual consumption and production will also depend upon the growth of real income over this period, and whether the present plans for food crops (especially sugar and wheat) and livestock developments are successfully implemented.

Although, the food balance sheet analysis shows that food supply will not be very critical over this period this does not imply that nutritional adequacy will also be achieved. The achievement of national nutritional adequacy will depend upon the growth and distribution of incomes, the success with which current nutritional education programmes will be successfully implemented and whether the supply situation will be guaranteed. The supply problem hinges on the overall

Table 3
Food demand and supply for selected products, 1972, 1973 and 1978

Product	1972 Consumption	1973 Production	1978 Consumption	1978 Production
Maize (million tons)	1.5	2.1	1.9	3.3
Wheat ('000 tons)	160.8	136.2	217.6	170.0
Sugar ('000 tons)	159.6	140.0	235.4	195.0
Rice ('000 tons)	22.8	31.6	29.6	55.4
Meat ('000 tons)	215.2	218.3	346.5	355.4
Milk	0.9†	279.6‡	1.4†	400.0‡
Beans & Pulses ('000 tons)	240.0*	82.0**	321.3*	258.1**
Edible oils & fats ('000 tons)	36.0	n.a.	53.3	n.a.
Starchy roots (million tons)	1.4	n.a.	1.9	n.a.
Sorghum & millets ('000 tons)	87.6	n.a.	112.5	n.a.
Eggs ('000 tons)	6.0	n.a.	8.9	n.a.

† Milk and milk products in '000 tons
‡ Milk only in million litres
* Pulses
** Beans only
n.a. = not available

Source: L.D. Smith, 'Food situation in Kenya, 1969–75' and *Kenyan Development Plan*, 1974–78.

strategy the government has taken to stimulate the development of the small farm sector and hence must depend upon the incentives (price, credit, extension) that will be provided to the farmers.

A study of nutrition in relation to income distribution in Kenya by B. Jones and E. Osundwa reveals that most Kenyans are undernourished and that most receive very low incomes that would prevent them from achieving nutritionally adequate diet [13]. Using adjusted FAO Food Composition Tables they show that an adult Kenyan needs 2,589 calories and 70.6 grams of protein a day and that a Kenyan child needs 1,891 calories and 55.6 grams of protein a day. These required intakes are costed for 1970. For that year they found that the 'minimum cost of adequate diet' for an average Kenyan household comprising 5.6 members needed Kshs. 221 per month and for 1973 (after price adjustments) Kshs. 224 per month. Allowing for 20 per cent price inflation it would seem that at 1975 prices household expenditure on food per month has to be Kshs. 292 in order to achieve the 'minimum cost of adequate diet'. Therefore, in order that a household should get the annual nutritional adequacy their nonmonetary and monetary disposable income must be above K£175.

The majority of Kenya households, as the ILO report shows, received less than K£100 per annum in 1972. In fact they found that out of the 2.34 million households, 2.04 million (87 per cent) earned less than K£200 per annum and that 1.47 million households (60 per cent) earned less than K£60 per year. Conditions have changed dramatically since 1973, such that with existing rates of inflation and the slow growth in income, the majority of the rural population cannot afford the 'minimum cost of adequate diet'.

What comes out of this is the fact that a lot has to be done to stimulate agricultural/rural development so that people receive higher incomes. To bridge the gap between increasing food demand and supply and to solve distributional problems there are several measures that have to be taken. Some of these include land reform, agricultural extension, marketing and credit programmes, pricing incentives and proper nutrition education and family planning.

Nutrition policy and family planning

Kenya does not have, as yet, a clearly worked out nutrition policy although in the current Development Plan it was hoped that national nutrition policy regarding production, marketing and distribution of foodstuffs, food technology, the improvement of nutritive quality, nutrition education and research would be formulated and that a National Food and Nutrition Council would be formed to co-ordinate and implement that policy. A major step taken in this direction is the organisation of a nutrition workshop early in 1975 under the auspices of the Institute for Development Studies and was intended to provide the framework for national nutrition policy. The workshop findings [14] and recommendations are now being scrutinised by government. What is currently available in the field of nutrition are the various nutrition intervention programmes which can be divided into three categories. The first are the direct programmes which include the School Feeding Programme and Pre-School Feeding Programme under the Ministries of Health and Social Services, Mother-Child Health activities under the Ministry of Health and Famine Relief under the Office of the President. Second are the Public Education Programmes under the Ministries of Health and Agriculture. Third are the various nutrition education and training programmes now undertaken at Karen College for nutrition field workers and the agricultural training colleges for the training of agricultural extension personnel, social workers and Community Development workers. One of the most serious difficulties with these programmes are their limited coverage and lack of co-ordination.

Apart from the programmes outlined above designed to increase food availability and nutritional adequacy, it is important that in order to ease the population/food situation something must be done to limit the rate of population growth. In Kenya the attempt is made through the family planning programme. This programme is primarily intended to enhance the health and welfare of mothers and children in general and in particular to reduce in some way the rate of population growth through the introduction of various methods of fertility control including contraceptive devices. These programmes have not produced measurable impact on population control and the conclusion of Professor Livingstone with regard to his assessment of the programme's impact in Vihiga seem to be justified. He says [15] that from the general analytical point of view we may conclude that the calculation of costs and benefits of an avoided birth for Kenya would be an extremely hazardous business, from the point of view of the response factor alone.

The 1974–79 Kenya National Family Planning Programme, financed by the Government of Kenya, the World Bank, United Nations Fund for Population Activities, Swedish International Development Authority and the US Agency for International Development, aims at averting some 150,000 births and reducing Kenya's rate of population growth from the present 3.3 per cent per annum to 2.8 per cent by year 2000. It is increasingly realised that attitudes towards family planning are influenced by education, shortages of land, the cost of providing for children and exposure to information about family planning.

From the point of view of population policy in Kenya, as Livingstone has pointed out, the overall conclusion should not be the abandonment of the programme despite the difficulty of demonstrating a substantial impact but, first, a reformulation of the programme to attack the problem of non-continuation, and second, in the face of the increasingly serious population situation, the acceptance of the fact that controlling population growth is likely to be a long haul, with the size of the problem becoming worse the longer the delay in coming to grips with it.

Major constraints on agricultural development and food supply

Generally, one would expect that the nature of economic activity in a country should closely reflect its natural resource endowment. The largest resources Kenya has are its people and the land, which includes the minerals and the flora and fauna it contains. Kenya in its development has not fully utilised the principal resources of land and people, and future development strategies have to address themselves to this fact. The development of any resource must however be achieved at a price. Below is a summary of the resources available and some of the major constraints that have to be considered.

Land

Compared to other countries in the world Kenya's land/population ratio seems reasonable. Kenya's population density is only 19 persons per square kilometre compared to 280 for Japan, 318 for Netherlands and 170 for India. By African standards land/population ratio however, seems to be moderately high; the overall population density is only 11 persons per square kilometre.

This, however, hides the fact that Kenya is by and large a land scarce country and also that there are wide differences in population densities for various districts in the country. For example, population densities for 1969, varied between one person per square kilometre for Tana River, Isiolo, Marsabit, andGarissa to 307, 222, 194 and 193 persons per square kilometre for Kisii, Kakamega, Kiambu and Kisumu districts respectively. Given the rate of population growth of 3.3 per cent per year the land/population ratios will rise dramatically over time. Availability of good agricultural land has in fact reached critical proportions and already rural/ rural migration from high and medium potential lands to marginal agricultural land has continued rapidly. This problem is likely to get more acute as years go by. Agricultural production will be severely limited by the scarcity of good land, unless intensive usage and changes of technology intervene to overcome this constraint.

Climate

Climate in Kenya is largely determined by altitude; lowlands tend to be dry while highlands are cool and have plenty of rainfall.

The climate of the highlands has two distinct zones separated by the Rift Valley. The Western Highlands and the Western slopes of the Mau Range receive the greatest amount of rainfall particularly in the Central altitudes. Kitale, which typifies the zone at 1,900 metres above sea level, has an annual rainfall of 1,130 millimetres. Temperatures over Trans Nzoia and Uasin Gishu Plateau vary very little with mean maxima between 23°C and 29°C and minima between 10°C and 13°C. Further west, average annual rainfall is 1,275 millimetres for Kisumu at 1,157 metres above sea level with marked peaks in April and November. Temperature ranges between maxima of 30°C and 34°C and minima between 14°C and 18°C. The area around Kisii and Kericho shares climatic characteristics similar to Kitale.

East of the Rift a high rainfall zone covers the Aberdares and Mt Kenya. South Kinangop and Nairobi, for example, receive 2,600 mm and 1,800 mm annually. Machakos, which is at the Southern end of the highlands at an altitude of 1,680 metres, receives 620 mm. This pattern also covers Isiolo and the Narok areas.

A narrow band at the coast receives adequate rainfall for crop farming. Mombasa at sea level has an annual rainfall of 1,040 mm with a pronounced peak in April/May. Further North at Lamu rainfall declines to 899 mm per year. Relative humidity in this zone is generally around 80 per cent.

The remaining part of the country (over half of the country) receives less than 500 mm of rainfall annually. The Northern parts are the driest. A belt between Lake Turkana and Wajir in fact receives less than 250 mm of rain. Over much of the year the area is dry and hot.

Soils

Although detailed soil data are not available, because the ongoing soil survey is not yet completed, a broad soil classification is possible.

In general the soils over much of the highlands are well-drained, deep and dark clays. They are, however, phosphate deficient and acid. These are the typical soils of the tea and coffee areas and are derived from volcanic and basement complex soils. At higher altitudes, particularly on the Mau and Aberdare Ranges and Mt Kenya, dark brown loams occur. These are derived from volcanic activity.

On the plateau and below the highland ranges, soils have a laterite horizon which leads to impeded drainage. Agriculturally, the most significant are the Uasin Gishu Plateau, parts of Western Province and much of Nyanza except for the Kisii Highlands. Also suffering from impeded drainage are the 'black cotton soils' of the Kano plains and the Trans Mara area in Narok district. They also occur over much of the potential commercial ranching areas of Athi Plains and Laikipia.

At the coast dark red loamy sands derived from sedimentation occur. Elsewhere along the coast sand predominates with broken clays frequently occurring in the depressions.

The soils of the plains between the coastal belt and the highlands are mainly dark red loamy soils derived from volcanic basement complex rocks. Soils of the North Eastern parts of Kenya are dark reddish brown sandy loams derived from sediments of basement complex rocks. The balance of the North Plain has shallow stony soil interspersed with areas predominantly covered by lava boulders.

Water resources, irrigation potential and fisheries

As we have shown above less than 40 per cent of Kenya receives high rainfall that can support forests and natural vegetation and give rise to permanent streams. This explains why water conservation is of paramount importance.

Although most of the country does not receive much rainfall the basic problem in Kenya is one of storage and distribution. Total rainfall on the land areas is estimated to be 289,500 million cubic metres in an average year. The mean annual discharge of rivers and streams is estimated at 14,836 million cubic metres. Ground water availability has not yet been fully assessed but its importance for the development of the drier low potential areas is enormous.

The domestic requirement of the present population is about one per cent of the average annual precipitation and slightly more than one per cent of annual run off. The long term objectives of water development and conservation aim at providing water to thirty million people by the year 2000. The new Ministry of Water Development is charged with the responsibility of accomplishing this task.

As far as food production is concerned, the availability of water for irrigation purposes may be relevant. Though complete assessment of water resources available for irrigation is not made, potential irrigation areas have been identified. One is the Lake Victoria basin where irrigation potential is about 35,000 hectares and includes 12,000 hectares in the Kano plains and 17,000 hectares in Yala Swamp. The second is the Rift Valley drainage area. This area of internal drainage into Lakes Turkana, Natron, Naivasha, Nakuru and Baringo has limited irrigation potential. The third is the Athi River drainage system where very little is known about the irrigation potential though about 6,000 hectares at Taveta has been identified as usable. The fourth is the Tana River Basin where the irrigation potential is about 100,000 hectares in the Upper Basin and about 120,000 hectares in the Lower Basin. Tana River has got major hydropower development potential and hence irrigation possibilities might be linked to hydropower developments in the future. The fifth is the Ewaso Nyiro drainage area which has the least development potential. Total irrigation potential is estimated to be around 700,000 hectares.

The full exploitation of Kenya's irrigation potential will be constrained by lack of finance. Hence, its contribution to the food situation will also be limited by that factor. Development expenditures on irrigation (including minor irrigation schemes) will amount to K£5.7 million during the current plan period.

Fish is no doubt a very importance source of protein, the consumption of which needs encouragement. Like most developing countries fishing makes a very small contribution to national income. Yet even for Kenya the full contribution of fisheries can only be assessed after taking into consideration the value added in processing, distribution and other related industries attributed to fishing operations [16].

About seventy-five per cent of the tonnage of fish landed in recent years comes from freshwater fisheries. Lake Victoria alone accounts for over half of the national catch, the remaining amount comes from Lakes Turkana, Naivasha and Baringo, the deep sea fisheries and numerous other lakes, rivers and fish ponds [17].

Fish consumption varies considerably among population groups, being traditionally greatest among the communities living adjacent to the principal fisheries of Lake Victoria, Lake Turkana and the Indian Ocean seaboard. For the country as a whole estimates of fish production and trade suggest that *per capita* consumption of fish is about 3 kilogrammes per person per year [18]. This is very low indeed for a country that has the fish and is suffering widespread protein deficiency, especially among the young children. In terms of the whole population of Kenya and considering nutrition status, animal protein contribution of fish to the diet is not significant.

Although one of the factors that prevent widespread consumption of fish is the different customary practices, the other factors include high prices, poor distribution and marketing channels and the simple fact that some of the fisheries have reached the absolute limit of their potential. This is particularly so for the inland lakes. Deep-sea fishing offers the greatest potential if people can be persuaded to consume deep-sea fish and if investments can be provided for this difficult operation. However, fish farming is one area where on the farm consumption of fish can be improved.

Capital and financial constraints

The brief survey of the natural resource position given above shows clearly that in order to guarantee food and employment to the majority of the people currently either unemployed or earning very low incomes, a lot has to be done to increase the productivity of the land. The population/resource position has very important implications for economic development in general and the choice of agricultural strategy in particular. What seems crucial in the present economic environment is the fact that whatever strategy is chosen, capital, manpower and financial constraints have become acutely binding.

In order to deal with unemployment and its attendant problems, the government had, at the time of the current plan preparation, a strategy that involved structural transformation of the economy and which would require the continued flow of resources into industrial and service sectors (modern sector) and with a pattern of investment that should be labour-using. Secondly, more resources (human and financial) should be directed to the agricultural sector in such a manner as to encourage easy adoption of innovations and the use of modern agricultural practices, consistent with the small farmer socio-economic environment.

What this strategy means is that more resources would be provided to small farmers to enable them to use fertilisers, pesticides, animal and mechanical power and to exploit and conserve available soil and water resources.

Agriculture is the only sector whose development makes moderate demands upon financial resources. In Kenya, it has the greatest development potential at least cost. The policy of large-scale industrialisation would be difficult to attain due to lack of sufficient demand and, much more important, would face very serious constraints imposed by the low level of domestic savings, the problems that limit increased foreign investment and foreign exchange constraints that are decisive in this context.

At the time the current plan was being prepared, it was envisaged that a total of K£455.9 million would be spent on all central government development projects. Out of this agriculture and water would take K£66.7 million or 14.6 per cent of total development outlay [19]. At the same time recurrent expenditure over the plan period was to amount to K£986.6 million, of which K£55.9 million would be spent on agriculture and water development. This is 5.7 per cent of total recurrent expenditure allocations. It was assumed at that time that with improvements in the tax system and with increased revenues from other sources such as sales tax and import duties, total domestic revenues would amount to K£24.8 million and external financing would amount to K£45 million and both short-term and long-term borrowing would bring in K£15.0 and K£28.0 million respectively. The terms of trade facing Kenya were assumed to remain favourable and the balance of payments position would not become worse compared to the situation towards the end of 1972.

However, as a result of the 'oil crisis' and the consequent inflationary trends the balance of payments position and foreign exchange availability became critical. Planned expenditures were thrown out of balance and plan figures and targets have had to be revised.

As shown in the Sessional Paper No. 4 of 1975, major revisions were made [20].

Total development expediture is to be maintained at K£455.9 million. This would be a smaller figure, taking account of price inflation. The situation calls for a more efficient utilisation of domestic resources and the only sector where this can be achieved with relative ease is the agricultural sector. This is dictated by the totally new environment Kenya is facing because, since independence in 1963, Kenya was able to maintain a favourable balance of payments position and availability of foreign exchange was not a serious problem. Although the trade deficit had increased from K£10.7 million in 1963 to K£80.0 million in 1973, it was off-set by increases in net receipts from other current account items (e.g. tourism) so that the deficit remained relatively small. From 1971 there has been a gradual deterioration in the balance of payments position. As a result of very tight import and credit controls, foreign exchange reserves increased from K£6.8 million at the end of 1973. The situation got much worse after the 'oil crisis'. Various corrective measures were taken, including assistance from the IMF of K£1.9 million for easing the balance of payments difficulties. Yet the reserve stood at K£6.8 million by the end of 1974; equivalent to merely two months of imports [21].

To deal with the situation, the government has introduced additional fiscal and monetary policies and measures including increased taxes, higher interest rates and a ceiling on the expansion of credit to the private sector. Government borrowing from the Central Bank has also been reduced. In addition more restraints on imports have been imposed and measures have been taken to expand exports and private sector consumption is to be compressed in order to release resources for increased local production of import substitutes and exports [22].

What seems clear is that Kenya is facing a more severe foreign exchange constraint than ever before. What this implies is that Kenya's highly capital and import intensive growth cannot be sustained any longer. As emphasised by the World Bank in their report of 1974, the only way out of this situation is to make fuller use of domestic resources through greater emphasis on agriculture and industries based on local resources.

Experience has shown, in Kenya and elsewhere in the developing world, that in order to stimulate small farm activity, an extension package of credit, research, extension, training and marketing programmes are needed. In Kenya the importance of these have been recognised. The marketing system, that is largely based on co-operatives and statutory boards, has been found to be slow in responding to the needs of increased production from the rural areas. It is now under special study by experts from FAO and UNDP [23].

Kenya's agricultural credit system includes financial institutions which may be classified into three types. The first consists of the relatively new institutions and programmes serving smallholders. The second type includes older structures oriented towards large scale agriculture; and the third is composed of a series of programmes formed to support the transfer of agricultural land from European to African ownership. The current institutional distribution of funds outstanding by source and term are as follows.

Credit type	Institution	Proportion of all credit (%)
Long term	Agricultural Settlement Fund	19
	Agricultural Finance Corporation	6
	Commercial Banks	4
Medium term	Agricultural Finance Corporation	18
	Agricultural Settlement Fund	14
	Commercial Banks	11
	Government Programmes	2
Short term	Commercial Banks	13
	Merchant Supplies	9
	Guaranteed Minimum Return (GMR)	3
	Co-operative Societies	1

These data show that most of the farm credit is provided by a few major institutions, notably the Agricultural Finance Corporation (AFC), Agricultural Settlement Fund and the commercial banks [24].

For a long time most of the available credit went to the large farm sector and it is only recently that attention has been given to the small farm sector. Up until 1973 out of the 1.2 million smallholders only 250,000 were able to get some form of credit. Most of the 23,000 large farms and ranches received the bulk of institutional credit in Kenya.

The most significant short term lenders to smallholders include the AFC, and the Co-operative Bank through the Co-operative Production Credit Scheme. In order to correct this imbalance the Government of Kenya has entered into an agreement with the World Bank for the finance of an Integrated Agricultural Development Programme and with USAID for an Agricultural Sector Programme Loan that are primarily designed to meet the small farmer's needs. The IADP is in two phases. Phase one starts in 1975 and will cost K£9.25 million. At project maturity, the net incremental annual output is estimated to be K£3.99 million from crops and K£5.25 million from livestock [25]. The USAID loan programme during the first phase will cost K£6.4 million. It is anticipated that most of the farmer participants will be able to receive net additional incomes ranging from K£97 to K£144 per year [26]. The basic purpose of these loans is to provide a practical and operational means of reaching the small farmers and to bring about changes in the existing practices which tend to limit small farmer access to inputs and markets. These include size of farm loan, security and other eligibility requirements for credit, risks to be assumed by the agencies providing inputs and marketing arrangements for the outputs. The basic components of these loan programmes which depart from the usual government approach to this sector include training, marketing and storage, rural access road improvement and various forms of institution building.

In spite of these programmes the traditional problems in the area of small farm credit will not be easily solved. First, the credit system will still remain fragmented with the co-ordinating mechanism yet to be worked out. Secondly, loan payment by many farmers will still be difficult to achieve.

Regional imbalance

Regional disparities in the level of economic development can come about due to uneven factor endowment. In this regard, the critical factor in a predominantly agricultural country is the regional distribution of rainfall [27] and good agricultural land. Land in Kenya is classified into four categories:

1. High potential land with adequate rainfall (889 millimetres or more);
2. Medium potential land with 635 to 889 millimetres of rainfall a year;
3. Low potential land receiving between 508 and 635 millimetres and suited mainly to ranching, except for irrigation;
4. Nomadic pastoral land with less than 508 millimetres of rainfall [28].

An indication of the distribution of high potential land by administrative districts is given in Table 4. Some districts in the Central, Coast, Rift Valley, Nyanza and Western Provinces are well endowed with agriculturally good land, most of the Eastern and North-East Provinces are not so favourably endowed.

Natural or geographical drawbacks can be mitigated by deliberate government policy and action. For some time now, 'balanced economic development' [29] has been a declared government policy and 'in the allocation of funds for agriculture, greater attention will be paid to less developed agricultural areas and to range areas than before' [30]. For a comprehensive picture of the regional development scene, one would have to look at such things as the effect of the taking up by the central government from the local governments of education and health services, the activities of the National Irrigation Board, the work done by the Range Management Division of the Ministry of Water Development and local initiatives by way of self help (*Harambee*) activities. While unable to do justice to all these, some indication of the distribution of public social and economic services is to be found in Table 4 where are shown length of road per 1,000 square kilometres and ranking of districts in terms of educational expenditure. An index of both government and communal effort is given by the proportion of the population in primary school and percentage of land devoted to cash crops.

The conclusion is inescapable that:

> 'There are enormous regional disparities ... the percentage of the total population in primary schools varies widely between provinces and districts. Even greater disparities are found in the provision of secondary schools. Wide differences also exist in the availability of other services such as water and electricity supply, roads and health services.' [31]

Table 4
Selected indicators of regional disparities, 1969–70

Province and district	A	B	C	D	E	F	G	H
	Population (thousands)	Population per km²	Km of road per 1,000 km²	Ranking in terms of educational expenditure	Percentage of population in primary school	Area under cash crops as % cultivated area	Percentage of high-potential cultivated area	Availability of good agricultural land (hectares per person)
Coast								
Kilifi	302	24	56.7	19	7.6	66	8.4	0.5
Kwale	206	25	60.7	21	7.1	42	15.3	0.8
Lamu	22	4	22.2	32	4.6	–	1.1	3.3
Mombasa	247	–	200.5	n.a.	10.6	–	–	n.a.
Taita	111	6	22.5	20	16.7	66	2.5	0.5
Tana River	51	1	14.1	25	7.7	–	1.9	2.4
North-Eastern								
Garissa	64	1	11.8	31	2.5	–	–	–
Mandera	95	4	10.6	33	1.5	–	–	–
Wajir	86	2	17.9	29	1.5	–	–	–

(table continued overleaf)

Table 4 (continued)

Province and district	A	B	C	D	E	F	G	H
Eastern								
Embu	179	62	123.3	17	17.2	7	24.4	0.6
Isiolo	30	1	13.6	30	8.3	—	—	n.a.
Kitui	343	11	40.8	14	12.4	16	2.2	0.9
Machakos	707	50	65.6	3	17.8	24	8.8	0.4
Marsabit	52	1	13.7	27	3.9	—	0.05	n.a.
Meru	597	63	69.0	7	13.3	35	24.3	0.4
Central								
Kiambu	476	127	267.3	1	20.9	41	48.1	0.4
Kirinyaga	217	146	151.2	15	14.5	23	68.5	0.5
Muranga	445	178	204.1	4	21.9	18	84.0	0.5
Nyandarua	177	54	127.6	18	19.5	86	75.0	1.5
Nyeri	361	108	130.5	5	23.8	37	48.6	0.4
Rift								
Baringo	162	15	61.2	13	9.8	—	15.6	1.2
Elgeyo Marakwet	159	57	99.8	8	9.7	23	38.1	0.7
Kajiado	86	4	39.0	23	9.0	—	1.1	n.a.
Kericho	479	97	139.3	11	11.2	16	77.7	0.8
Laikipia	66	7	55.3	22	12.1	—	13.4	2.1
Nakuru	291	40	127.1	13	9.8	—	41.5	1.0

(table continued below)

Table 4 (continued)

Province and district	A	B	C	D	E	F	G	H
Rift (continued)								
Nandi	209	75	133.7	8	9.7	8	85.4	1.1
Narok	125	7	46.3	24	5.0	—	49.0	7.3
Samburu	70	3	20.2	28	3.3	—	6.7	2.2
Trans-Nzoia	124	50	134.6	8	9.7	—	84.2	1.7
Turkana	165	2	13.2	26	0.9	—	0.2	n.a.
Uasin Gishu	191	50	135.8	8	9.7	—	86.5	1.7
West Pokot	82	16	71.8	8	9.7	—	28.2	1.3
Nyanza								
Kisii	675	304	212.1	9	12.6	31	100.0	0.3
Kisumu	401	192	173.4	6	10.8	21	93.7	0.6
Siaya	383	151			12.9	9		0.9
South Nyanza	663	114	149.5	10	7.2	20	99.1	
Western								
Bungoma	345	113	138.0	12	16.8	13	82.1	0.7
Busia	200	119	196.9	16	13.9	20	100.0	0.8
Kakamega	783	220	176.1	2	12.4	13	92.3	0.4

na. = available — = magnitude negligible.

Source: ILO, *Employment Incomes and Equality*, Geneva, 1972, Table 28, p. 78 and Table 1, p. 35.

The existence of regional imbalance makes it possible to divide the country into six ecological zones [32] which have differing land use potential. A comprehensive study of the economic potential of the various ecological zones was undertaken by the World Bank team [33]. They estimated the area and type of activity that would guarantee an annual income of K£70, which they defined as the 'minimum acceptable income' at 1973 prices. Prices in general have gone up 30 per cent since then but the analysis brings out the limitations population growth, natural and other factors are putting on the economic use of available land.

Zone 1:

This ecological zone covers 801 sq. kilometres and lies at high altitudes above the treeline. Vegetation is moorland or grassland and use is limited to water catchment, tourism, forestry and animal life.

Zone 2:

This covers about 53,000 sq. kilometres and embraces most of Kenya's forest land, both indigenous and exotic. Agricultural potential of this zone is high and tea, coffee and pyrethrum are important cash crops. Macadamia nuts can be grown in the higher altitudes and cotton in the lower altitudes. For this zone, the area and type of activity that can provide the 'minimum income' of K£70 would be the following:

Enterprise	*Area employed (ha.)*	*Gross margin (Kshs.)*	*Labour requirements (man-days)*
Maize/potatoes	0.8	550	140
Cash crops	0.4	350	275
Grade dairy cattle	1.0	475	50
House & gardening	0.1	50	75
	2.3	1,425	540
Allow 10 per cent for other uses	0.3		
Average farm size required for K£70	2.6		

It is important to note that this is the zone with the highest population density and where the demand for land is most acute. Pressure is being put upon the government to allow part of the 100,000 hectares of planted forests to be excised and the area put to agricultural use. This pressure has been resisted because these forests are also very important as water catchment zones.

Zone 3:

Covers 53,000 sq. kilometres and has medium agricultural potential. The zone contains the largest mixed farming areas in the country. Maize would be the main crop for subsistence and for sale. Pulses and vegetables, cotton and livestock would also be important cash earners.

Enterprise	Area employed (ha.)	Gross margin (Kshs.)	Labour requirements (man-days)
Maize	0.8	620	120
Beans	0.4	160	60
Livestock	4.0	280	100
Cotton	0.5	310	225
House & vegetables	0.1	50	75
	5.8	1,420	580
Allow 10 per cent for other uses	0.6		
Average farm size required for K£70	6.4		

Zone 4: (including drier parts of zone 3)

This zone also covers about 53,000 sq. kilometres and is marginal for agricultural purposes. Commercial ranching on well managed pastures can support one stock unit per four hectares or less. Drought resistant Katumani maize can be grown. Crop diversity is a great problem in this zone.

Enterprise	Area employed (ha.)	Gross margin (Kshs.)	Labour requirements (man-days)
Maize	1.25	625	150
Beans	0.4	160	60
Cotton	0.75	220	190
Livestock	14.00	380	140
House & vegetables	not significant		
Average farm size for K£70	16.4	1,385	615

Zone 5:

This zone covers 300,000 sq. kilometres and is largely not suitable for cropping. This zone is the main focus of the livestock development programmes. Subsistence crops would include millet and pulses.

Enterprise	Area employed (ha.)	Gross margin (Kshs.)	Labour requirements (man-days)
Cereals	1.6	340	160
Pulses	0.8	130	80
Livestock	60.0	900	300
House & vegetables	–	–	–
Average farm size for K£70	62.4	1,370	615

Zone 6:

This zone covers 112,000 sq. kilometres and is true range area covering much of Northern Kenya with low and erratic rainfall and is the home of nomadic tribesmen. Livestock production is the only possible economic activity. However, land carrying capacity varies greatly from 10 to 15 hectares per livestock unit.

Enterprise	Area employed (ha.)	Gross margin (Kshs.)	Labour requirements (man-days)
Livestock	90–135	1,350	450

It will be noticed from the foregoing (i) that the amount of land required to generate a given income level increases as land potential declines, (ii) that the amount of employment generated per unit area declines as land potential declines, and (iii) that crop diversity diminishes with low potential of land so that a poorly endowed region cannot be expected to produce adequate and balanced foodstuffs. The moral is that meaningful programmes on income, employment, food and nutrition have got to be area specific.

Rural employment

Table 5 gives time series of employment in agriculture and forestry. The two — agriculture and forestry — are treated together because for most years the data are not disaggregated. It will be noticed that between 1954 and 1960, employment in agriculture and forestry climbed from 223,100 to 271,800; this was in keeping with the general expansion of the primary sector and the economy in general. In 1961, however, employment in this sector declined to 252,000 persons. The decline continued to 1964, when employment was 201,200. This downturn was due primarily to the crisis of confidence that permeated the economy around the time of independence. A slight gain was recorded in 1965 when 202,400 people were employed. This was partly due to the 1964 Tripartite Agreement whereby the government undertook to increase its labour force by 15 per cent and private employers by 10 per cent. Clearly that arrangement did not have lasting benefits for in 1966 employment declined sharply to 188,000. The decline continued to 1967 but between 1968 and 1973 we notice increases in the numbers employed.

One striking feature of the employment picture in agriculture and forestry is that in 1973 there were fewer people employed in this sector (220,600) than there were some twenty years before. Employment declined both absolutely and proportionately. As Table 5 brings out, the proportion of people engaged in agriculture as a proportion of total employment declined from about 0.4 between 1954 and 1965 to about 0.3 between 1966 and 1973. It is tempting to conclude that this phenomenon supports Kuznets' and other economists' contention [34] that the proportion of the labour force in purely agricultural activities declines as any economy grows. This may be so, but one should not lose sight of the fact that our analysis has relied entirely on recorded wage employment in the so called 'formal' or 'modern' sector agriculture [35]. Self employed persons and family workers who do not receive regular wages or salaries are excluded. So are persons engaged in small farms. This means that there is an underenumeration of people supported directly by the land. For example, in 1972, there were, in addition to the people recorded in Table 5, some 3,875,000 self employed in rural non-agriculture and 222,000 people employed in rural non-agricultural activities and in small farms and settlement schemes [36].

It is this kind of situation that gives rise to the optimism that 'some 650,000 additional persons have to be found employment in the rural areas during this plan either as farmers, family workers, self employed or wage employees' [37]. A prime objective of policy should be to make workplaces cheap enough, on the average, so that they can be created in large numbers without imposing an undue strain on the economy's level of savings, imports, skilled manpower and other scarce resources. Some policy options to achieve this end are considered here.

There is evidence to suggest that small farms are more labour intensive than large farms. Table 6 reveals that small farms use more men equivalents per 1,000 acres than large farms; they are also less dependent on machinery cultivation than their larger counterparts. Therefore, from the point of view of creating employment, there is a *prima facie* case for the promotion of small scale land tenure than large scale. The case is even stronger when it is realised that gross output per acre is, by and large, higher for small size farms. A holding that is 'small' by the standards of one ecological zone may be 'large' by the standards of another. What should be done is to determine the smallest viable farm unit in any ecological zone and institute land policy to foster that farm size.

Another thrust to boost employment in agriculture is to promote those crops that have high labour requirements per acre. Table 7 shows that different crop enterprises have different labour—land coefficients. To cash in on this, it is incumbent on planners to ascertain labour input requirements for all crops that can grow in a certain area and to encourage those that maximise the number of people employed.

Thirdly there is an urgent need to evolve a labour intensive farming technology. Research and development in the field of farm mechanisation should lead to the

Table 5
Recorded employment in agriculture and forestry

Year	Employment in agriculture and forestry ('000)	Total employment ('000)	Proportion employed in agriculture and forestry
1954	223.1	544.4	0.41
1955	247.9	615.1	0.40
1956	235.2	596.7	0.39
1957	253.4	614.4	0.41
1958	249.5	593.2	0.42
1959	251.7	596.9	0.42
1960	271.8	622.2	0.44
1961	252.0	596.8	0.42
1962	245.5	579.8	0.42
1963	215.7	539.2	0.40
1964	201.2	575.4	0.35
1965	202.4	582.1	0.35
1966	188.1	585.4	0.32
1967	172.7	597.5	0.29
1968	173.0	606.4	0.29
1969	178.7	627.2	0.28
1970	183.7	644.5	0.29
1971	189.6	691.2	0.27
1972	197.9	719.8	0.27
1973	202.6	761.6	0.29

Source: *Statistical Abstract*, various years.

introduction and promotion of prototypes of small tractors and other farm implements. In particular, serious attention should be given to the promotion of cattle-drawn ploughs and other intermediate farm machinery.

All these emphasise that 'low cost labour-using, rather than capital-using techniques must be employed to the greatest extent possible in agriculture' [38].

Even labour intensive agriculture is unlikely to provide year-round full employment in rural areas due to the seasonal nature of agriculture. Employment-generating minor development works with high labour content should be carried out with underemployed and seasonally unemployed rural labour [39]. Construction of feeder roads, irrigation and other works, flood control such as school houses and clinical buildings should be phased in the slack during the rainfall and agricultural activity cycle. These activities contribute directly or indirectly in boosting agriculture. Local materials should be used wherever possible to provide

Table 6
Output, employment and farm size

Farm size (acres)	Gross output (Sh. per acre)	Labour inputs (men equivalents per 1000 acres)	Expenditure on machinery cultivation (Sh. per acre)
10 or less	635	808	6
10 – 19.9	250	399	11
20 – 29.9	156	234	9
30 – 39.9	161	159	28
40 – 49.9	113	124	21
50 – 59.9	98	111	19
60 – 69.9	98	109	12
70 or more	111	70	10
All small farms*	156	190	14
250 or less	248	93	135
250 – 499	161	62	140
500 – 749	133	43	136
750 – 999	113	44	146
1,000 – 1,249	89	34	119
1,250 – 1,499	149	46	167
1,500 – 1,999	128	28	155
2,000 – or more	65	14	131
All large farms**	117	36	143

* 1967/68
** 1970/71

Source: *Kenya Statistical Digest*, vol. X, no. 1, March, 1972, Tables 3 and 4, pp. 7 and 8.

employment and reduce transport costs.

Small-scale, labour-using light industries [40] with low capital requirements should be established in rural areas to supplement employment opportunities in agriculture and provide supplemental incomes to small cultivators and landless agricultural workers. Certain light industries are better than others. Obvious cases are (1) the processing of agricultural commodities produced in the areas concerned which might include fruit and vegetable canneries, flour and rice mills, wood working factories, slaughter houses, creameries and milk powder plants,

Table 7
Labour/land coefficients for individual enterprises, 1969/70

Enterprise	Mean annual labour input (man-days per acre)			
	Nyeri	Kiambu	Nandi	Nyandarua
Coffee	190.7	105.5	–	–
Mature tea	187.6	–	193.2	–
Unimproved dairy cattle	178.6	69.4	–	–
Improved dairy cattle	144.7	50.1	10.4	18.4
Other livestock	135.3	51.1	–	13.0
Pyrethrum	80.8	55.6	–	66.5
Maize	49.3	76.8	36.2	63.0
Hybrid maize	–	12.8	24.7	61.7
Wheat	–	–	–	4.9

Source: *Kenya Statistical Digest*, vol. X, no. 1, March 1972, Table 7, p. 9.

sugar refineries, processing units for cotton ginning and edible oils; (2) the fabrication of inputs for agriculture such as cattle, pig and poultry feed mills, fertiliser mixing plants, small tool making shops, clay, brick and tile works; (3) production of consumer goods and building materials for capital construction and infrastructure inputs.

In setting up such industries the criterion should be economic feasibility. Agro-industries of the type using agricultural inputs may involve weight or bulk losing processes and therefore have locational advantage if established near their sources of raw materials. Those producing products intended primarily for the farmers in an area have transport advantages when located near their markets. This is especially true if products are heavy, e.g. brick, tile and concrete blocks; or bulk gaining, e.g. harrows, chicken brooders, wheelbarrows, water tanks, etc.

A study [41] in 1969 concluded that 'non-agricultural activities are still extremely weak in rural areas. They provide very few employment opportunities and generate very little income' [42]. But there is a growing realisation that rural small scale industries have a role to play in promoting rural welfare, in industrial deconcentration for regional balance and in creating employment [43]. In fact the Kenyan Government has committed itself to the expansion of rural non-agricultural enterprises. According to the current Development Plan, 'efforts will be made to encourage development of small-scale industries. There is a great potential for small-scale rural manufacturing which has promise of producing, cheaply and profitably, goods both for import-substitution and for export... Government programmes will be undertaken during the plan period to encourage development of small scale industries, especially in rural areas' [44].

An institutional set-up which can be used to foster labour-intensive agriculture, labour using minor development works and agriculturally oriented small-scale light industry using labour intensive techniques already exists. The Special Rural Development Programme (SRDP) and Rural Industrial Development Programme (RIDP) are being implemented with a view to experimenting, replicating, doing research and evaluation designed to achieve increased standards of living in the countryside. These two programmes aim at co-ordinating and synchronising on a continuing basis the related activities of the different ministries, departments and agencies concerned with rural development in Kenya.

Income distribution

One of the policy goals in Kenya is 'to improve the distribution of rural income' [45]. An approximate estimate of rural incomes in 1969 is given in Table 8. About 40 per cent of the K£231 million was derived from sources other than agriculture as such.

In Table 9 we present the distribution of earnings among people employed in formal sector agriculture and forestry. It will be noticed that over 90 per cent of the employees earn less than KSh. 200 per month suggesting a skewed income distribution. When all economic groups in rural areas are considered as in Table 10, the picture of skewness in income distribution is similarly supported. The majority of rural households are poor.

In the absence of firm data on personal income, some researchers have resorted to an assessment of the distribution of such income-related items as consumer durables, tea acreage and cattle. Michael Cowen's study of Mathira Division in Nyeri District and Diana Hunt's study of Mbere Division in Eastern Province reveal 'unequal distribution of economic status' [46].

The ILO report [47] talks of there being a high degree of income inequality in both rural and urban areas because 'the dispersion around the average ... is enormous' [48], but concludes that in terms of absolute numbers, the great majority of the poor in Kenya are to be found in the rural areas [49]. So whatever is to be done about the overall strategies of mitigating inequality, most of the target groups will have to be the rural poor.

Migration

We should distinguish two kinds of migration: rural-to-rural migration and rural-to-urban migration. Both are causally the same because they are necessitated by differences of what origin and destination have to offer. There is a relative 'pull' of the area of in-migration and 'push' of the area of out-migration.

There is a tendency in Kenya for people to migrate from rural areas to urban centres. This 'involves a rapid shift of people towards the larger towns, especially Nairobi and Mombasa. The movement is massive and involves all kinds of people – young, old, male, female, the educated and the illiterate, the landless and those with large holdings' [50].

Table 8
Rural incomes, 1969

	£ million
1. Gross domestic product at factor cost outside the monetary economy:	
Agriculture	89.0
Other	26.1
2. Contribution of small-scale agriculture to the gross domestic product in the monetary sector at factor cost:	
Accruing to owners	20.7
Other items	9.1
3. Estimate of contribution of African-owned part of large-scale agricultural sector to the gross domestic product in the monetary sector, at factor cost (net of worker's earnings)	8.7
4. African agricultural wages in the modern agricultural sector	10.6
5. Assumed remittances from the urban sector (20 per cent of the remainder of the African wage bill)	18.3
6. Contribution of small-scale rural non-agricultural enterprises to gross domestic product in the monetary sector:	
Accruing to owners	13.6
Accruing to hired workers	4.6
7. Earnings from wage employment in rural non-agricultural industries in the modern sector	30.7
Total	231.4

Source: ILO, *Employment Incomes and Equality*, p. 333.

This situation exists because, as at least one expert has pointed out 'the countryside is failing in its traditional function of holding the labour surplus until industry is ready to absorb it ... A widening differential between town and country, whether in wages, social services or infrastructure; then the very fact that there is work to be had in the towns, especially casual labour, brings in more and more people' [51].

An insight into the reasons why people move from rural to urban areas in Kenya is had when one refers to the data in Table 11. The fact that work could not be found and that land was not available are the most powerful reasons for moving.

But clearly, the situation is not characteristised by a lack of memory. Sooner or later, people realise that by going to towns they may not always get a job. They may be spurred to move not by the absolute differential in real welfare, but by a differential weighted by the probability of securing a job. This is the basic idea underlying the path breaking work of Michael P. Todaro on a probabilistic model of labour migration [52].

Table 9
Distribution of income in agriculture and forestry, 1970

Income groups (Sh. per month)	Percentage of employees
100 and less	61.5
100 – 149	19.9
150 – 199	9.9
200 – 299	3.3
300 – 399	1.6
400 – 599	1.1
600 – 999	0.7
1000 – 1499	0.7
1500 – 1999	0.5
Over 2000	0.9

Source: ILO, *Employment, Incomes and Equality*, Table 60, p. 354.

Table 10
Household income, 1968–70

Economic group	Annual income (£)
Big farmers	1000 and over
Less prosperous big farmers	600 – 1000
Prosperous smallholders and better-off owners of non-agricultural rural enterprises	200 – 600
Significant proportion of smallholders and most owners of non-agricultural rural enterprises	120 – 200
Employees in formal sector agriculture and a small proportion of owners of non-agricultural rural enterprises	60 – 120
Workers employed on smallholdings and in rural non-agricultural enterprises; sizeable number of smallholders	20 – 60
Smallholders; pastoralists in semi-arid and arid zones; unemployed and landless persons in rural areas	20 or less

Source: ILO, *Employment, Incomes and Equality*, Table 25, p. 74.

Table 11
Reasons for migration among male migrants aged 15–50, 1970

Reason	Total
Could not find work	80.9
Land was not available	3.2
Could not enter school	4.4
Schools not available or of poor quality	0.6
Lack of social amenities	0.2
Other	10.7
	100.0

Source: ILO, *Employment, Incomes and Equality*, Table 9, p. 46.

A study [53] by Mbithi and Barnes deciphered that rural-to-rural migration may come about for several reasons. There is migration due to famine, drought and land pressure in home areas. This is the kind of migration that has led to squatting within the ten mile coastal strip by tribesmen from drier hinterlands. There is migration due to political manoeuvring to gain possession of unoccupied special reserves, state land, margins of game parks, land owned by a pastoral tribe, or on large scale farms. There is also temporary migration when crop failure occurs and people are forced back into the more prosperous areas for short term employment [54].

Rural-to-rural migration is determined by (1) the carrying capacity of a given piece of land as determined by the level of technology and physical characteristics of the environment, (2) rate of population growth, (3) alternative non-farm employment, and (4) land tenure policies. These factors, operating in any one given setting, will determine occupational opportunities, food supply and population movements [55].

Hence, it is clear that migration, of whatever category, is in response to differential earning power, social amenities and unemployment. These factors are closely connected with uneven development between various areas and regions. A diagnosis should be made of the various 'pull' and 'push' forces and action taken accordingly.

Political and social constraints [56]

Agriculture as the prime mover in the Kenya economy suffers from its historical – colonial structures. The most significant elements of the historical structure of agriculture [57] was first European ownership, second its location in the white highlands and, third its relative capital intensity. These first two elements led to important political constraints after independence as the government spent valuable resources to Africanise the ownership of European — owned agricultural land in the white highlands. There were two approaches to this. These were to allow individual Africans to buy the land and the other was to settle 'landless' Africans in the white highlands [58]. The impact of the policies related to Africanisation of white highlands was to continue the relatively capital intensive 'tractor' based agriculture which was practised by Europeans. Colin Leys [59] estimates that there may be as many as 500,000 Africans in the former white highlands. On the whole they have led to the peasantisation of plantation agriculture. This probably has not led to an increase in inter-regional labour mobility but rather it has transferred labour (family labour mainly) from the former African areas to the former white highlands. It also transferred inter-tribal political competition for land into the Rift Valley Province.

A parallel process has been the increase in cash crop production in the smallholder sector in the former African areas [60]. This has been remarkable especially for tea and dairy production. This has led to seasonal labour shortages in some high potential districts and the consequent increase in migrant labour. The extent of this is hardly quantified although many people have working estimates [61].

The Africanisation of European agriculture and the growth of smallholder cash crop production in high potential areas has led to fantastic regional inequalities compared to the medium and low potential districts. These non-high potential areas can be considered as potential labour reservoirs. But given the socio-political constraints, particularly ethnicity which does not allow the migrating labour to own land (the perceived critical production variable to most of the population), there are several interrelated issues. First, it is not easy for minority tribes to get access to former white highlands, e.g. there are few Pokots in settlement schemes. Second, land in the marginal/low potential minority areas is being also bought by relatively richer migrants from high potential areas who can break the ecological parameters by utilising higher technology, e.g. Kikuyus and Kambas buying Digos and Durumas out in Kwale District. Thirdly, low potential areas are less organised [62] to have access to the political system, e.g. the number of schools, business loans to North-Eastern Province are insignificant compared to the same in Central Province or even Eastern Province. In reviewing factors such as the above one gets a feel of the impact of agriculture on access to food and nutrition.

The major social and political constraints to future food policy pertain (a) to distribution and (b) patterns of consumption.

Taking political constraints first one should note that the recent political history of Kenya shows that local large scale farmers have, as an item of their priority in accumulation, pushed up the farm gate prices of basic foodstuffs. Thus, as is clearly illustrated in maize and milk policy they get fantastic prices for their commodities. This is so since they are organised and some also control the instrumentalities of the state which initiate, debate and execute the policy. Since these commodities are distributed by statutory monopolies there is not a framework for consumers, be they urban, labour or small scale producer/consumers to force the statutory boards to change policy in their favour.

Another aspect of the political constraint is the regional nature of access to the political system as a factor in distribution of basic foods. Surplus maize comes essentially out of Western Province (which is relatively unimportant in national politics) and the large scale farmers in former white-highlands. If Western Province was perceived as important nationally it could be rewarded by opening its maize reserves for speculation in other regions. The large scale farmers have essentially been interested in farm gate prices to bale themselves out of the farm loans and not in trading/speculating on the grain. Thus, there has not developed a marketing system to distribute the regional surpluses to the areas of shortfall in production. These areas mainly in Eastern, Coast and North-Eastern provinces have not been able to force the political system to allow them to import the maize surplus from the regions of surplus. The same point about the relative unimportance politically of regions can be shown by looking at the sources of milk and the areas of dumping. Milk from Rift Valley and Central Province is usually processed but when Kenya Cooperative Creameries (KCC) has a surplus it is the Sotik plant which dumps rather than Naivasha or Kiganjo. Probably feeding school children with the milk may serve a more useful purpose to society whatever the politics of price support.

Social constraints operate to act as constraints on food and nutrition. They do not act independently of the political constraints but in tandem. Clearly the fact that there is no systematic research on agriculture and horticulture of traditional foods, e.g. finger millet and assorted vegetables, is a political variable. When low income families in arid areas change their consumption patterns to follow what they consider as good (*ustaarabu*) food, e.g. rice, maizemeal rather than finger millet, etc., then we are in the realm of social constraints, i.e. copying the consumption patterns of the elite although from a nutrition point of view mixtures of finger millet, eluisine and arrowroots etc. can be shown to be more nutritious than maize/beans mixtures. Of course when the low income groups change to *ustaarabu* food they also create demand on some foodstuffs which are short, e.g. rice.

The other aspect of social constraints which has perhaps received undue emphasis is the fact that some foods are not acceptable to some peoples, pork to Moslems, maizemeal to Somalis, Masais etc. This may not be as important now, as the traditional structures of food and nutrition are collapsing. Whereas a group like the Masai had a healthy balanced diet based on meat and blood (usually of small stock) as more of them are marginalised by land consolidation, and the encroachment on grazing land by commercial agricultural production (usually not controlled by the Masai) their diet patterns have become poorer and they have moved into the maize/beans pattern. International teams have made a great deal of fish and wildlife as protein sources. The evidence is conflicting on fish but the traditional fish eaters now complain that they cannot get enough since people who never used to eat it are appropriating this resource. Wildlife in the rural areas is still an important source of protein. Those who stress game cropping only pay attention to the monetisation.

In summary then, sociological and political marginal groups have not been able to have access to the political system and thereby insure that basic foodstuff research, production and distribution is in their favour. The political system has in its pricing mechanism, structure of agriculture and monopoly marketing insured high returns to the large-scale producers. Monetisation leads to less easily available food which to some extent is less nutritious. To break this constraint would entail fundamental reorientation on distribution of foods and a new policy on especially protein sources.

Suggestions for further work on food, population and rural development

In the course of our investigation in this area we came across several topics and sub-areas where we felt more investigation is required. We group these into those topics that relate to:

1. agriculture and rural development;
2. food and nutrition;
3. population and family planning; and
4. general coverage.

Agriculture and rural development

(a) There is need to assess land carrying capacity, paying special attention to dry land research and dry farming methods, optimal land use plans and strategies.
(b) Research into optimum farm size for the various ecological zones should be carried out, bearing in mind the constraints imposed by resources (natural or otherwise) and laudable objectives like regional balance, employment and equitable income distribution.
(c) Research and development (R & D) should be accelerated in the area of small farm implements for various terrains and soil texture.
(d) A comparative study of large and small farms is called for so as to assess the relative contribution of each and how 'efficiently' each can be used as an instrument to achieve various social and economic objectives.
(e) Construction of Water Balance Sheets and development possibilities should be undertaken with a view to highlighting the various sources and applications and their related dynamics.
(f) Research is needed into the 'pull' and 'push' forces of the various areas, regions and centres. Ways and means to reduce the 'potential difference' between the 'poles' are required so as to achieve a balance of job opportunities and development activities within the nation.

Food and nutrition

(a) There is need for research into optimum food baskets with respect to nutritional objectives and related economic and other costs.

(b) An urgent line of action is research on traditional foods such as finger millet, arrowroots, grams, eluisine (peas, njahi), etc. This would help in assessing whether to phase them in or out as farm activities.

(c) A thorough study of food habits would provide a basis for inducing diversification of food intake. Such a survey would help establish nutritional status among various communities and population groups.

(d) A plank in the food agenda should be fisheries research: the stocking and harvesting of rivers, lakes and ocean should help in boosting protein adequacy.

(e) Cases of the effects of food processing should be documented with respect to, say, maize, wheat, fruits, vegetables, etc. and, if necessary, compulsory fortification of, for example, bread with soybean or other oilseed and of salt with iodine, should be required by statute.

Population

(a) Research into the determinants of population growth in an African situation is urgently required. In particular we need to know: is there such a thing as a desired or optimum family size?

(b) More research ought to go into family planning — its desirability and its delivery programme.

General

(a) Research is required into the optimal combination of agricultural and non-agricultural activities that would achieve the multiple objectives of nutritional adequacy, employment creation, income generation, minimisation of risks, etc. Perforce, such studies would be area-bound.

(b) There is need to establish how effectively to co-ordinate the activities of the agricultural extension worker, the nutritionist and adult literacy worker in rural areas. Is it better to have several workers with different skills or all workers trained in all skills?

(c) To what extent can the price mechanism be used to discourage the consumption of some items and encourage the consumption of others?

(d) A large scale statistical survey should be undertaken to provide data on the magnitude of the unemployment problem and the distribution of income in rural areas. Parallel with this should be a census of capital assets in these areas.

(e) A relatively neglected area in the whole sphere of food, population and rural development is the differential roles of men and women. A comparative study of the two sexes should be a matter of priority. What is their roles in making important and critical decisions, bearing the costs and sharing the benefits?

Notes

[1] See Table 19(a), *Statistical Abstract, 1974.*
[2] See *Statistical Abstract, 1974,* pp. 42 and 43.
[3] Table 59(c), *Statistical Abstract, 1974,* p. 63.
[4] Kenya, *Development Plan: 1970–74,* p. 2. See also Chapter 6, pp. 168–178.
[5] Kenya, *Development Plan: 1974–78,* p. 91.
[6] Ibid., p. 197.
[7] See Central Bureau of Statistics, *Economic Survey 1975,* pp. 5 and 86.
[8] T.R. Masaya, 'Spectral Analysis of Coffee, Maize and Wheat Production in Kenya', Working Paper No. 218, Institute for Development Studies, University of Nairobi, May 1975, p. 6.
[9] John W. Mellor, *The Economics of Agricultural Development,* Cornell University Press, 1969, p. 37.
[10] See J.C. Likimani, 'Report on Nutrition in Kenya' (1969), and M. Buhdal, N.E. Gibbs and W.K. Simmona, 'Nutrition Survey' (1971).
[11] L. Smith, 'Food situation in Kenya, 1969–75' (mimeo). Earlier Food Balance Sheets for Kenya have been constructed by USDA (1960–61) and FAO (1964–66).
[12] IBRD, Report No. 254 (a) – KE, Annex 2.
[13] B. Jones and E. Osundwa, 'Nutrition in Relation to the Distribution of Incomes in Kenya' (mimeo, 1973).
[14] See *Food and Nutrition Strategy for Kenya,* IDS Occasional Paper No. 14, 1975.
[15] Ian Livingstone, 'Prospects for Population Limitation in Kenya: a Statistical Evidence from Vihiga Programme', IDS Working Paper No. 214, 1975.
[16] FAO, *Fisheries in the food economy,* Basic Study No. 19, Rome, 1968.
[17] *Kenya Development Plan 1974–78,* pp. 226.
[18] For *per capita* consumption data see Table 1, FAO Basic Study No. 19.
[19] Sessional paper No. 4 of 1975 on *Economic Prospects & Policies,* Republic of Kenya, 1975.
[20] Ibid.
[21] Central Bank of Kenya, *Financial and Economic Review,* March 1975. Statutorily, the Central Bank is supposed to hold foreign reserves worth at least four months' imports.
[22] Sessional Paper No. 4, 1975.
[23] Work has already started on the FAO/UNDP supported Marketing Development Programme – Project No. KEN 75/005, 1975.
[24] See J.D. Von Piscke, 1973, 'A Survey of Major Agricultural Credit Programmes and Institutions operating in Kenya', IDS, November 1973.

[25] See IBRD, Integrated Agricultural Development Programme Report 1975.
[26] USAID, Agricultural Sector Programme Loan, 1975.
[27] For rainfall patterns in Kenya, see earlier section.
[28] S.H. Ominde, *Land and Population Movements in Kenya*, Heinemann Educational Books, 1968, p. 28.
[29] *Kenya, Development Plan for 1970–74*, p. 2.
[30] *Kenya, Development Plan for 1974–78*, p. 18.
[31] International Labour Office, *Employment, Incomes and Equality: A Strategy for Increasing Productive Employment in Kenya*, ILO: Geneva, 1972, p. 81.
[32] The six ecological zones coincide with the four categories into which land is classified earlier. Ecological zones 1 and 2 correspond to the high potential land with adequate rainfall; ecological zones 3 and 4 correspond to medium potential land, zone 5 to low potential land and zone 6 to nomadic pastoral land.
[33] See IBRD Report No. 254 (a) – KE.
[34] Simon Kuznets, *Economic Growth and Structure*, London: Heinemann, 1966.
[35] This includes large-scale farms as well as establishments of the public sector engaged in agricultural activities.
[36] *Development Plan for 1974–78*, table 3.3, p. 95.
[37] Ibid., p. 109.
[38] Albert Waterston, 'A Viable Model for Rural Development', *Finance and Development*, vol. 11, no. 4, December 1974, p. 23. The next three paragraphs rely heavily on this article.
[39] The experience gained in the SRDP roads indicates clearly that conditions exist under which large-scale employment of a local work force can be cheaper than the application of a capital-intensive technology. See Chapter 12 of the *Second Overall Evaluation of the Special Rural Development Programme*, IDS Occasional Paper No. 12, 1975.
[40] For an examination of the interaction between industry and agriculture, see Bruce F. Johnston, 'The Agriculture Industry Continuum'. Discussion Paper No. 215, IDS, University of Nairobi, December 1974, and also Bruce Johnston and Peter Kilby, *Agriculture and Structural Transformation*, Oxford University Press, 1975.
[41] Judith Heyer, Dunstan Ireri and Jon Moris, *Rural Development in Kenya*, IDS, October 1969, mimeo.
[42] Loc. cit., p. 55.
[43] See L.P. Mureithi, 'Non-farm Economic Activities in Rural Areas', in Frank Child and Mary Kempe (eds), *Small-Scale Enterprise*, IDS, Nairobi, Occasional Paper No. 6, 1973.
[44] *Kenya, Development Plan for 1974–78*, p. 19.
[45] *Kenya, Development Plan for 1974–78*, p. 197.
[46] See Diana Hunt, 'Methodological Issues and Selected Findings of an Analysis of the Distribution of Wealth and Income in Mbere Division, Eastern Kenya', IDS Working Paper No. 212, March 1975; and Michael Cowen, 'Concentration

of Sales and Assets: Dairy Cattle and Tea in Magutu, 1964–1971', IDS Working Paper No. 146, 1972.
[47] ILO, *Employment, Incomes and Equality*.
[48] Ibid., p. 77.
[49] Ibid., p. 76.
[50] ILO, *Employment, Incomes and Equality*, p. 45.
[51] W. Arthur Lewis, 'Summary of a Symposium on Economic Research for the World Employment Programme', *International Labour Review*, vol. 101, no. 5, May 1970, p. 551.
[52] See Michael P. Todaro, 'A Model of Labour Migration and Urban Unemployment in Less Developed Countries', *American Economic Review*, March 1969, pp. 138–48.
[53] Phillip M. Mbithi and Carolyn Barnes, 'Spontaneous Settlement in the Context of Rural Development in Kenya', IDS, June 1973, mimeo.
[54] For more on this, see P.M. Mbithi and B. Wisner, 'Drought and Famine in Kenya: Magnitude and attempted solutions', IDS Discussion Paper No. 144, July 1972; and George D. Gwyer, 'Trends in Kenyan Agriculture in Relation to Employment', *Journal of Modern African Studies*, vol. 11, no. 3, September 1973.
[55] Mbithi and Barnes, op. cit., pp. 2–3.
[56] This section was ably put together by Gideon M. Mutiso of the Department of Government, University of Nairobi.
[57] There are many studies of European Agriculture. Among the best are M.P.K. Sorrenson, *Origins of European Settlement*, 1968; R. Van Zwanenberg, 'Primative Colonial Accumulation in Kenya 1919–1939', D. Phil. Thesis (Sussex University), 1971.
[58] See (a) (Lawrence Report) Report of the Mission on Land Consolidation and Registration in Kenya 1965–66, Nairobi, 1966; (b) (Stamp Report) Report of the Mission appointed to advise on proposals for Further Transfer of European Farmers in Kenya, 1965 (mimeo); (c) Government of Kenya, Department of Settlement Five Year Review and Annual Report, 1969; (d) Government of Kenya Economic Surveys 1963–1975; (e) H. Ruthernberg, African Agricultural Production Development Policy in Kenya 1952–1965 (Berlin) 1966; (f) (Van Arkadie Report) Report of the Mission on Land Settlement in Kenya (mimeo) 1966, for the policy debates and figures of year to year Africanisation. See Colin Leys, *Underdevelopment in Kenya*, London, 1975; and G.C.M. Mutiso, *Political Economy as a Constraint to Equitable Distribution*, (mimeo) 1973, for details of the political impact of white highlands transfer.
[59] Colin Leys, op. cit., p. 63.
[60] Ministry of Agriculture Annual Reports 1963–1975.
[61] See, for example, G.D. Gwyer, 'Trends in Kenyan Agriculture in Relation to Employment', *Journal of Modern African Studies*, vol. 11, no. 3, September 1973.

[62] M. Godfrey and G.C.M. Mutiso, *Politics, Economics and Technical Training: Kenya's Institute of Science and Technology* (Forthcoming) reviews the structure of inequality even in Harambee education.

Achieving food and population balance in Nigeria: priorities in decision making

S.M. Essang

Introduction

The objective of this paper is to consider the Nigerian government's policy measures for achieving a balance between population and food supply in the 1970s and beyond. It will be argued that (i) Nigeria faces a considerable and growing food deficit which should be eliminated or reduced to a minimum before it reaches crisis proportions, (ii) the present food situation is largely a result of the fact that, though food—population imbalance has been evident since the 1960s, policy makers did not give top priority to food production until a few years ago, (iii) there is a tendency for Nigerian decision makers to view the food situation exclusively in terms of increased output of agricultural products and to ignore the obvious influence of demographic patterns, (iv) though no empirical evidence exists in support of the appropriateness of the strategy, major emphasis is being placed on the role of governmental institutions/organisations as well as large scale private farms and that (v) there is increasing pressure on agricultural scientists in both the universities and the research institutes to orient their research and other functions to the achievement of the national objective of increased food production.

Evidence of food—population imbalance in Nigeria

The first piece of evidence of food—population imbalance is provided by the data in Table 1 which shows the growth (in indices) of population [1] and food in Nigeria for the period 1960—1974. According to the data in Table 1, the growth rate of food supply has lagged behind that of Nigeria's population since 1963. While the population growth index increased at an annual compound rate of 5.2 per cent between 1960 and 1974, that of food production registered a growth rate of only 2.5 per cent during the same period.

Another piece of evidence is presented in Tables 2 and 3 which compare the growth of consumers and food price indices. In Table 2, the food price index increased more than the general consumer price index for most of the period. In Table 3, it is easily seen that though both the consumer and the food price indices were increasing at very high rates, the rates registered by the food price indices were higher in all the five towns. This situation reflects, to a large extent, the imbalance between the supply of and the demand for food during the period under

Table 1
Indices of growth of population and food supply in Nigeria,
1960–1974

Year	Indices (1960 = 100)	
	Population	Food
1960	100	100
1961	101	110
1962	104	114
1963	159	124
1964	163	121
1965	167	122
1966	171	109
1967	173	110
1968	180	113
1969	184	127
1970	189	130
1971	193	133
1972	205	137
1973	206	140
1974	211	143

Sources: (i) Federal Digest of Statistics, 1960, 1965, 1970 and 1975.
(ii) Agricultural Development in Nigeria, 1973–1985, FMANR, Lagos, 1974.

consideration. The third and most glaring evidence of food—population imbalance is given in Table 4 in which estimated food deficits and surpluses are presented for the years 1970, 1975, 1980 and 1985. From the information in Table 4, it is clear that Nigeria faces deficits in the supply of all the major food crop items except rice. While rural—urban migration, labour shortage in the rural areas and land tenure problems have been variously blamed for the situation, it is the view of knowledgeable observers of the Nigerian economic scene that government attitude lies at the heart of the current food shortage.

Government policy and food — population imbalance

Government policy is central to the existing food—population imbalance in two respects. First, there is the attitude which, until 1970, conceived of agricultural development exclusively in terms of the promotion of export crops. Second, there is the belief in government circles that it is possible to solve the food problem by

Table 2
Consumer and food price indices in Nigeria, 1960–1974

Year	Price indices (1960 = 100)	
	Consumer	Food
1960	100	100
1961	106	109
1962	112	118
1963	108	106
1964	110	106
1965	114	110
1966	125	133
1967	120	119
1968	120	112
1969	132	133
1970	150	164
1971	175	211
1972	180	217
1973	191	225
1974	215	259

Source: (i) Federal Digest of Statistics, 1960–1975.
(ii) Annual Abstract of Statistics, 1960–1975.

Table 3
Growth rates of consumer and food price indices in selected Nigerian towns, 1966–1972

Town	Annual growth rate of price index (%)	
	Consumer	Food
Lagos	6.5	6.8
Ibadan	4.9	7.6
Benin	6.7	7.6
Port-Harcourt	5.3	7.0
Enugu	5.3	5.4

Source: Computed from Federal Digest of Statistics, 1968, 1970 and 1973.

Table 4*
Nigeria: Estimated food deficits and surpluses ('000 tons)

	Commodity	1970	1975	1980	1985
1.	Maize	− 23.916	− 200.836	− 407.784	− 833.889
2.	Millet	− 87.950	− 705.818	−1503.521	−2946.225
3.	Sorghum	− 143.040	−1142.503	−2435.849	−4753.344
4.	Rice	+ 6.287	+ 67.546	+ 311.680	+ 820.160
5.	Wheat	− 3.759	− 38.544	− 52.778	− 101.329
6.	Yams	− 157.234	−1271.209	−2784.377	−5621.761
7.	Potatoes	− 2.917	− 21.639	− 51.815	− 104.915
8.	Cassava	− 162.743	−1316.065	−2882.757	−5820.729
9.	Cocoyam	− 16.138	− 130.509	− 285.859	− 577.237
10.	Plantain	− 29.684	− 222.174	− 483.174	− 973.537
11.	Cowpeas	− 0.454	− 4.133	+ 65.032	+ 145.180
12.	Groundnuts	− 6.934	− 55.450	− 117.722	− 230.730
13.	Soyabeans	− 0.389	+ 3.607	+ 13.217	+ 28.687
14.	Melon seed	− 1.167	− 9.542	− 20.218	− 41.699
15.	Vegetables	− 33.572	− 297.084	− 561.829	−1168.408
16.	Fruits	− 4.666	− 42.000	− 77.548	− 161.675
17.	Palm oil	− 33.148	− 265.376	− 561.654	−1092.898
18.	Poultry	− 2.009	− 19.986	− 32.472	− 67.621
19.	Beef	− 12.574	− 111.350	− 225.117	− 461.155
20.	Fish	− 46.146	− 407.908	− 836.224	−1702.000
21.	Eggs	− 3.759	− 36.365	− 62.844	− 131.451
22.	Milk	− 26.314	− 235.848	− 472.028	− 959.091

Source: S.O. Olayide, 'The Food Problem: Tractable Or the Mere Chase of a Mirage?' (mimeo), University of Ibadan, 1975.

concentrating only on measures that increase output in utter disregard for the role of the population variable.

That Nigerian agricultural policies were until 1970 exclusively export-oriented is now frankly acknowledged by policy makers themselves. For while the government set up several commodity research institutes and introduced an array of regulatory measures for the benefit of the export crop producer, practically nothing was done to boost food crop production. Among the reasons for the emphasis on export crops were the need for capital and foreign exchange, the lack of popular awareness that a food problem existed, the remarkable stability of food prices in

---

* For details on the techniques of estimation, see Olayide, S.O. *et al.*, *'Quantitative Analysis of Food Requirements Supplies and Demands in Nigeria, 1968–1985*, Federal Department of Agricultural, Lagos, 1972.

the 1950s and the early 1960s and the belief that the peasant producer could be counted upon to supply adequate food given the existence of 'abundant' land in the country. Whatever the explanations for government attitude, the results were lack of infrastructural investment in the food crop subsector and the tendency for farmers to concentrate on the more remunerative investments in export crop production.

Like most Third World countries, Nigeria is faced with a demographic situation characterised by a high growth rate which averages between 2.5 and 3.0 per cent per annum. In addition, the country is experiencing an explosive growth of urban population. According to a recent estimate, the population of the twenty largest urban centres increased at the rate of 8.3 per cent per annum between 1953 and 1973 [2]. Yet policy makers and their advisers pay scant attention to population as a variable affecting the food situation in Nigeria. One reason for ignoring the population variable is the fact that population is a very sensitive and explosive issue in Nigeria. Another reason is the fact that proposals for regulating population growth are very unpopular with influential Nigerians who view the problem mainly in terms of electoral and revenue considerations [3]. Moreover, it is believed that under peasant conditions characterised by labour intensive farming operations, rapid population growth could have a positive effect on farm output through increase in family hands. Finally, those who do not question the validity of the theory of demographic transition stress economic development as the key to the solution of whatever problem is posed by rapid population growth.

There can, however, be no doubt that rapid population growth aggravates the present imbalance between food supply and demand especially when this is coupled with growing *per capita* income. Apart from the demand effect, the current demographic pattern has several implications for food supply. It is associated with a rapidly declining land/man ratio. For example, a recent publication [4] indicates that for Nigeria as a whole, the land/man ratio declined from 1.86 hectares *per capita* in 1961 to 1.48 hectares in 1970. Within the same period, the size of arable land *per capita* fell from 1.39 to 1.10 hectares. For some states, the decline was even more dramatic as Table 5 illustrates.

The implication of this decline in land/man ratio is the inevitability of diminishing returns and the need to invest heavily in yield increasing innovations. Second, Nigerian population is very unevenly distributed, a situation which leads to the coexistence of areas with very high population densities with those characterised by low densities. The result is a sharp variation in land/man ratios among the states in the federation. This variation in land/man ratios has important implications for the strategy of food production. Among these is the need to relate farm size and the degree of labour intensity to the prevailing demographic and land situation within each state instead of relying on approaches dictated by such *a priori* considerations as economies of scale. Where the ratios are high as in Benue Plateau state (1.70), Kwara (1.90) and North Western (2.54), large scale farming could be an appropriate strategy for increasing food production. But where the ratios are very low as in the South East, East Central and Kano states

Table 5
Changing arable land/man ratios, selected states in Nigeria, 1961 and 1970

States	Land/man ratios (hectares per capita)		% decline
	1961	1970	
East Central state	0.25	0.19	24
Lagos state	0.82	0.64	22
Kano state	0.59	0.46	22
Rivers state	0.93	0.73	22
South Eastern state	2.78	0.62	78
Western state	0.63	0.49	22
Nigeria	1.39	1.10	21

Source: Computed from *Agricultural Development in Nigeria, 1973–85*, Federal Ministry of Agriculture and Natural Resources, 1974, p. 13.

(Table 5) appropriate strategy would appear to be small scale production units based on the intensive use of high yielding varieties of seeds and chemical fertilisers. The disparity in land availability among the states also suggests the need to discourage any attempt at state self sufficiency in food production. Rather, policy measures should aim at maximum food production in land abundant states such as Kwara, and North West where this could be done relatively cheaply. Finally, the fact that both land and population are unevenly distributed underlines the vital importance of measures aimed at fostering rural labour mobility throughout the country and end the present embarrassing coexistence of areas with overcrowded and over cropped land within the same region.

Current strategies for achieving food–population balance

Emphasis on government institutions and organisations

In the view of Nigerian policy makers and their advisers, the establishment of government or quasi-government food production organisations is a crucial element in the strategy for increasing food production. Accordingly, in the Third Development Plan, 1975–1980, government food production schemes will absorb ₦114.2 million or forty-five per cent of a total capital expenditure of ₦252 million allocated in the plan for food crop production [5]. In the southern states, government food projects are to account for ₦67.35 million out of a capital expenditure estimate of ₦131.38 million on food crops.

As usual, a number of arguments have been advanced in support of direct government involvement in food production. Among these are the need to supplement inadequate private efforts and promote a fuller utilisation of land and labour resources by establishing government food plantations in the land abundant parts of the country where there is considerable underutilisation of land. Direct government involvement in food production is also defended on the grounds that it is a strategy for large scale introduction of modern technology into food production. While a critical evaluation of the arguments presented above will not be undertaken in this paper, it should be noted that these arguments in no way imply that government direct entrepreneurship is the least costly approach to the solution of the food problem. On the contrary, this strategy is associated with a highly unproductive use of resources and entails a high opportunity cost to the Nigerian economy in many ways.

First, experience shows that the execution of government agricultural projects often ties down a very high proportion of administrative and technical manpower in the management of these projects. Consequently, only a small proportion of such manpower can be released to work on private smallholders' agricultural projects although the latter account for virtually all the food produced in the country. Second, government agricultural projects have very unenviable records because of political interference, a high incidence of corrupt and fraudulent practices and bureaucratic inertia. Third, using the data in the Third Development Plan document, it has been shown that the current emphasis on direct government involvement in food production will entail considerable foregone earnings. A calculation performed on the data shows that if the governments of the Rivers, South East, East Central and Western States were to devote all their capital estimates for food production to smallholder food projects, output of food would increase by ₦50 million at 1973 wholesale prices over and above what is likely to be achieved under the current strategy which biases allocation of the capital estimates heavily in favour of governmental projects [6].

Predilection for large scale farming

Apart from emphasising the role of governmental institutions, policy makers also display considerable predilection for large scale farming as a solution to the current food problem. It is believed that large scale farming holds the key to increased food production at lower production cost. The faith placed on large scale farming can be explained, though not justified, by a number of considerations. First is the widely held view that large farming facilitates the introduction of radically new production methods and organisational arrangements in the food producing subsector and thus could speed up the transformation of agriculture. Second is the desire to take advantage of economies of scale which are believed to arise from the use of indivisible inputs such as tractors, specialised managerial/supervisory staff and the integration of production and marketing. It is widely assumed that these economies will not only be appreciable but will necessarily be passed on to consumers by way of reduced product prices. Further, it is claimed that unlike the peasant smallholder system, large scale farms have considerable labour absorptive potential because of their much higher productivity and the tendency to employ labour all the year round at wages comparable to those prevailing in urban industries. Also, policy makers believe that a large scale agricultural production unit will facilitate mechanisation and, by eliminating the drudgery associated with manual operations, should make food production attractive to school leavers and thus stem the tide of rural—urban migration.

For all these reasons, emphasis is placed on large scale food farms especially in the discussions which preceded the launching of the Third National Plan, 1975—1980. At present, six of the twelve [7] states have large scale food farms while arrangements have already been concluded to involve foreign capitalists in large food farming projects.

Yet this emphasis on large scale farming as a strategy for dealing with current food deficits is misplaced for a number of reasons. First, it is based on an erroneous view which regards farm size as the crucial determinant of productivity and innovation in agriculture. That small farmers can be highly productive and innovative is shown by the experience of Japan, Taiwan and Korea. On the other hand, experience of large farms in some Latin American countries does not support the view that innovations and high labour productivity are the sole prerogatives of large farms. In Nigeria, the export crop sector has experienced dramatic productivity increases based on new high yielding varieties and the application of chemicals, even though the smallholder remains the backbone of the export economy. It is indeed surprising that policy makers fail to realise that the determinants of productivity and innovation in agriculture are appropriate price policy and massive capital investment in rural education, research, infrastructural facilities and credit. Second, the economies of scale argument in support of large food farming is based more on a faulty analogy with industrial production than on hard empirical evidence. A number of economists have advanced theoretical reasons why such economies are of limited significance in agricultural production [8]. It is, therefore, not surprising that empirical evidence hardly supports the economies of scale hypothesis. Third, even if economies of scale were to exist in food farming, there is no reason for believing that they would be reflected in lower product prices, given the tendency of large corporate firms to keep prices rigid by administrative action. Fourth, the adoption of innovation argument is hardly convincing. For one thing, the green revolution experience has shown that yield increasing technologies are not only very divisible but are also neutral to the scale of farming operations. In other words, as long as credit, water and adequate supporting services are available, the size of farm unit poses no insuperable barrier to the use of modern inputs. Finally, even if all the arguments in support of large scale food farming were both theoretically sound and empirically valid, they would hardly constitute a sufficient case for a food production strategy based on large farms. The issue of farm size transcends the question of economic efficiency, however defined. It involves the question of income distribution and the distribution of political power.

Food production programmes

In addition to the strategy of direct government entrepreneurship in food production and the encouragement of large scale farming, the attention of the policy makers and the Nigerian public is at present sharply focused on two programmes of an emergency nature. These related programmes are the National Accelerated Food Production Programme and Operation 'Feed the Nation'. The former, which is an attempt to apply the 'green revolution' agricultural strategy to food production in Nigeria, seeks to combine research, extension, the production and distribution of high yielding new seed varieties, heavy application of fertiliser and the provision of storage and marketing facilities. It differs from previous government efforts in several respects. It is the first national and co-ordinated effort to solve the food problem in the country. Also, unlike previous attempts, the current programme attaches considerable importance to research aimed at testing and adapting new crop varieties to different local conditions. The programme encourages production by each state of those food crops which are ecologically suited to it and can, therefore, be produced at least cost.

At the time of writing, the programme is still in the first phase of testing and establishing the adaptability of new varieties to local conditions. It is the view of this writer, however, that though the motive behind the programme is laudable and the financial resources for successful implementation readily available, the National Accelerated Food Production Programme has a limited chance of ushering in a green revolution in Nigeria, for many reasons.

First, is the very inadequate infrastructural investments in the food producing villages. Second, is the fact that, unlike the situation in India, Pakistan, the Philippines and Mexico where the green revolution was preceded by massive investments in research and the training of food crop scientists, investments in these areas have not been appreciable in Nigeria, notwithstanding the presence of IITA (International Institute of Tropical Agriculture). Nor is there a nationwide organisational and institutional framework to facilitate the rapid distribution of the new biological, chemical and mechanical technologies. On the contrary, the programme rests on the initiative and efforts of the Ministry of Agriculture and is, therefore, likely to suffer the fate of government directed agricultural projects [9]. Moreover, the institutional and cultural obstacles inherent in the Nigerian system of land rights are still evident and will continue to constrain food production.

The other programme, Operation 'Feed the Nation' is clearly an imitation of a similar programme which enabled Ghana to dramatically increase food production and cut down food imports. It seeks to involve every institution and person in food production and related activities and, therefore, could be regarded as the implementation phase of the National Accelerated Food Production Programme. In view of the fact that the programme was launched only recently, evaluative comments would seem very premature at the time of writing. Nevertheless, there can be no doubt that this is a classic example of episodic economic measures characteristic of the development process in the less developed countries. Moreover, the programme must be regarded as an acknowledgement by Nigerian policy makers of the failure of government directed large scale food projects which were a prominent feature of the 1970-1974 development plan. Further, in view of the fact that the launching of the programme was not preceded by detailed and careful planning of the input as well as the administrative and logistical framework, there is a strong probability that its implementation will involve considerable waste of resources.

The role of scientists and research institutions

Although past government policies did not place as much emphasis on the training of food crop scientists as on that of those working on export crops, existing food crop experts and related institutions are playing a significant role in the war against food shortage. In IITA scientists have embarked on a variety of research and have come up with high yielding seed varieties, disease and insect pest resistant cow-peas with a yield potential quadrupling that of the traditional variety and the production of yams from seeds which will in due course replace the present vegetative propagation method associated with a 25 per cent seed rate. In the universities, technical research activities oriented to food production include analysis of soil properties, fertiliser trials, the designing of suitable diets for maximum livestock growth and research on the biology, ecology and integrated control of major pests affecting food crops. Complementary economic research efforts are directed towards the identification of managerial practices essential to realising the yield potential of the new seed varieties, estimation of the production elasticities with respect to major inputs, designing the least cost feed mixes for livestock and analysis of marketing problems of food producers. In addition, many members of the academic staff of Nigerian universities are actively involved as consultants in the conception and planning of a number of food production and other related programmes. Such is the demand for the services of university academic staff by government agencies that the university authorities will sooner rather than later face up to the problem of deciding the optimal allocation of efforts between teaching/research which determines the professional advancement of their staff and food production-oriented extracurricula activities.

Notes

[1] For the purpose of this paper, the population data from which the indices were derived were obtained from (i) official records (1960-1963), (ii) projection of the 1963 census data at the rate of 2.5 per cent per annum (1963-1970) and (iii) projection of the 1963 census data at the rate of 3.0 per cent per annum (1971-1974). For the basis of the projections see 10, 11 and 12.

[2] S.O. Olayide, 'Policy for Dealing with Urban Sprawl in Nigeria', (mimeo), 1974.

[3] The share of Federal revenues which accrue to the states in Nigeria is based in part on population. For the politics of Nigerian Population see R.K. Udoh, 'Population and Politics in Nigeria' in *The Population of Tropical Africa*, Cadwell and Okonjo (eds), London, 1968.

[4] *Agricultural Development in Nigeria 1973–1985*, Federal Ministry of Agriculture and Natural Resources, 1974.

[5] Third National Development Plan, 1975–1980, Ministry of Information, Lagos, 1975.

[6] S.M. Essang, 'Pattern of Estimated Agricultural Expenditures in the 1975–80 Nigerian Plan: Some Implications', Forthcoming paper.

[7] Since February 1976, seven additional states have been created, bringing the number to nineteen.

[8] J.M. Brewster, 'The Machine Process in Agriculture and Industry', *Journal of Farm Economics*, vol. 32, February 1950.
A.M. Ekhusro, 'Returns to Scale in Indian Agriculture', *Indian Journal of Agric. Economics*, vol. 19, 1964.

[9] Already, the reasons given for the delay in moving from research/testing to the production phase are unavailability of new inputs and untimely arrival of the inputs which is a result of lack of forward planning and bureaucratic bottlenecks. See (i) NAFPP, Annual Progress Report for 1975/76, Western State, 1975 and (ii) NAFPP, Annual Progress Report, 3rd April, 1975, page 1.

[10] Cadwell and Okonjo, op. cit.

[11] A. Igun, 'Nigerian Population Projection 1969–1985' (Personal communication).

[12] S.O. Olayide, D. Olatunbosun, Idusogie and D. Abiagum, 'Quantitative Analysis of Food Requirements, Supplies and Demands in Nigeria 1968–1985'.

Discussion on papers by Mureithi and Otieno and by Essang

O.A. Hakim

Dr Hani Affifi in opening the discussion, doubted the practical ability of the land reforms advocated by the authors as a means of narrowing the gap between food demand and supply and solving the distribution problem and also the recommendation to increase employment by promoting crops (without specifying them) having a high labour requirement. He also wished to know more about the non-agricultural sources that were reported to contribute 40 per cent of rural incomes in 1969. He felt that both papers neglected demographic factors as important elements in the solution of the problem.

Dr Andah drew attention to the uncertainty attaching to the statistical data on food production, stressing the fact that the majority of food crops do not pass through any point where they are recorded. Consequently a check on absolute levels is lacking. He spoke of the place of export crops in the colonial era in African countries, the demand for such crops by the industries of mother countries, and the continuance of the emphasis on export crops after independence because of the compelling need for capital and foreign exchange. The consequent neglect of domestic food needs might, he suggested, be solved by some degree of regional specialisation, which would, at the same time, reduce interregional competition for certain resources. In the course of general discussion the marketing efficiency in Kenya was criticised, together with the marketing policy of the maize marketing board, the latter being seen as contributing to price rigidity to the point that prices failed to reflect the forces of supply and demand. In reply it was argued that, though the board's price policy needed revision, the board's original purpose when established was simply to build a maize reserve against disaster years.

The question of encouragement of small farms and its effect on productivity and on migration attracted extended discussion. It was noted that the ILO report of 1970 indicated higher productivity on large farms. Creating more small farms might then be expected to reduce productivity. Moreover there was a tendency for small farm promotion to have the effect of moving agriculture out of the commercial sector which was, in the long term, imprudent. On the other hand it was held that support for the creation of more small farms really stemmed from its contribution to solving the problem of migration; it was not envisaged that large farms would be abolished.

The speaker's view of both production increase and population reduction as contributing to a solution of the problem brought the comment that the data which had been tabled suggested that family planning could reduce the Kenya population by only 150,000 people. In reply it was argued that family planning could at least be seen as an insurance against a marked increase in the population.

On a technical point coffee and tea were seen as perhaps the most significant labour intensive crops in Kenya. Was an argument for their promotion tantamount to the authors advocating the neglect of maize in Kenya notwithstanding the shortages which that country had suffered and the place of maize in the diet of the majority of the people?

The comment to the effect that too many African countries concentrated on industrialisation led to a general discussion on this issue. It was argued that, since this was not an unnatural tendency all things considered, it could be usefully channelled into the development of food processing industries. However this development was not without its problems. The local consumer was not accustomed to processed foods and price did not encourage their consumption locally. Relations with mother countries after independence did not encourage import substituting industries. A slightly contrary comment that the deficit on the Nigerian food balance reflected Nigerian demand consequent on high income after the discovery of oil brought the reply that food imports were high even before that point.

Various facets of the subject of migration were explored. Some saw the causal factor as primarily the higher incomes which could be got in the cities compared with the countryside. Others wished to stress either in addition to this, or possibly instead of it, the idea that it was the quality of life as a whole which attracted them. The private land ownership and the after effects of civil war which made movement across tribal lines less attractive were among the restraints on migration.

SPECIAL SESSION II

Achieving a Balance Between
Population and Food

ASIA

Achieving a balance between population and food: the Indian case

V.M. Dandekar

The purpose of the present paper is to review briefly the growth of population and the expansion of food production in India in the past quarter century and to assess the prospects of achieving a balance between population and food in the near future. It will be evident that, in spite of vigorous official action on both fronts, namely population and food, a balance between the two is by no means in sight.

Population—food balance in the past

In Table 1 are given the basic data for 1951 to 1974. It shows, for each year, the estimated population, the estimated output of foodgrains, net imports of foodgrains, and changes in stocks of foodgrains held by the government. A simple calculation gives the estimated supplies of foodgrains to the public. There would also be stocks in the hands of the public and changes in them from year to year as producers, traders, and consumers would all build up stocks in good years and carry them into the next year; and, in a bad year, withdraw from the previous stocks. No estimates are available of changes in stocks with the public. We should suppose that in years in which the production is much below the normal, the stocks would be low. In particular, we shall assume that at the end of 1952, 1953, 1958 and 1967, the stocks in public hands were near zero and that at the end of 1974, they were very small. On this basis, the average *per capita* consumption, including all uses such as human consumption, seed, animal feed and wastage, amounted to 181.80 kgs. *per capita* per annum between 1954 and 1958; 184.87 kgs per annum between 1959 and 1967; and 188.0 kgs per annum between 1968 and 1974. The estimated changes in stocks in public hands, on the assumption that the *per capita* annual consumtpion between 1954 and 1958 was in fact 181.80 kgs, between 1959 and 1967 in fact 184.87 kgs and between 1968 and 1974 in fact 188.0 kgs, are given in column 7 of the table. These are of course hypothetical but they are not implausible. For instance, it may be noted that the maximum stocks with the public (at the end of 1965, fully unloaded in 1966 and 1967) constituted about 20 per cent of the supplies of foodgrains with the public during the year. This amounts to carrying less than two-and-half months' requirements from one year into the next and should be quite normal. It is possible, therefore, that the actual *per capita* annual consumption during 1954–58, 1959–67, and 1968–74 was in fact about 181.80 kgs, 184.87 kgs, and 188.0 kgs, respectively.

Table 1
Population–food balance

Year	Population (million)	Output of foodgrains (million tonnes)	Net imports (million tonnes)	Changes in government stocks (million tonnes)	Foodgrains supplies with the public (million tonnes)	Hypothetical changes in stocks with the public (million tonnes)	Per capita consumption (kgs)
(1)	(2)	(3)	(4)	(5)	(6)=(3)+(4)−(5)	(7)	(8)
1951	363.211	55.011	4.801	+ 0.589	59.223	—	163.05
1952	369.231	55.603	3.926	+ 0.618	58.911	—	159.55
1953	375.633	61.784	2.035	− 0.483	64.302		171.18
1954	382.438	72.326	0.832	+ 0.202	72.956	+ 3.427	181.80
1955	389.668	70.739	0.513	− 0.746	71.998	+ 1.155	181.80
1956	397.334	69.335	1.372	− 0.602	71.309	− 0.928	181.80
1957	405.450	72.457	3.620	+ 0.856	75.221	+ 1.509	181.80
1958	414.021	66.629	3.210	− 0.269	70.108	− 5.163	181.80
1959	423.052	78.803	3.851	+ 0.492	82.162	+ 3.951	184.87
1960	432.543	77.120	5.119	+ 1.403	80.836	+ 0.871	184.87
1961	442.372	82.326	3.486	− 0.165	85.977	+ 4.195	184.87
1962	452.212	82.397	3.629	− 0.355	86.381	+ 2.780	184.87
1963	462.027	80.330	4.536	− 0.022	84.888	− 0.528	184.87
1964	472.132	80.699	6.252	− 1.243	88.194	+ 0.910	184.87
1965	482.530	89.367	7.439	+ 1.063	95.743	+ 6.537	184.87
1966	493.209	72.347	10.311	+ 0.137	82.521	− 8.660	184.87
1967	504.162	74.231	8.659	− 0.260	83.150	−10.056	184.87
1968	515.414	95.052	5.671	+ 2.035	98.688	+ 1.790	188.00
1969	526.986	94.013	3.824	+ 0.462	97.375	− 1.698	188.00
1970	538.881	99.501	3.547	+ 1.116	101.932	+ 0.622	188.00
1971	550.822	108.422	2.010	+ 2.568	107.864	+ 4.309	188.00
1972	562.467	105.168	−0.498	− 4.694	109.364	+ 3.620	188.00
1973	574.216	97.026	3.587	− 0.309	100.922	− 7.031	188.00
1974	586.056	103.611	4.827	− 0.456	108.894	− 1.285	188.00

Source: Bulletin of Food Statistics 1975. Directorate of Economics and Statistics, Ministry of Agriculture & Irrigation, Government of India, New Delhi.

We may neglect the very low *per capita* consumption in the early years of 1951, 1952 and 1953. Even if we do that and consider the situation since 1954, there is a clear evidence of a certain, though a small, improvement in the *per capita* consumption of foodgrains. It increased from 181.80 kgs in 1954 to 188.0 kgs in 1974, which is an increase of about 3.4 per cent over a period of 20 years. This came about partly because of increased production and partly increased imports. The position is summarised in the following:

Period	Production	Net imports net of change in govt. stocks	Consumption	Column (3)/(4)
		(kgs per annum per capita)		(%)
(1)	(2)	(3)	(4)	(5)
1954–58	176.72	5.08	181.80	2.795
1959–67	172.33	12.54	184.87	6.785
1968–74	182.31	5.77	188.00	3.070

Thus, in 1954–58, 2.8 per cent of the consumption was supported by imports. The improvement in the *per capita* consumtpion in 1959–67 was entirely due to increased imports; production of foodgrains *per capita* declined from 176.62 kgs in 1954–58 to 172.33 kgs in 1959–67 and imports were increased from 5.08 kgs in 1954–58 to 12.54 kgs *per capita* in 1959–67. The imports supported 6.8 per cent of the consumption in 1959–67. The improvement in 1968–74 was almost entirely due to increased production though *per capita* imports were also somewhat higher than in 1954–58. Compared to 1954–58, the level of *per capita* consumption in 1968–74 was higher by 6.20 kgs. Of this, 5.59 kgs was contributed by increased production and 0.069 kgs by increased imports.

Targets and prospects for food supply

The Draft Fifth Five Year Plan (1974–79) has proposed a target of 140.0 million tonnes of foodgrains in 1979. The projected population in 1979 is 636.8 million. This gives an output of 219.85 kgs of foodgrains *per capita* which is more than enough to achieve a balance between population and food. In fact, it seems that at the level of development and *per capita* consumption envisaged in the Fifth Plan, 200.0 kgs of foodgrains *per capita* should be adequate for the purpose. In the following, we shall examine the prospects of achieving this in the near future.

The targets of food production envisaged in the Fifth Plan were much influenced by the record production in 1971, namely, 108.4 million tonnes. Consequently, the Planning Commission estimated that the output of foodgrains in 1974 would be 114.0 million tonnes and targeted the output in 1979 to be 140.0 million tonnes. The estimate of 114.0 million tonnes in 1974 has turned out to be very much an overestimate; the actual production in that year was 103.6 million tonnes. Moreover, an increase from an assumed 114.0 million tonnes in 1974 to 140.0 million tonnes in 1979 is an increase of 22.8 per cent which is equivalent to an annual rate of growth of 4.1 per cent. This is a growth rate in the production of foodgrains never achieved in the past over any period of five years, including the period of the new strategy of agricultural production based on high-yielding varieties of foodgrains and intensive application of water and fertilisers. Both the potential and the limitations of the new strategy have now become evident. The chief inputs are the research in high yielding varieties and pests and diseases to which they are liable; irrigation water and fertilisers. The high yielding varieties have to be extended and new varieties have to be continually developed. Except for sheer good luck, the progress in this matter cannot be more rapid than in the past few years. Expansion of irrigation is both expensive and inevitably a slow process. The world-wide oil crisis and consequent rise in the prices of fertilisers have caused new problems in the supply of and expansion of use of fertilisers. A large part of agriculture in India is still at the mercy of the monsoon and the output is liable to wide fluctuations from year to year. Because of these circumstances, a more realistic assessment of future prospects should be based on the whole experience of the past two decades.

In Table 1, we have already presented the estimates of output of foodgrains from 1951 to 1974. The increase in the output in the initial years up to 1954 was largely due to expansion of cultivation of which there is little possibility any more. Hence, to assess the future prospects, it is advisable to consider the period beginning with 1954. The annual rate of growth obtained by fitting an exponential curve to the estimated output from 1954 to 1974 turns out to be 2.13 per cent ($r^2 = 0.74969$). There are four years in which the actual output deviates from the exponential trend by a large magnitude: in 1958, 1966 and 1967, the output was exceptionally low; in 1971, the output was exceptionally high. The four years illustrate the vagaries of the monsoon; but they are not useful in determining the growth rate over a period. If we omit them, the annual growth rate turns out to be 2.08 per cent with greatly improved coefficient of determination ($r^2 = 0.94128$). We are inclined to accept this growth rate for assessing the future prospects of food production.

In Table 2, along with the estimates of actual output of foodgrains are given the estimates of the trend output determined by fitting an exponential curve to the data for 17 years from 1954 to 1974 omitting 1958, 1966, 1967 and 1971. As mentioned above, the annual growth rate so determined is 2.08 per cent. Also given are the deviations of the actual output from the trend output expressed as percentage of the latter. It will be noticed that except in the omitted years, the deviations of the actual output are more or less within 5 per cent of the trend output. In the omitted years, the deviations are of course much larger. In 1958, 1966 and 1967 the actual output fell below the trend output by 11.5, 18.5 and 18.1 per cent respectively; in 1971, the output was above the trend output by 10.2 per cent.

Table 2
Exponential trend fitted to output of foodgrains, 1954–74
(omitting 1958, 1966, 1967 and 1971)

Year	Output of foodgrains (million tonnes)	Exponential trend output (million tonnes)	Deviation of actual output as per cent of trend output
1954	72.326	69.328	+ 4.324
1955	70.739	70.770	− 0.044
1956	69.335	72.241	− 4.023
1957	72.457	73.743	− 1.744
1958	66.629	75.277	− 11.488
1959	78.803	76.842	+ 2.552
1960	77.120	78.440	− 1.683
1961	82.326	80.070	+ 2.818
1962	82.397	81.735	+ 0.810
1963	80.330	83.435	− 3.721
1964	80.699	85.170	− 5.250
1965	89.367	86.941	+ 2.790
1966	72.347	88.748	− 18.480
1967	74.231	90.594	− 18.062
1968	95.052	92.477	+ 2.784
1969	94.013	94.400	− 0.410
1970	99.501	96.363	+ 3.256
1971	108.422	98.367	+ 10.222
1972	105.168	100.412	+ 4.736
1973	97.026	102.500	− 5.340
1974	103.611	104.631	− 0.975

Annual rate of growth = 2.08 per cent (r^2 = 0.94128)

Earlier it was suggested that an output of 200.0 kgs *per capita* would be adequate to achieve a balance between population and food. If a trend output of 200.0 kgs is reached, we may expect that in all years, except the very bad years which might occur once in seven or eight years, the actual output will be above 190.0 kgs *per capita* and that would be adequate to achieve the balance between population and food. In Table 3, the trend output is projected for 1981 and 1986. In parallel columns are given estimates of projected population and projected output of foodgrains *per capita* of the projected population. Thus it will be seen that even in 1986, that is ten years hence, the *per capita* output will barely reach the level of 190.0 kgs, provided the population does not grow faster than is projected. It is obvious, therefore, that the growth rate of output of foodgrains derived from the trend in the past 21 years since 1954, namely 2.08 per cent, will prove

Table 3
Projected population and output of foodgrains

Year	Population (million)	Ouptut of foodgrains (million tonnes)	Output of foodgrains per capita (kgs)
1974	586.056	104.631	178.53
1981	657.329	120.843	183.84
1986	705.200	133.940	189.93

inadequate to achieve a balance between population and food even in 1986. For this purpose, the growth rate of output of foodgrains must be immediately stepped up to at least 2.52 per cent per annum. Taking the trend output of 104.6 million tonnes in 1974 as the base, if the output grows at 2.52 per cent per annum, it will reach 141.0 million tonnes in 1986 which, with the projected population of 705.2 million, gives 200.0 kgs *per capita.* A growth rate of 2.52 per cent per annum in the output of foodgrains is not impossible but, judging by the past experience, is not easy and cannot certainly be taken for granted. Much greater effort in the expansion of irrigation and fuller utilisation of available water will be needed. While efforts on the agricultural front are thus intensified, sustained efforts must be made to ensure that the population in 1986 is no more than the projected 705.2 million.

Population growth

In Table 4 are given decennial estimates of population of India for 70 years from 1901 to 1971 and also estimates of crude birth and death rates for the several decades. It will be seen that India did not have much of a population problem until 1921. In the two decades, 1901–1921, the population grew by only 5.4 per cent. But, since 1921, as a result of a gradual improvement of the medical and health services, the death rates began to fall without a corresponding fall in the birth rate. In the three decades, 1921–1951, the death rate fell by about 20 per thousand but the birth rate fell by only 8 per thousand. In consequence, the population increased by 11 per cent in 1921–31, by 14.2 per cent in 1931–41; and by 13.3 per cent in 1941–1951. Thus, in 1951, India already had a recognisable population problem on her hands.

In 1951, India entered the era of planned economic development and, as an essential and integral part of that process, rapidly expanded her medical and public health services. As a result, the death rate declined rapidly, from 27.4 per thousand in 1951 to 22.8 per thousand in 1961, to 15.1 per thousand in 1971. On the other hand, the birth rate declined by only 2.7 per thousand, from 39.9 per

Table 4
Trends in population, birth and death rates in India

Year	Population (million)	Decadal growth (%)	Annual growth (%)	Rate per annum per 1000		
				Crude birth	Crude death	Natural growth
1901	238.337	⎫		–	–	–
1911	252.005	⎬ 2.67	0.26	49.2	42.6	6.6
1921	251.239	⎭		48.1	47.2	0.9
1931	278.867	11.10	1.05	46.4	36.3	10.1
1941	318.539	14.23	1.34	45.2	31.2	14.0
1951	360.950	13.31	1.26	39.9	27.4	12.5
1961	439.073	21.64	1.98	41.7	22.8	18.9
1971	547.950	24.80	2.24	37.2	15.1	22.1

Source: Pocket Book of Population Statistics, Registrar General of India, Census Centenary, 1972.

thousand in 1951 to 37.2 per thousand in 1971. In consequence, the population increased at an unprecedented rate of 1.98 per cent per annum between 1951 and 1961 and at 2.24 per cent per annum between 1961 and 1971. Thus the process of economic development greatly accelerated population growth and seriously aggrevated the population problem.

In 1951, the Government of India enunciated the official policy on population and explicitly recognised the need to reduce the birth rate along with the decline in the death rate; but it mainly relied on the 'natural' methods of contraception, namely, abstinence and rhythm. In 1956, a major change in policy occurred; sterilisation was officially accepted and an active programme of family planning was initiated. The programme is now well established. It is an entirely voluntary programme actively supported by extension education and persuasion. In the service centres, all effective methods of contraception are made available for the individual to choose from. These include the conventional contraceptives such as the condoms, diaphragms, jelly/cream and foam tablets; the intra-uterine device (IUD) and finally sterilisation of the male (vasectomy) and of the female (tubectomy). Acceptors of IUD and sterilisation are offered small monetary incentives partly to cover the incidental costs and partly to compensate possible loss of wages for a few days because of forced rest.

By the end of March 1975, the estimated number of married women of reproductive age effectively protected from conception was as shown on page 126. The number of married women of reproductive age (15–44) in March 1975 is estimated to be 102.2 million. Of these, 14.97 million, that is 14.6 per cent, were effectively protected from conception. It will be seen that sterilisation has proved

	Number of women of reproductive age (15–44) (million)
Sterilisation	12.533
IUD	1.223
Conventional contraception	1.215
Total	14.971

to be the main instrument of protection from conception; it accounts for 83.7 per cent of the contraceptive protection provided in March 1975. The balance is equally divided between IUD and the conventional contraceptives.

Population prospects

The population projections accepted by the Planning Commission in the Draft Fifth Five Year Plan are based on the following assumptions regarding decline of birth, death and growth rates in the coming decade:

Year	Birth rate	Death rate	Growth rate
	(per thousand of population)		
1973–74	35.57	15.23	20.34
1978–79	29.57	12.81	16.76
1983–84	24.82	11.14	13.68

Thus it is expected to bring down the birth rate by 1.2 per thousand on an average every year in the first quinquennium 1973–74 to 1978–79 and by 0.95 per thousand on an average every year in the second quinquennium from 1978–79 to 1983–84. On this basis the birth rate is estimated to decline to 26.69 per thousand in 1981–82 and to 22.09 per thousand in 1986–87.

The birth rate during 1951–61 was estimated to be about 40.0 per thousand and we might take this to be the level of birth rate prior to the initiation of the family planning programme. As we have seen, as a result of the operation of the family planning programme over 20 years from 1956 to 1975, 14.6 per cent of the married women of reproductive age were contraceptively protected in March 1975. If the protected women were evenly distributed among different categories of women with different levels of fertility, the contraceptive protection of 14.6 per cent of the women would bring down the birth rate by about 14.6 per cent, that is by about 5.86 per thousand (14.6 per cent of 40.0 per thousand). In fact, a majority of the protected women are found to have three or more living children. Taking into account the distribution of women according to the number of living children and the live-birth order-specific fertility rates, it seems that the contraceptive protection of 14.6 per cent of the married women of reproductive age would cause a decline of about 4.89 per thousand in the birth rate. We may generalise this and say that, to cause a decline of one per thousand in the birth rate, three per cent of the married women of reproductive age must be contraceptively protected.

The implications of this for the future family planning programme are as under:

	1981–82	1986–87
Targeted birth rate per thousand	26.69	22.09
Decline per thousand from the pre-family planning level of 40.0 per thousand	13.31	17.91
Per cent of married women of reproductive age that must be protected	39.93	53.73
Estimated population at the beginning of the year in million	657.329	705.200
Estimated number of married women of reproductive age (172 per thousand of population) in million	113.061	121.294
Number of married women of reproductive age that must be contraceptively protected at the beginning of the year in million	45.145	65.171

In short, while in March 1975, only 14.97 (say 15.0) million married women of reproductive age were contraceptively protected, this number will have to be raised to 45.145 (say 45.0) million in March 1981 and further to 65.171 (say 65.0) million in March 1986. This will require immediate expansion, more than doubling, of the family planning programme. The computational details are shown in Table 5.

In Table 5, column (2) gives the number of married women of reproductive age that must be protected at the end of each year. Column (3) gives the addition to this number each year. Besides this additional number, the number of protected cases which become inoperative each year will have to be replaced. This is estimated in column (4) assuming that 5 per cent of the protected cases at the beginning of each year become inoperative during the course of the year. This is approximately correct in the case of sterilisation which becomes inoperative only in the event of death or widowhood of the mother or her reaching the end of her reproductive period, namely, age 45. In the case of IUD insertion, the proportion becoming inoperative each year is much higher, estimated to be about 30 per cent, because, in addition to the above mentioned circumstances, allowance has to be made for the removals and expulsion of the IUD. We may neglect it because, as we have seen, sterilisation accounts for over 80 per cent of the contraceptive protection presently provided. This proportion is likely to increase in future. Column (5) which is the total of columns (3) and (4) thus gives the number of

Table 5
Family planning programme for the decade: 1975–76 to 1985–86

Year	Number of women to be protected at year end	Additional number of women to be protected	Replacement of inoperative cases	Total number of new women to be protected during the year
		(figures in million)		
(1)	(2)	(3)	(4)	(5) = (3)+(4)
1974–75	15.00			
1975–76	20.50	5.50	0.750	6.250
1976–77	25.80	5.30	1.025	6.325
1977–78	30.90	5.10	1.290	6.390
1978–79	35.80	4.90	1.545	6.445
1979–80	40.50	4.70	1.790	6.490
1980–81	45.00	4.50	2.025	6.525
1981–82	49.40	4.40	2.250	6.650
1982–83	53.60	4.20	2.470	6.670
1983–84	57.60	4.00	2.680	6.680
1984–85	61.40	3.80	2.880	6.680
1985–86	65.00	3.60	3.070	6.670

women which will have to be given new protection each year. This number is 6.25 million in 1975–76, gradually rises to 6.68 million in 1984–85 and gradually declines thereafter.

To judge the feasibility of achieving these targets, one should examine the performance in the past. Though the programme was actively initiated in 1956, it picked up only after 1966. The progress in vasectomies was particularly impressive. But after reaching a peak of 2.6 million vasectomies in 1972–73, it suddenly collapsed. Vasectomy is amenable to mass campaigning. This was done on a large scale in 1971–72 and 1972–73 with added financial incentives. It showed some immediate results but, for good reason, the practice was given up. The number of vasectomies performed in 1974–75 was only 608,000. In comparison, the progress in tubectomies has been slower but steadier. The number of tubectomies performed in 1971–72, 1972–73, 1973–74 and 1974–75 are 567,000, 509,000, 539,000 and 720,000, respectively. Tubectomy appears to be preferred to even the IUD insertion. In fact, after a promising start, the IUD seems to have lost ground, reportedly because of numerous post-insertion complaints. Since 1971–72, the number of tubectomies has steadily exceeded the number of IUD insertions.

Thus it seems that sterilisation by vasectomy and tubectomy will remain the main item in the family planning programme in the immediate future. In 1972–73, the Family Planning Programme in India performed over 3.0 million cases of vasectomy and tubectomy. With some strengthening, it may be able to perform over 6.0 million cases each year.

The crucial question is whether the targets can be achieved under a voluntary programme as it operates at present. It may be noted that a reduction in the birth rate from a pre-family-planning level of 40.0 per thousand to 22.1 per thousand in 1986–87 is a reduction of 44.8 per cent. It means that of the births ordinarily occurring in a year, about 45.0 per cent must be prevented. Of the live births occurring in a year, it is estimated that about 45.0 per cent occur to mothers who already have three or more living children. Hence, the programme must aim at sterilising all mothers, or their husbands, who have three or more living children. It is doubtful whether this can be done, at any rate for some years to come, under a purely voluntary programme. It is not without reason that serious consideration is being given to making sterilisation legally compulsory for all couples having three or more living children, in spite of certain obvious dangers and difficulties of compulsion.

Conclusions

In spite of the serious efforts being made by the Government of India on both fronts, it seems that balance between population and food is not easy to reach much before 1986. Even to reach it in 1986, the efforts on both fronts will have to be further intensified. The rate of growth of production of foodgrains in the past two decades has been only 2.08 per cent per annum. It must be stepped up to at least 2.52 per cent per annum. This is not impossible but cannot be taken for granted. On the population front, the family planning programme must be expanded to perform at least 6.0 million sterilisations every year. The aim must be to sterilise all married women of reproductive age, or their husbands, who already have three or more living children. If this cannot be achieved by education and persuasion under a voluntary programme, compulsion may have to be contemplated.

It is thus obvious that the battle will have to be fought on both fronts – food and population. Fortunately, the two programmes are operationally independent and they do not compete for the same real resources. It is also evident that, in the process of economic development, the two programmes will mutually strengthen each other. Hence, both the programmes can and must be pursued simultaneously and vigorously. Between the two, the family planning programme is presumably capable of a more rapid expansion because the real-resource constraint on this programme is less rigid than in the case of expansion of food production.

Population and food production in Indonesia

Syarifuddin Baharsjah [1]

Population growth and food consumption

Presently Indonesia is importing rice to meet its consumption needs, despite its successful efforts to increase domestic production through intensification programmes. Several reasons had been put forward for the delay in achieving self-sufficiency. One is the rapid increase of the population. The annual rate of population growth has been estimated at 2.55 per cent. Although a family planning programme has been implemented in an intensive manner since 1967, its impact will not assume significant proportions until the 1980s. Based on past achievements several projections are made with regard to domestic rice production. When these are compared to consumption projections under different sets of assumptions concerning the effectiveness of the family planning programme, the growth of *per capita* income and consumption habits, it becomes clear that with the same performance in food production as in the past few years self-sufficiency conditions could only be maintained if the family planning programme succeeds in lowering the rate of population growth significantly.

Another factor which contributed to the delay in achieving self-sufficiency was the rise in consumption due to rises in *per capita* income. There is no accurate estimate of the income elasticity of demand for rice in Indonesia. It is believed that for the greater part of the population which is currently enjoying but a low level of income, the income elasticity was underestimated when targets were set and self-sufficiency was predicted in the past. Similar underestimation of the income elasticities in the demands for sugar and cloves were suspected when it was discovered that instead of obtaining surpluses as targetted, the country had to increase the imports of these commodities.

Table 1 shows the above mentioned production and consumption projections. The low estimates shown in this table were obtained by assuming that the family programme could effectively lower the rate of population growth from the current 2.55 to 2.49 per cent, while *per capita* income was assumed to increase steadily at about 4 per cent a year. The high estimates were obtained on the assumption that the family planning programme failed to lower the rate of population growth and that at the same time due to better health conditions the rate of population growth increases, reaching about 3 per cent by the end of the century. The *per capita* income was assumed to increase at an optimistic rate of 4 to 6 per cent per year. On both estimates, the income elasticity in the demand for rice was estimated at 0.4.

Table 1
Projections of domestic production and consumption of rice,
Indonesia, 1978–1998

Year	Estimated production* ('000 tons)	Estimated consumtpion	
		Low estimates ('000 tons)	High estimates ('000 tons)
1978	18.183	18.766	18.766
1983	22.353	22.832	25.611
1988	27.494	27.779	32.686
1993	33.818	33.797	51.390
1998	41.596	41.120	68.771

* Based on performance in first and second five year plan.

Source: Directorate General of Food Crops, Ministry of Agriculture, 1975.

A closer look at the estimated production will also reveal a high degree of optimism with respect to the performance in increasing rice production. With the current harvested acreage of almost 9 million hectares the projected production figures imply yields of about 3.5 to 4 tons per hectare compared to the current 1 ton per hectare. On the other hand, with present yields they imply an increase of harvested acreage of up to 400 per cent.

Most of the need for rice will arise in Java, where most of the population of Indonesia live. A prominent feature of the demography of Indonesia, beside the size of the population, is that the population is quite unevenly distributed. Java and Madura, in which land area is but 6.95 per cent of the total land area of the country, are inhabited by about 64 per cent of the total population. Consequently, the regions in Java belong to the world's most densely populated, while those in the outer islands are sparsely populated.

Even if it is assumed that the family planning programme is to be directed only to the densely populated regions in Java and that this programme is successful in lowering the rate of population growth, the population density in Java will still reach over 1,000 persons per square kilometre by the year 2000. If the family planning programme is not as successful, the population density may be as high as 1,300 persons per square kilometre. In the outer islands, even without a successful family planning programme the population densities are considerably lower, namely 115 persons per square kilometre in Sumatra, 117 in Sulawesi and only 23 in Kalimantan by the year 2000.

Transmigration of part of the population from the dense regions to the outer islands had long been regarded as one means of improving the uneven population distribution. The resettlement programme has been in existence since 1905 when the first organised resettlement project was started at Gedong Tataan Lampung. Since then, the transmigration programme has attempted to move farm families from Java and resettle them in the thinly populated outer islands. The programme was interrupted briefly by the Second World War and was resumed after independence.

The outflow of farmers from Java to the outer islands under the government sponsored transmigration programme does not give the complete picture of the migration which occurs between Java and the outer islands. Each year there is a steady, if not increasing, flow of people who migrate from these thinly populated outer islands to Java. Young men migrate to look for training and employment opportunities which they believe are more plentiful in Java. Once settled their families may follow. Many a disappointed transmigrant may drop out of the programme and return to more familiar situations in Java. On the other hand there are also the spontaneous, non-supported transmigrants who voluntarily left Java for the thinly populated regions. News of prospering transmigration areas may reach home and attract relatives to join. In many cases the spontaneous transmigrants would become the more successful farmers in the new areas. There is no accurate information about the numbers of persons migrating between Java and the outer islands. An estimate placed the net-outflow from Java at 50 persons per year [2].

The resettlement programme and future food production

The main effort to increase food production has been the intensification programme which was directed chiefly to the high potential regions mostly situated in Java and Bali where physical infrastructure, notably irrigation is not a limiting factor. In these areas, packages of new technology consisting of high yielding varieties, fertilisers, pesticides, insecticides and improved cultivation methods are made available to the farmers. The intensification programme has been quite successful. Still, at the end of the first five year development programme, as was stated earlier, some basic problems remain unsolved. Looking into the future, it became also apparent that the intensification programme alone could not solve the food problem. Expansion of cultivated agriculture land in particular for food production becomes crucially important.

In the densely populated regions in Java and Bali, practically all land suitable for agriculture has been utilised, in some places even exceeding the ecologically suitable level. Most of the land resources for the expansion of agriculture are found in the outer islands. In these regions, agriculture, particularly food production, is also conducted by smallholders, however mostly in a much less intensive manner. Land potentials have not been fully utilised, and those which are now under cultivation are not being utilised to the full and in many instances cropping intensities are quite low.

Although inadequate data does not permit precise estimation of the existing unexploited land resources, figures such as 15 to 20 million hectares are mentioned, describing the vastness of these land potentials. It should be noted that a large part of the potential land resource consists of soil types, particularly the Red-yellow Podzolic Soils (Ultisols) and the Organosols (Histosols), categorised as problem soils. These soils are acid and have low fertility. They are considered marginal soils with regard to food production. Careful studies of their properties in order to formulate suitable cultivation practices becomes necessary, since agricultural expansion in the future will have to be directed to regions with these soil types.

A large part of these soils have already become unproductive waste lands. Although no accurate data exist on the size of the waste land, it is agreed that it has reached serious proportions. The shifting cultivation methods, under the population pressure contributed much to the formation of these waste lands. In addition, poor management of forest exploitation also resulted in the increase of these unproductive waste lands. More importantly, however, are measures which could prevent their increase.

A programme to utilise the land resources in the outer islands will necessarily be multi-sectoral. An important part of the overall effort is the transmigration programme.

Transmigration of people from the densely populated core regions to the outer islands is expected to play an important role in the agriculture expansion programme. A resettlement programme was started before World War II. The two main objectives of this pre-independence programme were (1) to lessen population pressure in densely populated Java and at the same time improve population distribution through the country, and (2) to provide plantations situated in the thinly populated outer islands with labour. Resettlement projects have been continued after independence under the national transmigration programme. Meanwhile the objectives of the resettlement programme have changed. Even though demographic considerations remain important, transmigration is now considered as a part of the total effort to develop regions outside the core. Just as the old resettlement programme would supply labour to the plantations, the national transmigration programme would supply the regions with the labour force needed for their development. The difference is of course that regional development is a much more complex undertaking compared to running a plantation. It also has much more far reaching consequences to the national economy, including the aspect of providing enough food in the future for the population.

One of the better known and revealing examples of pre-war resettlement projects is the Pringsewu project, in Lampung, Sumatra. Two conditions prevailing in the years 1927—1931 provided the main reasons for the first large scale resettlement programme. One was the general depression which caused great sufferings to the Sumatran farmer whose agriculture was mostly oriented to the world market. The rice price increases resulting from famines in India and Burma (1927 and 1931) intensified the sufferings. The second reason was the lack of labour to exploit the huge land resources in Sumatra through the production of world market oriented crops. In Lampung, which was the largest pepper producing area in the archipelago, the scarcity of labour was acutely felt during harvest time. Hired labour, mostly from West Java, created serious social problems. The Dutch government acted to solve this problem through a massive resettlement programme. The basic idea was to resettle several thousand Javanese farmers in Lampung who could also earn additional income as pepper pluckers. The scheme was to serve several purposes: (1) it would lessen population pressure in Java and at the same time improve upon the distribution of the population throughout the country, (2) it would provide labour and (3) it would improve rice self-sufficiently in Sumatra.

One of the basic features of the Pringsewu project is that the resettlement farmers were expected to cultivate their land in the new location according to their Javanese method of cultivation, primarily sawah rice production. Hence, an irrigation network was constructed in Pringsewu prior to the actual resettlement of the farmers. After completion in 1936 about 10,000 Javanese families were settled. The Pringsewu project was quite successful and its design and approach became a standard for future resettlement projects.

The colonisation and transmigration programme in Luwu, South Sulawesi would provide another revealing case. Luwu has long been regarded as a potential area which could grow into a prominent rice bowl. The area is located at the southern arm of Sulawesi, facing the Bay of Bone. It is thinly populated (in some areas as thin as 9 persons per square kilometre) and has vast unexploited land resources. Large tracks of land situated in the plain area are suitable for sawah rice production and the system of large and small rivers would provide good quality irrigation water.

A colonisation programme was initiated in Luwu in 1938 and established the villages of Lamasi, Sidomukti and Katulungan. Between 1938 and 1969 no transmigration projects were undertaken due to the War and the security conditions prevailing in the area following independence. Between 1969 and 1973 a total of about 1,900 families were resettled in the three colonisation villages and in other villages. Following the pattern of Pringsewu in Lampung, irrigation projects were the main components of the resettlement undertakings in Luwu. A total of 2 hectares of potentially irrigable land and upland were allotted to the transmigrant families.

In addition to the government supported colonisation and national transmigrants, local, spontaneous transmigrants are also moving into the region. Most of these migrants come from the neighbouring Tana Toraja area, also in South Sulawesi. The population of North Luwu can therefore be grouped into four categories, namely, the local indigenous people, the local transmigrants, the pre-War colonisation transmigrants and the more recent national transmigrants.

Information on the four groups of the population with regard to their performance in agriculture reflects the performance of the transmigration programme in this area.

A characteristic of the agronomy of the region is the low cropping intensity even in the colonisation and transmigration areas.

Table 2
Cropping intensities in three districts in North Luwu, 1975

District	Cropping intensity (%) Sawah	Upland
Bone-Bone, including colonisation transmigration villages	162	202
Lamasi, including colonisation villages	162	259
Kalaena, including transmigration villages	100	190

Source: Micro Economic Study of North Luwu, IPB, 1976.

The above figures indicate that even the colonisation farmers had not been able to fully utilise the land resources allotted to them. These cropping intensities are lower than those in similar areas in other well developed regions. Unlike the current transmigrants, the colonisation transmigrants have had ample time to accumulate capacity to utilise their land.

Another feature is the low agricultural yields obtained in the transmigration areas. Crop failures due to pests and diseases contributed much to the poor performance. The tunggro disease of rice is a very serious problem in Luwu. Some areas have not produced a significant crop for several years due to the disease. Rats, unattended roving cattle and wild pigs are also problems.

There is little application of the higher levels of technology that are used in many other areas in Indonesia. Fertiliser utilisation is almost entirely restricted to urea application to rice on a small percentage of the total irrigated sawah.

Although the region is thinly populated the average farm size is not significantly larger than in other parts of the country. Table 3 shows the average farmland utilised per farmer family amongst the different groups of population in transmigration areas in Luwu.

Table 3
Average farmland utilised by different groups of farmers
in North Luwu, 1975

Farmer group	Sawah (ha)	Upland (ha)
Local indigeneous farmers	0.47	0.74
Local transmigrants	0.18	0.90
Colonisation transmigrants	0.76	0.22
Current national transmigrants	0.41	0.77

Source: Micro Economic Study of North Luwu, IPB, 1976.

The above figures show that among the government supported transmigrants, both pre-War and current, the actual utilised farm land is smaller than that allotted to them. In the case of the current transmigrants this indicates the inability of the farmers to utilise all the land allotted to them due to limitations on investment capital.

It is interesting to note that among the groups, the colonisation farmers are the ones which increase their land utilisation by all possible methods, implying that they had attempted to enlarge their farm size by opening virgin forests (outside the transmigration project) and through land purchase. Still they end up with an average farm size which is below the size of land previously allotted to them.

The level at which the family labour force in the transmigration areas is being utilised appears to be low, as shown by Table 4.

Table 4
The average number of days utilised in a year in farm and non-farm activities by the family labour force, North Luwu, 1975

Areas	Farm activities	Non-farm activities		Total work days
		Direct income earning	Gotong Royong	
Lamasi	111	20	10	141
Bone-Bone	85	67	15	167
Kalaena	187	12	10	109

Source: Micro Economic Study of North Luwu, IPB, 1976.

It is strikingly evident that job opportunities outside the farm are scarce. The 'Gotong Royong' activities refer to community mutual help, in which neighbours assist in soil preparation, rehabilitation of irrigation ditches, and so on, no wages being earned from these activities.

The low productivity and the small average farm size are reflected by the levels of income received by the farmers in the transmigration areas as shown in Table 5. Comparing farmer groups, the colonisation transmigrants evidently enjoyed the largest farm income. It is to be noted however that even this group's income is below those obtained in other regions with a similar agricultural pattern. Moreover, the low farm income could not be supplemented by income earned from other sources which are also quite low. It is obvious that the transmigration programme which has been implemented in North Luwu for a long time has not been able to help develop the region into a prominent food bowl for the country.

Detailed soil and water surveys revealed that even though the soil fertility is low and the physical characteristics might cause some problems in irrigation and drainage, large pieces of land in the region could become good sawah and upland

Table 5
The average family farm income by farmers' groups,
North Luwu, 1975

Farmers' groups	Lamasi (Rp)	Bone-Bone (Rp)	Kalaena (Rp)
Local indigenous farmers	83,339	25,727	33,401
Local transmigrants	–	19,011	51,062
Colonisation transmigrants	96,847	32,751	64,871
Current national transmigrants	–	17,084	29,298

Source: Micro Economic Study of North Luwu, IPB, 1976.

agriculture land. With careful, responsible and improved cultivation methods a high yielding agriculture, mainly of food production, would be possible.

The preceeding sections show that while vast unexploited land resources exist in the outer islands, the transmigration programme has not been able to utilise these resources for agricultural development and food production. Several reasons have been identified:

(1) During the preparation and planning stage the design of a particular project has not been rigorously based on the specific conditions of the location, there is too much reliance on general standards and patterns which may or may not fit these conditions;
(2) During the implementation stage effective coordination between agencies has yet to be developed with the result that development of the infrastructure such as roads and irrigation and expansion of marketing facilities lags behind;
(3) During the first years in the new location the transmigrants are under direct guidance and support of the transmigration agency, in many cases the projects are in fact isolated activities which have limited connection with the economy of the region, so that withdrawal of the agency's support caused serious setbacks to the progress of the project.

Problems of increasing food production in the crowded regions

The transmigration programme, which attempts to move farm families from the densely populated regions and resettle them in the outer islands with their vast unexploited land resources, is but a part of the overall population reallocation problem in Indonesia. Its performance in the past has not had any significant effect on the uneven distribution of the population. Indeed, the goals have been wisely shifted from demographic to regional development. However, this also implies that the crowded regions can not realistically expect that the resettlement programme would ease their population problems in the future. In these regions future increases in the production of food have to be realised under ever increasing population pressures.

One factor which will be seriously affected by the population increase is the average farm size. Practically all food crops are grown on small farms. Table 6 indicates the small average farm size in Java.

Table 6
Size of farms in Java, 1963

	Size of farm	
	Less than 0.5 Ha	More than 0.5 Ha
Number of farms (millions)	6.1	3.8
Percentage of total number of farms	62.0	38.0
Average farm size in class (hectares)	0.2	1.2
Total class hectarage (million hectares)	1.2	4.5

Source: Sajogyo. ANP Evaluation Study. Lembaga Penelitian Sosiologi Pedesaan. IPB, 1973.

We have shown in the preceeding sections that in these regions all increases in food production have to be realised through an intensification programme which involves the use of new high yielding varieties, heavy doses of fertilisers, pesticides and insecticides. The figures in Table 6 show that most of the farmers in Java will be seriously handicapped by their small operations in realising production increases. If we arbitrarily take 0.5 Ha as a dividing line, already 62 per cent of the farmers in Java will have to be categorised as those seriously handicapped in their effort to benefit from the new technology. This means that we cannot expect significant production increases from as much as 6.1 million hectares out of the total 9.9 million hectares under food production in Java.

The rapid population increase aggravates the situation. Recent surveys showed that in many places in Java, notably in Central Java, the class of landless agricultural labourers and those with farms less than 500 square metres have increased in prominence.

Looking at food production as a subsector of agriculture, some plan has to be designed which would regulate the systematic and purposeful reallocation of people hitherto engaged in this subsector among other subsectors in agriculture as well as among other sectors in the economy. The intensification programmes themselves provide possibilities of establishing a rural based agriculture-supporting industry and service sector which can be expected to create employment possibilities and thereby absorb a part of the rural population. The two main intensification programmes are the BIMAS and the INMAS programmes. The BIMAS programme is a packaged, supervised credit programme where the credit extended consists of high yielding seeds, fertilisers, pesticides and insecticides at subsidized costs. INMAS is likewise an intensification programme, where the modern input factors such as fertilisers and pesticides are provided at subsidised costs, however on a cash payment basis. The intensification programmes are directed by boards set up at the various levels of government. The area under intensification is divided into village units, each covering an area of 600 to 1,000 hectares of rice fields. These village units are urged to equip themselves with the following four supporting institutions: a village unit rural bank, an extension service, a processing plant and a retail shop supplying seeds, fertilisers, pesticides and insecticides. As modernisation of food production proceeds it is expected that the need by each individual farmer for the supporting activities and services will also grow, creating new employment possibilities in the rural industry and services sector.

The ease with which a part of the population find new employment in the rural industry and services sector is affected by the effectiveness of education programmes. During the year 1973 only, a total of 6,000 primary school buildings were built, providing facilities for about 720,000 children. Many of these schools are in Java. In addition to the formal education programme, there is also the adult education and extension programmes. Moreover, since the first five year plan was initiated in 1969, investments by domestic and foreign firms have been encouraged with the result that socio-economic interactions are being established with inroads even to the rural areas. Nevertheless it is felt that the education programmes could be made more effective in facilitating the reallocation of the population between sectors, when more emphasis is placed on vocational training.

Unless the necessary steps are taken to make possible the creation of a vigorously developing farmer class in Java, unencumbered by the Lilliputian farm size, this crowded region cannot be expected to grow enough to feed itself, let alone provide for the other regions of the country.

Notes

[1] A revised version of a paper by the same author appearing as Chapter 3 'Indonesia' in D. Ensminger (ed.), *Food Enough or Starvation for Millions*, Tata McGraw-Hill, New Delhi, 1977.
[2] World Bank, Agricultural Sector Survey, Indonesia, 1974.

Achieving a balance between population and food: the Korean case

Sung-Hoon Kim [1]

The sheer size and menacing character of population growth in the developing countries today has resulted in widespread demands for action. The rapid growth in population in many nations implies that even more scarce resources will be required for the production of food.

The Republic of Korea is a leader in rapid industrialisation and successful implementation of family planning programmes by the international community. During the decade of the 1960s and the early 1970s, Korea's real GNP increased at an average annual rate of around 10 per cent and the rate of population growth dropped from 2.9 per cent in 1960 to 1.6 per cent in 1974. Despite the fact that the rate of population growth declined significantly, total population increased from 25 million in 1960 to about 33.5 million in 1974 with the growth of large concentrations in the country's urban-metropolitan areas. Population density has reached 'serious' proportions with 339 persons per Km^2. This ranks the Republic of Korea as one of the most densely populated countries in the world. Furthermore, even with a sharp decline in the rate to 1.3 per cent by 1986, the most optimistic projections show that the total population of Korea will increase to 41 million. This means that Korea will have to invest about 5–7.5 per cent of her GNP simply to maintain the same level of living standards as in 1974. As population expands and the economy develops, there is an increasing use of and competition for the nation's scarce resources for different ends. The conversion of land on a large scale from farmland to industrial sites, highways, housing developments and other purposes is occurring rapidly. An average of 20 thousand hectares of agricultural land is lost per annum to competing uses. Such uncontrolled conversion seriously affects potential increases in food production and has touched off heated land speculation. The agricultural labour market is experiencing a structural change as rural to urban migration proceeds rapidly. The seasonal shortage of agricultural labour becomes a serious obstacle to increased food production, even though farm mechanisation is slowly substituting for human labour requirements.

Thus, population growth as a whole has caused an expansion of the economic base and correspondingly greater demands for food, shelter, recreation and government services, especially for rapidly growing urban centres. The quantity and quality of given resources, however, are not sufficient to satisfy the increasing demands of all the sectors of the economy at the same time. The increased competition between sectors for land, water, minerals and the environment brought about by a dynamically growing and shifting population may generate substantial bottlenecks to future economic growth.

In view of these prospects, the economic meaning of population growth and its structural changes should be thoroughly reviewed to provide a sounder basis for long-run economic, social, and population planning. In particular, agricultural development planning needs answers to such questions as: Can we effectively control the future course of population growth? Is the food producing sector of Korea capable of increasing the supply of food enough to keep up with the demand for food arising from the rapid growth in the population and the economy? If not, what are the most significant constraints to increasing food production? To what extent can scientific research contribute to ease those constraints?

Of course it is not easy to discover the full range of consequences that may occur as a result of the interaction between population growth and food consumption and production. However, the illustration of future alternatives and consequences can help to stimulate an increased awareness of the problem. Such awareness is the first step in fostering more intensified biomedical and socio-economic research and in formulating the appropriate development programmes.

Population

Analysis of population growth

Population trends in Korea since 1920 have been documented by means of censuses taken about every five years, as summarised in Table 1. The data indicates that population grew rapidly during the early 1920s but slowed between 1925 and 1944. A very large increase occurred during the period from 1944 to 1949, with a small increase between 1949–1955, and the return of rapid growth between 1955–1960. Rapid growth continued from 1960 to 1966, after which growth had become more modest.

Some of the above fluctuations can be linked to migration and do not reflect the balance of birth and death rates alone. A sizeable emigration of Koreans to Japan, Manchuria and the northern portion of Korea resulted in relatively low rates of population growth from 1925 to 1944. On the other hand, the large jump beteeen 1944–49 can be explained by the repatriation of Koreans from overseas and by refugee movements from North Korea after World War II. Population growth during the 1949–55 period was curbed by a drastic rise in the death rate and a slight reduction in fertility due to the Korean war. These declines were more than offset by the large number of refugees that fled to the south during the war.

From 1953 to 1966, the population has exhibited a relatively high growth rate [2]. The post war baby boom pushed the natural birth rate during the 1955–60 period to 2.9 per cent per year. Since 1962, a series of national population control policies were adopted and incorporated into the nation's first and second five year economic development plans [3]. These, in conjunction with the rapid economic growth, fostered by the family planning and a rapid increase

Table 1
Census population of Korea, 1920—74

	Population in thousands		Intercensal increase in per cent	
Census date	Entire country	Republic of Korea (South)	Entire country	Republic of Korea (South)
1920 (October 1)	17,264	–	–	–
1925 (October 1)	19,020	–	10.2	–
1930 (October 1)	20,438	–	7.5	–
1935 (October 1)	22,208	–	8.7	–
1940 (October 1)	23,547	–	6.0	–
1944 (October 1)	25,120	16,244	6.7	–
1949 (May 1)	29,907	20,167	19.1	24.2
1955 (September 1)	30,532	21,502	2.1	6.6
1960 (December 1)	35,024	24,994	14.1	16.2
1966 (October 1)	–	29,476	–	17.9
1970 (Mid-year)	–	31,469	–	6.7
1974 (Year end)	–	33,459	–	6.3

Source: *Korea Statistical Yearbook*, Planning Board, 1975.

in rural—urban migration have resulted in a drop in the natural birth rate from 2.7 per cent per annum during the 1960—66 period to a more acceptable rate of 1.6 per cent a year during the 1966—74 period.

The decline in the natural birth rate has been attributed to a sharp decline in the nation's crude birth rate. In 1960 this rate stood at 42.9 births per 1,000 total population. By 1973 it had dropped more than 17 points to 25.3 per 1,000 total population. The total fertility rate, i.e., the average number of children born to a woman surviving to the end of the child bearing period, showed a similar decline from 5.9 to 1960 to 3.9 in 1973. The decline, however, was not uniform among all age groups within the child bearing range, the two most found age groups are 25—29 and 30—34, which show a relatively slow decrease during the same period. This overall reduction in fertility level can be attributed to three principal factors: an increased control of fertility within marriage, an increased number of abortions and a later average age at marriage. Fertility decline in rural areas is also noticeable but there still is a big gap in the fertility rate between urban and rural, i.e., 3.2 versus 4.7 in 1973. It seems unlikely that the gap will be overcome.

In every census up to 1974 the sex ratio has consistently favoured males. This has been true despite heavy casualties during the Korean War and the normally higher infant mortality rates associated with male births. Data from the 1974 census, however, seem to indicate a change in this ratio. The 1966 census indicated

		Total fertility rate	General fertility rate
1960:	Urban	5.3	180
	Rural	6.7	227
	Average	5.9	200
1970:	Urban	3.5	113
	Rural	5.5	145
	Average	4.5	129
1973:	Urban	3.2	103
	Rural	4.7	114
	Average	3.9	105

a sex ratio of 104.4. By 1974 this had declined drastically to 101.0.

Changes in both the birth and death rates have influenced the age composition of the population over the years as shown below, namely, compared with 1960, a smaller proportion of 'under 20 years' population and a greater percentage of '60 and over' class appeared in 1974 [4].

	1960	1966	1970	1974
Percent of 'under 20 years'	52.45	52.80	52.00	48.23
Percent of '20–59 years'	42.15	42.20	42.65	45.64
Percent of '60 and over'	5.45	5.10	5.35	6.13
Total (%)	100.0	100.0	100.0	100.0

Several evaluations have been carried out in the Republic of Korea since the national family planning programme began operation in 1962. The attitudes of Korean women concerning family size indicate a gradual decline in the ideal number of children that the average woman wishes to have; i.e., from 3.9 persons in 1965 to 3.4 persons in 1973. Despite this decline, the number of children that Korean women want to have still exceeds the goal of the government family planning programme, as expressed in the slogan 'Stop at Two'.

One of the most serious psychological barriers to changes in family size is the Korean strong preference for sons. Most Korean women regard the continuation of the male lineage and the dependence on children in old age as the most important considerations in determining the desired number of children [5]. Previous demographic studies, conducted at different times, have indicated that the long prevailing preference for boys has not significantly changed, although the desired number of children, whether sons or daughters, has slightly decreased. The persistence of a strong boy preference is evidenced in a recent study which found that, among women whose ideal number of children is three, 96 per cent wanted to have two sons and one daughter while only 1 per cent desired to have one son and two daughters [6].

Another study attempted to examine this preference for males using three social variables: education, economic status and residence. The results indicate that the preference for males is lowest among those women who have at least a high school education, are higher in economic status and reside in Seoul. The ideal number of children among this group is smaller than the national average of 3.56, and the actual number of living children is also smaller than the national average of 3.22. Although the number of living children is lower than the number of desired children for all groups, the difference is greater among those groups with low male preference attitudes. Male preference was highest among women who had no education, were residing in rural villages and enjoyed low economic status [7].

Employment and Migration

Changes in the structure of population growth by labour force participation between 1965 and 1974 are presented in Table 2.

Table 2
The population and labour force of the Republic of Korea, 1965, 1970 and 1974

Population classification	1965	1970	1974
	(in 1,000 persons)		
Total population	28,377	31,317	33,459
Economically active population	9,199	10,020	12,080
(%)	32.1	32.0	36.1
Total employed persons (A)	8,522	9,574	11,586
Agricultural and fishing workers (B)	5,000	4,834	5,584
B/A (%)	58.7	50.0	48.2
Mining and manufacturing workers (C)	879	1,369	2,062
C/A (%)	10.3	14.3	17.8
Social overhead capital & service (D)	2,643	3,371	3,940
D/A (%)	31.0	35.2	34.0
Unemployment rate:	7.4	4.5	4.1
Farm sector (%)	3.1	1.6	1.2
Non-farm sector (%)	13.5	7.5	6.8

Source: *Annual Report on the Economically Active Population*, EPB, 1975.

The high fertility rates of the 1950s and early 1960s are now being reflected in a rapid increase in the size of the working population. As the data indicates, the economically active population in 1970 numbered slightly over 10 million and has increased to 12 million by 1974. The ratio of the labour force to the total population has increased from 32.1 per cent in 1965, to 36.1 per cent in 1974. On the other hand, total employed persons increased from 8.5 million in 1965 to 9.6

million in 1970 and again to 11.6 million in 1974. Thus the unemployment rate was reduced from 7.4 per cent in 1965 to 4.1 per cent in 1974. It may be noted that more unemployment exists in the non-farm sector than in the farm sector. In 1974, 48 per cent of the employed persons were engaged in agriculture and fisheries, indicating the transition from a predominantly agricultural to a relatively industrialised economy. Between 1965 and 1974, the agricultural sector experienced both a relative and absolute loss of manpower, while both secondary and tertiary industries grew considerably. The figures indicate that the out-migration rate of the population exceeds the rate of natural growth in the farm sector by 1.5—2.0 per cent. The move away from agricultural dominance is also reflected in the changing occupational structure. The category of 'farmers, fishermen and related workers' has decreased in proportional terms rather sharply in recent years.

The rapid growth of the Korean economy during the 1960s was marked by rapid industrial growth, with a progressively stronger concentration of economic activities in several large cities. The concentration of rapid economic development in the modern industrial sector has stimulated a great number of rural people to flock to the nation's urban centres. In 1949, 17.2 per cent of the nation's population resided in urban areas. By 1966 almost 10 million people or 33.6 per cent of the total population lived in urban centres. During the last decade, urban population increased at a drastic rate so that by 1974 20 million people or 59.8 per cent lived in urban centres.

A striking aspect of this growth has been the rate at which the larger cities have grown relative to the smaller cities. The five largest cities with populations greater than 300,000 in 1974 grew at an annual rate of 4.2 per cent or more between 1960 and 1974. In contrast, small and medium size cities with populations of 100,000 or less grew at an annual rate of about 3 per cent. This trend is especially true for the capital city, Seoul. The population of Seoul was 6.1 per cent of the national total in 1955, 9.8 per cent in 1960, and 19.5 per cent or 6.5 million in 1974.

The situation of 'over-urbanisation' and the growth of large urban areas are viewed by many Korean scholars and policy makers as critical national issues. Whether or not a greater proportion of the population living in urban places than the proportion living in rural areas is justified by the degree of economic development, remains a controversial issue. It seems clear, however, from evidence collected in other developing nations that growth of one or a few gigantic cities may have a number of undesirable socio-economic side effects and eventually hinders policies of rural and regional development.

Kim, studying the causes of rural—urban migration, found no conclusive evidence to substantiate the hypothesis that the difference between urban expected income and rural expected income was solely responsible for 'pulling' rural people into urban centres [8]. He explains that the rapidly growing number of recent migrants is itself one of the most important determinants of further migration. Parents' strong desire to provide their children with a better education and with opportunities for a better life later on leads them to migrate or send their children to urban schools. Once rural children are well educated and settled down with a permanent job in an urban area, they provide channels for both their parents and their brothers and sisters to migrate to the urban centres.

As a consequence of the increased rate of rural—urban migration, the farm population has begun to decline. Farm mechanisation is viewed by many as the most practical means of replacing the farm labour lost through migration. Adapting Korean agriculture to mechanisation, however, will be a major challenge. Land consolidation and rearrangement, building of access roads, refinements in irrigation systems and improved guidance services are all taking on a greater urgency in the forthcoming period of rapid demographic and economic change. A recent study found that even though the growth of mechanised agricultural production has lagged behind comparable Far Eastern countries, it does constitute a viable and profitable programme over the next twenty years [9].

Another recent study has indicated that the heavy out-migration of farm labour has aggravated a critical labour shortage, particularly during the peak demand periods of June and October. During 1970 it was estimated that this deficit supply constituted 19.7 and 16.3 per cent of the total supply of labour employed in agriculture [10]. Such a supply situation has resulted in the doubling of agricultural wage rates between 1969 and 1974.

Population projections

An extensive study of the Korean agricultural sector by Michigan State University of USA and the National Agricultural Economics Research Institute of the Republic of Korea has been under way since 1972. Population growth and off-farm migration have received major emphasis in the population component of the study. In its original report, issued in 1972 [11], the MSU/NAERI group estimated an increase in population of approximately 30 per cent between 1970 and 1985 under the assumption that existing government policies would continue. During the same period, growth in the rest of the economy was expected to cause high out-migration from rural areas, particularly after 1975. Such out-migration would result in a doubling of the urban population during the 15 year period and a drop of 43 per cent in the rural population.

The impact on Korean agriculture of these changes can best be seen in the projected changes in the supply of farm labour. Following a slight rise to 1975 when farm labour will average slightly more than 2.0 adult male equivalents per farm based on the number of farms in 1971, it will decline to 1.3 by 1985. In other words, for every 100 farm labour units (in adult male equivalents) on farms in 1975, there will be only 65 by 1986.

Clearly, changes of this magnitude will face farm operators with major adjustments — in farm enterprises, in farm operations and in family living. At the same time, these changes will pose major problems for rural and urban educators and for urban and industrial planners if the rural migrants are to be prepared for non-farm occupations, absorbed into the non-farm work force, and accommodated satisfactorily in their new urban environment.

To arrive at valid estimates for the population projection, a simulation modelling [12] has been attempted using the three sets of different assumptions on fertility and migration rates with the adjusted 1970 census data and survival ratios [11] as the base figures. Single year survival ratios were calculated exogenously from the Coale-Demeny Life Table (West Model), with the following Coale-Demeny Levels used for the indicated years.

Year	Coale-Demeny level	Life expectancy Males (years)	Females (years)
1970	18.6	60.27	64.00
1975	19.5	62.44	66.75
1980	20.3	64.35	68.25
1985	21.0	66.02	70.00

The projected total fertility rates for selected years used in the new model were in two groups. The first one was officially employed by the government in the population estimation during the formulation process of the 4th five year plan. The other was arbitrarily added by the author because the foregoing official estimation seems to be too optimistic. They are:

	Total fertility rate (TFR)			
Year	Farm women		Non-farm women	
	Group 1	Group 2	Group 1	Group 2
1970	5.964	5.964	3.152	3.152
1975	5.076	5.350	2.699	2.930
1980	4.354	4.730	2.327	2.715
1985	3.763	4.100	2.121	2.500

Net movement between the farm household population and non-farm household population is specified exogenously for the years, 1971, 1976, 1981 and 1986 with the values for specific years interpolated from the following array of point values:

	Rate of net off-farm migration	
Year	Group 1	Group 2
1970	4.2%	4.0%
1975	3.5%	3.0%
1981	3.1%	2.0%
1986	2.8%	2.0%

By combining these fertility and migration assumptions, we can easily organise the three sets of alternative assumptions on the population aspect of the model, which mainly accounts for food demand pattern. The organisation of the alternative sets can be summarised as follows:

Alternatives	Fertility	Migration
I	Group 1 (low)	Group 2 (slow)
II	Group 1 (low)	Group 1 (fast)
III	Group 2 (high)	Group 2 (slow)

Alternative I is considered as the base line model by the MSU/NAERI working group and Alternative III deviates from it due to its higher fertility assumption and Alternative II deviates from it due to its faster migration assumption.

The results of the model for selective years are shown in Table 3. Under even the lowest fertility assumption the total population in 1986 is estimated to exceed 41 million. Alternative III shows a relatively faster growth rate with the population increasing from 34.7 million in 1974 to 42.8 million in 1986. This 8.1 million increase constitutes a 23.3 per cent rise over the period or a 1.74 per cent annual growth rate. Alternative I depicts a relatively slow growth rate. Under its assumptions the population grows from 34.6 million in 1974 to 41.4 million in 1986. This increase of 6.8 million constitutes a 19.7 per cent rise or 1.49 per cent per annum increase.

Most demographers believe that under current budget levels the family planning programmes will not be able to achieve the targeted annual growth rate of 1.3 per cent by 1986. At present, research has not been able to determine quantitatively the relationships between the different levels of government budgeting for family planning programmes and their respective consequences. The rather substantial decline in total fertility, from 5.9 children per woman in 1960–61 to 3.9 in 1973–74, has been partially attributed to the family planning programme. Further declines in the years to come will be much more difficult to accomplish. Unless new and innovative programmes are adopted in the near future with regard to farm population policies the 1986 goal of a 1.3 per cent net growth rate will not be realised. Estimates of the ratio of the farm population to total population in 1986 ranges from 24.7 per cent to 28 per cent in the model. The difference between the two extreme alternatives amounts to 1.4 million persons. If we adopt Alternative II as a probable growth path, nearly five million people will move away from agriculture in the next twelve years, requiring a substantial increase in agricultural mechanisation. Under these contingencies farm capital formation is unlikely to be able to provide sufficient capital for the scale of mechanisation required.

On the other hand, if government policies prove effective in decentralising the location of new non-agricultural employment so that more non-agricultural employment is available to persons in farm households, the rate of physical withdrawal from the farm sector is likely to be slowed. Moreover, the need for

Table 3
Results of simulation of population growth, 1974–86

Year	Alternative I	Alternative II	Alternative III
(1) Total population in 1,000 persons			
1974	34,616	34,617	34,737
1976	35,661	35,658	35,908
1981	38,390	38,346	39,136
1986	41,447	41,305	42,838
(2) Farm household population in 1,000 persons (percentage to total)			
1974	13,424 (38.8)	13,333 (38.5)	13,462 (38.8)
1976	12,955 (36.3)	12,742 (35.7)	13,024 (36.3)
1981	12,168 (31.7)	11,381 (29.7)	12,325 (31.5)
1986	11,606 (28.0)	10,201 (24.7)	11,855 (27.7)
(3) Net migrants in persons (net migration rate)			
1974	462,811 (3.37)	505,588 (3.69)	463,547 (3.37)
1976	397,320 (3.00)	458,155 (3.50)	398,821 (3.00)
1981	246,763 (2.00)	361,895 (3.10)	249,500 (2.00)
1986	235,360 (2.00)	292,247 (2.80)	239,934 (2.00)

large scale, capital intensive mechanisation will be reduced since non-agricultural workers living on farms are likely to be available for work in agriculture during the peak seasons — a phenomenon which now occurs in Japan and Taiwan.

Since 1970, the Korean government has encouraged the establishment of more industrial plants in the rural areas; this is called the Saemaul Industry Programme. If the target of the programme, 'one *myun* — one factory' is realised, then the farmers will have sufficient off-farm job opportunities to supplement their low level income and the number of part time farmers will increase.

Impacts of demographic changes on future patterns of food consumption

Three basic demographic trends which have surfaced in recent years are likely to affect food consumption in the future. Firstly, since the proportion of the adult population is expected to increase at the planned rate of natural population growth by 1990 [13], the trend will exert a strong upward pressure on the rate of growth of food demand. In the meantime, the expected trend of continuous rural–urban migration will result in a strong downward pressure on their *per capita* demand for the relatively low income-elastic food sources such as cereal and carbohydrate foodstuffs. As these demographic trends will be accompanied by an acceleration in the growth of *per capita* income, a rapid increase in the demand for income-elastic foodstuffs such as fruits, vegetable and livestock can be expected. An increase in the demand for this latter commodity will generate an increase in the demand for feedgrains.

The second demographic trend, rapid urbanisation, will influence the pattern of food consumption in two ways. One is that as urban centres expand, urban consumption habits will exert a stronger force on the pattern of rural food consumption. As rural residents become a minority, the probability of their emulating the dietary habits of urban residents will increase. This will result in a decline in the differences between urban and rural consumption patterns. In another way, as urban populations which have a higher propensity to consume more expensive and animal foodstuffs increase, the demands for foodgrains and intensive horticulture will increase. This will result in a shift in the demand for cereals for human consumption to animal consumption and a possible increase in imported food grains.

The above trends, if they occur, may pose some very serious challenges to Korean agriculture. The movement of large quantities of food grain from human to animal consumption may not be a viable long run solution to the country's food-short economy. The inefficient conversion of vegetable foodstuffs to human nutritional elements via animal products and an already high man–land ratio may require the adoption of plant breeding and fortification rather than livestock breeding as a viable solution to the country's protein deficiency problem.

Food supply

Economic development and agricultural production

Endowed with few resources except an abundant supply of human labour, the Republic of Korea adopted an industrialsation/export orientation development strategy during the last decade. This strategy, which was followed closely until the advent of the world food crisis in the early 1970s, expedited the rapid growth of export industries while maintaining low grain prices and wage rates through the importation of foreign farm products which were then abundantly available at concessional terms [14].

Recent food grain imports alone have amounted to 600–800 million US dollars a year. Paradoxically, the necessity of using scarce foreign currency for food imports has severely limited the continuous energetic push for economic development. This sharp increase in grain imports was largely due to increasing food grain consumption. During the 1962–74 period, consumption increased at an average annual rate of 5.6 per cent. This was almost double the average annual production rate of 2.9 per cent during the twelve years period. As a result the self-sufficiency ratio in food grains dropped from 91.6 per cent in 1962 to 69.3 per cent in 1974. Broken down by major commodity, the figures are given below. Production of food grains, except rice, decreased by an average rate of 7 per cent per year during 1962–74. In contrast, during the same period production of fruits and vegetables, respectively, grew at average annual rates of 16.5 per cent and 9.9 per cent. Imports of non-grain food were irregular and negligible.

	Rice	Barley	Wheat	Corn	Soybean	Other grain	Total food grain
1962:							
Production (1000 metric tons)	3,015	1,378	268	18	156	558	5,423
Imports (1000 metric tons)	–	47	398	36	16	2	499
Self-sufficiency (%)	100.0	96.7	40.2	33.3	90.7	99.7	91.6
1974:							
Production (1000 metric tons)	4,445	1,705	136	58	319	641	7,304
Imports (1000 metric tons)	206	299	1,591	567	66	–	2,731
Self-sufficiency (%)	95.6	85.1	7.9	9.3	82.9	100.0	72.8

On the production side, increasing demands for farm produce along with rapid industrialisation and urbanisation has begun the sector's transformation from a subsistence to a cash crop farming system. Many believe that this transition in part has contributed to relatively slow increases in food grain production. For example, during the seven years of 1967–74, the area planted to food grains including potatoes decreased by 1.9 per cent while that planted to cash crops increased by up to 8 per cent. Similar results appear when examining the ratio of area planted to food crops to the total area utilised in agricultural production. This ratio for grain declined from 90.4 per cent in 1962 to 81.8 per cent in 1974, while the ratio of area planted in cash crops rose from 9.6 per cent to 18.2 per cent. These shifts, in order of their magnitude of value production, are shown in the top table on page 152.

Factors likely to affect future production of foodgrain

A number of strategic factors are required to increase Korea's foodgrain production which formed about 72 per cent of total agricultural production in 1974. These include: seed and technology improvement, increased availability of such inputs as fertiliser and insecticides, farm mechanisation, irrigation and drainage, intensive use and expansion of agricultural land, adequate credit facilities and improved price and marketing systems.

	Rice	Barley & wheat	Other food grain	Livestock	Vegetables & fruit	Agri. by-products	Special crop	Total
1962:								
Current value (mil. won)	127,040	32,256	27,623	16,588	14,949	13,560	6,949	238,955
Rank	1	2	3	4	5	6	7	
1974:								
Current value (mil. won)	816,065	159,439	62,375	353,282	246,239	112,133	94,183	1,943,717
Rank	1	4	7	2	3	5	6	

	Total		Nitrogen		Phosphorus		Potash	
	Total (metric tons)	Per ha. (kg)	Total (metric tons)	Per ha. (kg)	Total (metric tons)	Per ha. (kg)	Total (metric tons)	Per ha. (kg)
			...Elements of fertiliser....					
1965	393,098	119.4	217,925	66.2	123,489	37.5	51,684	15.7
1970	562,902	171.0	355,550	108.0	124,354	37.8	82,998	25.2
1974	863,359	254.2	499,383	136.5	231,877	70.5	155,399	47.2

The emergence of new high yield rice varieties, such as Tongil (IR667) and Yushin in recent years has added new hope to achieving the goal of rice self-sufficiency. These varieties have increased yields per hectare by an average of 20–40 per cent over conventional seeds. In 1975 these varieties constituted over 41 per cent of the total paddy planted area in the country, and thereby raised per hectare yield from 2,850 kg in 1965 to 3,830 kg in 1975. However, further incorporation of the new varieties into the present crop production system appears to be highly limited by the availability of irrigation facilities.

In addition, the new high yielding varieties require rather larger amounts of fertiliser and insecticides. It is estimated that the present production of rice, barley and soybean could be increased by 20–40 per cent if farmers would apply the optimum level of fertiliser at the right time. At present, the average farm applies 254.2 kg per hectare. While the increase constitutes a doubling in the fertiliser application rate since 1965, it is still just over a half of what the average Japanese farmer applied in 1972. Nitrogen application rates, however, are comparable with those of Japanese farmers (see bottom table on page 152).

The use of agricultural chemicals provides another method of increasing crop production. Presently, disease and insect damage account for about 10 per cent of the average annual production of rice and barley. This is slightly double that which occurs in Japan. In 1974, the typical Korean farmer used 5.3 kg of agricultural chemicals per hectare. This was less than half of that amount used by Japanese farms during the same period. Broken down into component parts, 65 per cent of the 5.3 kg package of chemicals was composed of insecticides, 21.1 per cent fungicides, 11.8 per cent herbicides and 2.1 per cent miscellaneous chemicals. In 1974, if Korean farmers had applied chemicals at the same rate as their Japanese counterparts, it has been estimated an additional 267 thousand tons of rice and 85 thousand tons of barley could have been safely harvested.

A recent study [15] outlining the effects of farm mechanisation on Korean agriculture revealed that one power tiller with its attachments has the capability of handling the necessary agricultural functions in a timely manner on 3.5 to 5.7 hectares, depending on the crop and region. It was estimated that a mechanisation programme if adopted would generate a 10 per cent increase in the yield of rice; 5 per cent from power spraying, 3 per cent from better timing in planting and harvesting and 2 per cent from better seedbed preparation. Such an increase would have meant an additional 267 thousand tons of rice during the year. As of the end of 1974, there were 60,056 power tillers (mostly 10 HP), 388 farm tractors, 12 power driven rice transplanters, 73 power weeders, 704 power dryers, 116,065 power dusters and sprayers, 108,494 power threshing machines, 53 combines and 149 power sowing machines employed in crop production. In Japan more than 70 per cent of farmers own a power tiller, compared with 2.5 per cent in the Republic of Korea.

The importance of proper irrigation and drainage in rice production has been highlighted in a recent survey of Korean rice producers which compared yields obtained from well irrigated paddy land with those from rain fed paddy land. The survey indicated that the well irrigated paddy was almost 12 per cent more productive than the rain fed paddy. In 1974 there was 1204 thousand hectares of cultivated paddy land, 70.4 per cent being well irrigated, 22.7 per cent being partially irrigated and 6.9 per cent being rain fed. If drought could have been avoided over the past decade via adequate irrigation, it has been estimated that annual rice production would have been increased by 15 per cent, or 650 thousand metric tons per year [16].

Increased cropping rates, slope land development and tide land reclamation have been proven to be viable approaches to increasing agricultural production. Over the past decade the double cropping ratio on paddy land has declined from 158 per cent in 1965 to 147 per cent in 1974. A reverse of this trend could be accomplished by a little or no additional investment. The lack of price incentives, however, has made it less attractive for farmers to follow the traditional rice/barley double cropping sequence. In 1974, the Office of Rural Development estimated that 5.6 per cent of the total paddy land capable of double cropping in the southern part of the Republic of Korea was not employed in a double cropping system, mainly due to less incentives to do so. If double cropping practices were used, barley production could have been increased by 183 thousand tons (US $55 million) during the year.

Plans for increasing Korea's land base through slope land and tidal land reclamation are presently under way. A recent government survey of land resources indicates that there are 2,450 parcels or 32 thousand hectares of undeveloped slope land under 30 degrees in slope. During the period 1975 to 1980 the government plans to reclaim 112 thousand hectares, half through government programmes and half through private projects made compulsory by law.

Estimates supplied by the Agricultural Development Corporation suggest that an additional 400 thousand hectares of paddy land could be added through tidal land reclamation projects. The cost of reclaiming one hectare was estimated at about 4 million won (US $8,000), compared with the current average market price of 4.5 million won per hectare of paddy land. If the above reclaimed areas were added to the Republic of Korea's present agricultural land base, agricultural land would increase from 22.7 per cent to 30 per cent of all land in the country. By developing the suggested slope and tidal lands, agricultural production might be increased by as much as a third of the present production in the foreseeable future.

During the ealry 1970s short term production loans offered by various institutions (agricultural cooperatives and government) increased as farm operating expenses increased. The proportion of the production loans to farm operating costs rose from 5.4 per cent in 1970 to 7.4 per cent in 1974. A breakdown of yearly loans and production costs appears below. However, the proportion was so small that farmers were forced to borrow from private sources at relatively high interest rates. The annual rate of interest on institutional short term loan during the period ranged from 9 to 15.5 per cent. Private credit sources charged an annual interest rate from 36 to 60 per cent. A 1973 survey conducted by the MAF found that 76.8 per cent of a farmer's year end liabilities came from private creditors with only 23.2 per cent from institutional sources.

Production loan	1970	1971	1972	1973	1974
Total (billion won)	72	101	150	114	191
A – per farm loan (won)	2,900	4,100	6,100	5,900	7,800
B – per farm operating costs (won)	54,027	64,658	74,613	89,943	104,560
A/B (%)	5.4	6.3	8.2	6.6	7.4

An integral part of any long term increase in crop production is a well planned and administered price and marketing system. The so-called high purchase price programmes for rice and barley since 1968 have positively affected both the farm production and farm income. Recent estimates of the price elasticities of supply for rice and barley were established by the author at 0.34 and 0.38 respectively in 1975, based on the data of 1960–73. The Korean Agricultural Sector Simulation Team estimated them at 0.21 and 0.74 in 1972. Also, the effects of the government controlled grain price on farm household income were found to be substantial. If the rice price were increased in real terms by 10 per cent, overall farm household income would be increased 5.8 to 6.1 per cent based on the 1971–73 data [17]. Net receipts from rice alone comprise 48.3 per cent of total farm household income in 1973. The above results indicate that an increase in the farm purchase price of rice would induce a substantial increase in production and reduce the rural–urban income disparity by increasing farm household income.

Potentials for foodgrain production

A comparison of normal farm yields for rice, barley and soybeans with those obtained by Korean agricultural experiment stations and Japanese farmers indicates that potential yield increases are not only possible but tremendous [18].

Assuming that government programmes are adopted and strengthened to supply adequate amounts of strategic production factors previously mentioned, there is no reason to believe that present yields could not be increased to equal those of Japanese farmers. If this were the case in 1974, Korea would have produced an additional 290 thousand metric tons of polished rice. This would have allowed the country to gain rice self sufficiency and to export 84 thousand metric tons of rice a year. If the nation's farmers were able to attain yields comparable to 70 per cent of those obtained at experiment stations, an additional 800 thousand metric tons of polished rice would have been produced.

Emulating Japanese yields, similar results would have occurred for barley and soybeans. Barley production in 1974 would have been 130 thousand tons and soybean production at 160 thousand metric tons. The implication of this simple exercise is that Korean agriculture, small and poorly equipped as it is, can for a sustained period of time feed more than her population with self supplied grains by fully exploiting her hidden resources.

Annual production increase (1000 metric tons)	*To attain the level of Japanese normal average yields*	*To attain 70% level of Korean exp. stations results*	*Net imports in 1974*
Rice (polished)	290	880	206
Barley (polished)	130	780	299
Soybean	160	295	66

Prospects for food demand and supply in Korea

Using the most current version of Korean agricultural simulation model, a policy experiment was attempted to assess the respective consequences with respect to the demand and supply of food resulting from six different policy-assumption combinations [19].

On the demand side, the three types of population projection profiles developed earlier and the estimates of price and income elasticities were employed as the bases for simulating demand projections for individual commodities. The population models incorporated three basic assumptions for fertility and migration parameters: low fertility and slow migration for Alternative I; low fertility and fast migration for II; and high fertility and slow migration for III. The elasticities of price and income for demand were measured by time series and cross section regression analyses. The estimated elasticities of important food items are as follows:

Commodity	*Direct price elasticity*		*Income elasticity*	
	Rural	*Urban*	*Rural*	*Urban*
Rice	–0.40	–0.45	0.10	0.10
Barley	–0.20	–0.25	–0.19	–0.33
Wheat	–0.40	–0.50	0.20	0.31
Beef	–1.80	–1.40	0.94	1.55
Milk	–2.00	–2.00	5.40	5.80
Pork	–1.00	–1.10	0.59	0.55
Chicken	–1.00	–1.70	0.80	0.95
Eggs	–0.50	–0.80	0.86	1.10
Fish	–0.50	–0.40	0.31	0.72

For the projection of supply of food grain, two price policy alternatives together with the fixed schedules of government's intended investment in land and water development were defined in terms of monetary values. The first assumption for grain prices in the future is that the government will continue to pursue the artificial high grain price policy as has been since 1968 [20]. The assumed consumer and producer prices of major food grains to be pursued by the first price policy alternative are as follows:

Year	Rice Consumer price	Rice Producer price	Barley Consumer price	Barley Producer price	Wheat Consumer price	Wheat Producer price
			...won per metric ton...			
1974	102,800	113,613	52,093	57,882	42,275	39,233
1975	115,000	115,000	52,500	55,000	47,740	44,000
1980	120,000	115,000	52,500	55,000	47,740	44,000
1985	120,000	115,000	52,500	55,000	47,740	44,000

Because the rapid realisation of self sufficiency in food grain production is of major concern for policy makers and wheat is mostly imported in the Republic of Korea, the second price policy alternative assumes that the consumer price of rice decreased from 120,000 won to 116,000 won per ton during the period of 1980–85 while maintaining the same lower consumer price of barley, and that the consumer price of wheat is increased from 47,740 won to 52,000 won and the producer price of wheat also increased from 44,000 won to 52,000 won in the same period. The objective is to accelerate wheat production and to substitute rice for wheat consumption, thus consuming the expected rice surplus and reducing wheat imports. Prices of other than foodgrain such as beef, pork and milk are assumed to be determined by free market forces and are to be fed back to estimate the elasticities of the subsequent year.

The other variable, considered in projecting future food supply was an investment flow in land and water development. The input figures follow MAF's current plan (161 billion won per year) to 1980 plus additional activities to enlarge production capacity with 60 billion won investment per year after 1980. This calls for the completion of eight large scale investment projects, substantial investment in eight additional projects to be completed by 1985, plus completion of 122 thousand hectares of irrigation improvement, 19 thousand hectares of surface drainage, 107 thousand hectares of subsurface drainage, 180 thousand hectares of land consolidation, and 107 thousand hectares of slope land reclamation. No tidal land improvement is planned other than the acreage included in the large scale projects.

Combining these four variables, the six simulation runs of the policy experiments with respect to food demand and supply are summarised in the table shown on page 158.

The results of the policy experiments are presented in terms of production, consumption, self sufficiency ratio and the nutrition level as shown in Table 4. Out of the six experiments, 'Run 3' turns out to be the most recommendable policy

Policy experiments	Demand side		Supply side	
	Population projections	Price and income elasticities	Price policy alternatives	Land and water development investment
Run 1	Low fertility/ slow migration	Fixed as the above estimates	High grain prices (I)	MAF's plan to 1980 plus 60 bil. won per year after 1980
Run 2	Low fertility/ slow migration	ditto	Low consumer price of rice vs. high wheat prices (II)	ditto
Run 3	Low fertility/ fast migration	ditto	I	ditto
Run 4	Low fertility/ fast migration	ditto	II	ditto
Run 5	High fertility/ slow migration	ditto	I	ditto
Run 6	High fertility/ slow migration	ditto	II	ditto

combination, in that production of major important foods except wheat and beef meets the self sufficiency level for exceeding the food requirements by 1986. The status of nutrition reaches the highest level of 2,731 calories per person a day with the largest supply of total protein at about 88 grams per person a day. The import requirements of wheat and beef in 1986, however, account respectively for 83.3 per cent and 8 per cent of total consumption in 1986.

Second best policy combinations are either 'Run 1' or 'Run 4', both of which are to achieve self sufficiency in food production except for wheat. 'Run 4' does satisfy an adequate level of beef consumption requirements without imports but all other policy experiments do not. Of these two, 'Run 4' meets the higher level of nutrition in both per person calories and total protein than does 'Run 1', whereas the latter achieves higher self sufficiency ratios in production of major foods except beef.

Various implications flow from this experiment. In order to achieve the self sufficiency in production of major food in the decade to come, vigorous population control programmes should be continuously pursued from the point of view of

Table 4
Summary results of policy simulation experiments for 1986

	Item	Unit	Run 1	Run 2	Run 3	Run 4	Run 5	Run 6
Rice	Production	1,000 metric tons	5,696.0	5,696.0	5,697.0	5,697.0	5,696.0	5,696.0
	Planted area	1,000 ha	1,222.0	1,220.0	1,220.0	1,220.0	1,220.0	1,220.0
	Consumption	1,000 metric tons	5,528.3	5,595.8	5,507.3	5,566.8	5,717.4	5,803.6
	Per capita C.	kg/Cap/year	120.9	122.6	120.8	122.3	121.4	123.4
	Balance	1,000 metric tons	167.7	100.2	189.7	130.2	-21.4	-107.6
	Self sufficiency	%	103.0	101.8	103.4	102.3	99.6	98.2
Barley	Production	1,000 metric tons	2,510.0	2,265.0	2,495.0	2,270.0	2,510.0	2,265.0
	Planted area	1,000 ha	928.9	838.2	923.3	840.2	928.9	838.2
	Consumption	1,000 metric tons	2,356.0	2,214.0	2,326.5	2,267.3	2,442.8	2,329.7
	Per capita C.	kg/Cap/year	49.5	48.1	49.0	48.3	49.8	47.9
	Balance	1,000 metric tons	154.0	51.0	168.5	2.7	67.2	-64.7
	Self sufficiency	%	106.5	102.3	107.2	100.1	102.8	97.2
Wheat	Production	1,000 metric tons	376.4	57.6	394.2	57.8	376.4	576.5
	Planted area	1,000 ha	142.0	21.7	149.0	41.6	142.0	217.5
	Consumption	1,000 metric tons	2,292.4	1,755.6	2,358.2	1,763.8	2,331.4	2,311.5
	Per capita C.	kg/Cap/year	53.9	53.0	55.6	53.4	53.1	52.2
	Balance	1,000 metric tons	-1,916.0	-1,698.0	-1,964.0	-1,706.0	-1,955.0	-1,735.0
	Self sufficiency	%	16.4	3.38	16.7	3.38	16.1	24.9
Beef	Production	metric tons	100,500.0	100,900.0	100,900.0	110,400.0	100,500.0	100,900.0
	Consumption	metric tons	112,810.0	122,470.0	109,662.0	97,380.0	121,940.0	116,700.0
	Per capita C.	kg	2.67	2.66	2.82	2.82	2.68	2.67
	Balance	metric tons	-12,310.0	-11,570.0	-8,762.0	13,020.0	-21,440.0	-15,800.0
	Self sufficiency	%	89.1	89.7	92.0	113.4	82.4	86.5
Milk	Production	metric tons	851,200.0	854,600.0	843,900.0	846,900.0	851,400.0	854,800.0
	Consumption	metric tons	851,200.0	854,600.0	843,900.0	844,202.0	784,400.0	854,800.0
	Per capita C.	kg	19.8	19.9	19.7	19.8	19.2	19.2
	Balance	metric tons	0	0	0	2,698.0	67,200.0	0
	Self sufficiency	%	100.0	100.0	100.0	100.3	108.5	100.0
Nutrition	Calories	Cal/Cap/day	2,727.0	2,724.0	2,731.0	2,723.0	2,719.0	2,716.0
	Protein	Gr./Cap/day	87.29	87.08	87.95	87.68	86.90	86.62

moderating rapid increase in food consumption. In this respect, maintaining a low rate of fertility is essential. Assuming that there would be a steady and fast rural–urban migration through the decade, providing them with non-farm employment opportunities poses an immediate problem. Urban problems would increase as the process of migration continues. Also, shortage of farm labour plus rising wage rates would aggravate conditions for increased production unless the process of farm mechanisation makes up the gap caused by a heavy drain of agricultural labour. In this respect, certain measures to slow down the fast migration need to be immediately made, under the circumstances of low funds available to counter-measure the ill effects.

On the supply side, by all means, the current high grain policy should be continued in order to increase grain production on the one hand and to maintain the moderate consumption level on the other. By changing administrative prices, a considerable substitution between barley and wheat production may be expected without jeopardising the level of total production. Wheat imports can be reduced with shifts to higher producer and consumer prices of wheat while lowering consumer prices of substitutable food grain. However, the model test indicates that the reduction rate was unsatisfactory at the current demand conditions. Besides a higher price policy some other non-price measures may be needed to decrease wheat consumption to an acceptable level. If the Republic of Korea is able to reduce wheat imports by one million tons from the estimated amount of 1.7 million tons (Run 3) in 1986, the value will amount to 300 million dollars by applying the price of $300,00 per ton projected by Japanese economists [21].

With the limited number of variables plus rigidity in the use of assumptions the model, however, could not tell us how to economically tackle the problems, given limited amounts of resources and many alternatives to take.

Recommendations and research needs

Attempts to achieve self sufficiency in food production have been made on both production and consumption aspects in the Republic of Korea. The decline in population fertility has been experienced during the past decade, in part due to the vigorous family planning activities of both public and private agencies. It is likely that the 'Stop at Two' campaign now underway will be gradually permeating into the nation if strongly supported by the government. However, some more serious attention needs to be paid to problems arising from the rapid rural–urban migration.

The past investment programmes have placed stress relatively more on the industrial and services sector development until fairly recently, in the wake of the world food crisis. The economic feasibility of increasing agricultural production and rural development is likely to continue under present population pressures and world price trends. To assure continued success in these areas it is recommended that:

1. The government budget for the family planning programme not only be increased, but also the ideal family size of the average Korean be lowered in order to attain the ambitious target of a 1.3 per cent population growth rate by 1986. Particularly, the following policy measures are highly recommended:
   (a) raise the legal age for marriage;
   (b) modify inheritance laws to favour daughters as well as sons;
   (c) relax military draft regulations to exempt a man from military service if he is an only son and has no more than one sister, and thereby encouraging participation in the 'Stop at Two' campaign.
2. Various government ministries cooperate in formulating a basic set of policies concerning urban taxation, pollution abatement, zoning and industrial decentralisation in hopes of slowing down the present trend of rural–urban migration.
3. Research on the effectiveness of family planning communication and education be initiated because communication and education programmes should be mobilised for the purpose not only of transmitting knowledge of contraceptives but also of stimulating and fostering the psychological processes identified to be important.
4. A policy analysis be conducted in order to explore effective measures of decentralising the location of new non-agricultural employment creation, and in realising well balanced distribution of population among different regions of the country.
5. Self sufficiency targets for various commodities be incorporated in the Fourth Five Year Plan, beginning in 1977. This will assure that public investment in increased agricultural production will be dealt with at the national level on a par with other forms of public investment.
6. A comprehensive programme of land use controls and development be adopted. Such a programme should contain a variety of elements, such as the promulgation of a set of uniform laws to minimise the conversion of prime agricultural land to urban uses, and intensified farm land expansion programme including both upland and tideland reclamation and the development of improved irrigation and drainage facilities. Such an intensified programme would likely require a doubling of the government's investment in rural infrastructure development.
7. Large scale pasture development programmes for grazing livestock be expanded to reduce imports of feed grain. A continuance of shift of cereals to feeds as much as is needed for producing animal protein would not be the long-run solution to the problem especially in a land-scarce country. On the consumption side, plant breeding, increases in the production of protein plant and fish catches, fortification of cereals might be alternative solutions to tackle

protein deficiencies.

8. Efforts be intensified to increase the rate of farm mechanisation and to improve the farm produce distribution and marketing system.

   Peak seasons of labour shortages are already beginning to occur because of the rapid increases in rural–urban migration. To overcome these shortages farm machinery should be made available over a wider geographical area. To take full advantage of improved technology in agriculture, marketing infrastructures are also required. Research is urgently needed to minimise storage and processing losses associated with the farm to market distribution system, to design an effective and efficient foodgrain management system at the national level and to enhance the growth and modernisation of the food processing industry.

9. The current production price support system for rice and barley be continued since it has increased both farm production and income. However, to increase efficiency within the system, standard criteria for determining the government purchase price are required. To assure the maintenance of an efficient and viable private wholesale and marketing system the government should discard the present system of setting a fixed seasonal release price and adopt a sliding scale of release price mechanism. This would help to minimise the amount of government funds required to maintain the subsidy programme and provide increased incentives to private wholesalers to maintain larger stocks even during off season periods.

10. The government adopt measures to reduce the growing importation and consumption of wheat. The wheat-made food encouragement programme together with the price support system for accelerated consumption of wheat and wheat flour should be abandoned to foster an increase in demand for locally produced wheat substitutes. Even a higher producer/consumer price system needs to be introduced. Research aimed at developing indigenous varieties of high yielding wheat should be intensified to assure future wheat self sufficiency.

11. The government improve and expand the present farm credit structure to assure adequate long and short term credit facilities for farm modernisation. A streamlining of credit for small farmers with a doubling of the present funds available will be required.

12. A minimum of 1 per cent of the agricultural sector's GNP (approximately 15 billion won) be devoted to the support of agricultural research and experimentation. The payoffs from such research are widely known. For example, the development of indigenous Tongil rice varieties has alone accounted for an increase in rice production of 3,000 metric tons. This is equivalent to a foreign exchange saving of 150 million dollars.

Notes

[1] The major contents of this paper was presented at the FAO/IAAE/UNFPA co-sponsored Seminar on Population and Food and Agricultural Development held in Rome, Italy, December 1–5, 1975. The author wishes to acknowledge Mr Dong Min Kim and Dr Dong Hi Kim of the National Agricultural Economics Research Institute for their contribution to this paper, for which he is solely responsible.

[2] S.K. Ahn, 'The Korean National Family Planning Program' presented at the 'Summer Seminar on Population', Seoul, July 15–19, 1974.

[3] As of 1973, the size of the family planning programme can be elaborated as follows:

Annual total expenditure:	1,827.9 million won (US $4.5 million equivalent)
Proportion of GNP:	0.37%
Number of field workers:	2,353 persons
Coverage per worker:	13,384 persons

[4] Demographic sample surveys and various indirect information estimated that the crude death rate was about 13 deaths per 1,000 total population in 1960, 8.5 in 1970, and 6.6 deaths in 1974. The life expectancy at birth, estimated on the basis of data on children born before 1973, was 62.4 years for men and 66.7 years for women.

[5] H.S. Moon *et al.*, 'Recent Trends in Ideal Family Size', in *Population and Family Planning in the Republic of Korea*, Vol. II, Korean Institute for Family Planning, Seoul, 1974, p. 281.

[6] Sang Joo Lee, 'Psychological Research: Korea', in *Population and Family Planning in the Republic of Korea*, Vol. II, Korean Institute for Family Planning, Seoul, 1974, pp. 281–96.

[7] Chung-Ja Kong, and Jae-Ho Cha, 'Boy Preference in Korea: A Review of Empirical Studies Related to Boy Preference', in *op. cit., supra*, p. 324.

[8] Seyeul Kim, 'The Economic and Social Determinants of Rural–Urban Migration in Korea', *Korean Journal of Agricultural Economics*, Vol. XVII, July 1975, p. 48.

[9] Exotech Systems Inc., 'Farm Mechanization Program for Korea – A Study of the Feasibility of Mechanizing Agriculture in the Republic of Korea', Seoul, 1973.

[10] Population Studies Centre, 'A Study of the Effects of Rural Out-Migration on Rural Development and Their Measures', Seoul, 1971.

[11] George E. Rossmiller, *et al.*, 'Korean Agricultural Sector Analysis and Recommended Development Strategies, 1971–85', Michigan State University, East Lansing, Michigan, USA, 1972.

[12] See John Sloboda and Tom Carroll, 'Approaches to Modelling Off-Farm Migration' (mimeographed), Michigan State University, East Lansing, Michigan, USA, 1974.

[13]

Year	Proportion of over age 20 to total (%)	Annual average growth rate of over age 20
1981	56.4	2.7
1986	59.7	2.9
1990	61.2	2.2

[14] The agricultural sector being in a relatively low value added position has, however, grown at a modest rate of 4.3 per cent a year during 1962—74. Yet its contribution to GNP declined from 44.1 per cent in 1962 to 22.5 per cent in 1974, attributed to the faster growth of other sectors of the economy.

[15] Exotech Systems, Inc., *op. cit.*

[16] According to IAS Report of 1974, the yield of barley is also affected greatly by the amount of water consumed. That is, there was almost a double difference between the case of water consumption by 325 mm and that by 179 mm. However, this approach assumes overall standard input requirements being satisfied.

[17]

Total farm household income (A)	480,711 won
Income from rice production (B)	232,096 won
B/A (%)	48.3
Direct price-income effect (%)	4.8
Production increase effect (%)	1–1.3
Total income increase (%)	5.8–6.1

[18] For the detailed data on the normal production averages and the experimental results of foodgrains in Korea, Japan and USA, see S.H. Kim and D.M. Kim, 'Population and Food in Korea', Michigan State University, East Lansing, Michigan, USA, 1975, p. 47.

[19] Michael Abkin, *et al.*, 'Briefing Charts on the Korean Agricultural Sector Simulation Project', Michigan State University, East Lansing, Michigan, USA, 1975.

[20] Since 1968 the Korean Government has followed a high grain policy for the dual purposes of: firstly, providing farmers with good incentives for production increase and secondly, leading consumers to follow more economical food consumption patterns. However, the consumer price of barley has been lower than the producer price (government's purchase price) for the benefits of low income households' economy.

[21] Mitsubishi Research Institute, 'A Projection Model of Food Supply and Demand of the World in 1980 and 1985', Tokyo, Japan, May, 1974, pp. 115–116.

Discussion on papers by Dandekar, Baharsjah and Kim

W.G. Farmer

The discussion of the three Asian case study papers gave general recognition to the need to establish national balances between population and food supply in association with an appropriate balance between the agricultural and industrial sectors in the underdeveloped situation of these countries where the agricultural, industrial, and population growth rates are interlinked.

A minority were still concerned with the need for the population and food balance to be struck on a national and global basis. For the problem to be solved the national and local interest groups must perceive its nature and, once motivated, they will be in a position to respond to measures being taken to reach a balance. At the same time integrated programmes, first of population control linked with nutrition and health programmes and, second, of raising agricultural production with its impact on both the incomes and production of farmers, will be priority areas in attaining the simple balance between food and population.

The case studies made it apparent that in Asia there are immediate cost implications connected with raising agricultural production. Achieving self sufficiency will be characterised by increasing marginal costs as both the boundaries of cultivation are approached and cultivation is intensified. The state of development of the domestic agricultural industry and the range of innovations still to be taken up, will determine the extent to which achievement of balance can be based upon increased food production. This is directly linked to the nature of the internal balance between agricultural and industrial development, determined by the relative speeds of sectoral development resulting from, *inter alia* the respective choices of technology, inter-sectoral comparisons of wage rates and the income transfers involved. In the establishment of feed prices associated with the balances is, also, the possibility of foreign trade and its potential distorting effects.

In the discussion this was illustrated by the past dependence of the Republic of Korea upon food aid to sustain its industrial development during the mid-1960s and its subsequent trade-off decisions between self sufficiency, in the face of increased marginal costs of raising the domestic food output, and the importation of foodgrains. Aid flows and the restriction of Korea's foreign markets had disrupted the pattern of trade based upon comparative advantage and led to a change of emphasis in the economy and of proportional factor use. The resulting agricultural/industrial balance has then directly affected the food/population balance. While it was noted that there is an obvious link between investment in industry for agriculture and increases in production, the impact of this will be delayed in comparison with direct investment in the sector.

The need was underlined to give emphasis to the greater involvement of local people in the execution of production projects, with a view to increasing their effectiveness by taking better account of local factors and by subsequently promoting a multiplier effect from direct government inputs. As part of the complex of issues affecting the raising of agricultural production the importance of institutional reforms was recognised as being a necessary factor in attaining this.

Consideration was also given to the effectiveness of methods of mobilising resources for stimulating food production by way, for example, of raising the yield of a land tax, and thereby redistributing farm income. However, while the connection between growth and social justice was established, it was agreed that policies to extend this should minimise the risk of creating production disincentives.

Policies aimed at raising the productivity of the agricultural sector in conjunction with industrial growth were discussed, covering in particular the development of simple small scale, labour-intensive industries producing simple agricultural equipment. Coupled to a pattern of small farm holdings using this technology there will be a direct influence upon the pattern of demand for consumer goods which will be different from the influence of alternative strategies. Raising the effective levels of production by improvements in harvesting, marketing and storage methods to reduce the incidence of food wastage was also considered. There was some discussion of the possibilities of influencing the growth of population. Consensus was reached on the need to make control measures effective by restructuring the environment of the target group, particularly that of the farmer so that the new social setting would reinforce the programme. Integrated programmes involving population control in which there is mutual reinforcement by the constituent parts are particularly appropriate.

The balance to be achieved between food and population will be found not when their respective rates of increase coincide, but when total food supply equates to the population's total food demands. The achievement of this balance is only one aspect of the problem of under development, and efforts will not be effective if they are directed solely to reaching this balance without regard to the rest of the complex of economic and social development.

SPECIAL SESSION III

Increasing Agricultural Production on the Small Farm and Motivating for Family Planning

Increasing agricultural production on the small farm and motivating for family planning

F.C. Sturrock

In considering this subject, let us start with the basic facts. In 1970, there were estimated (World Economic Survey 1973, UN), to be 1,730 million people in the developing countries. Of these, 1,264 million or 73 per cent were rural – most of them living off the land. Overall, the population was growing at 2.7 per cent a year. The growth rate in town and country is however quite different. In rural areas, the annual increase is 2.8 per cent, reduced to 2.1 per cent because of migration to the towns. In towns, the growth rate is 2.5 per cent, increased to 4.3 per cent by migration.

In most developed countries, the growth rate is less and migration to the towns more than takes care of any natural increase. In consequence the rural population is declining and there is an incentive to save labour. There is therefore a tendency to amalgamate farms and mechanise cultivation so that output can be maintained with a smaller labour force. Output per man in agriculture is therefore increasing and the rural standard of living is rising steadily.

The developing countries have a much more difficult problem. The growth rate is much greater and on average only a quarter of the rural increase in population is being absorbed into the towns. As a result, the rural population is increasing and will continue to do so for many years to come.

Suppose that we project the figures already given. In twenty-five years, the national population will double and the town population will treble. The rural population will grow by 65 per cent but if they are to feed the towns they must double their output. To put the matter in another form, three rural workers are at present feeding themselves and one town dweller. In twenty-five years, the three rural workers will be feeding two town dwellers in addition to themselves.

If the population doubles in twenty-five years, how is it to be fed? Let us take first of all those countries fortunate enough to have land to spare. In many cases the land belongs to the tribe rather than the individual, but each family has a recognised area on which it can grow crops. If numbers increase a young couple can start a new household and expect to be given enough fresh land that they can clear and cultivate.

Thus if there is land to spare, food production increases automatically with population and food supplies present no problems. In these conditions there is no incentive to limit the size of the family because an extra child is not a burden. In the tropics very little clothing is required and it is easy to grow an extra row of maize or cassava to supply extra food. With aunts and grandparents at hand, the child can be cared for if mother is ill or attending to her market stall. Even when he is quite young, a child can be useful and can help to weed the crops. Within a few years, he is doing a man's work and as the parents grow old, they will depend on their children to look after them. The child is thus an asset, and propaganda for family limitation will have little effect on the farmer.

By contrast, a young married couple who migrate to the town are in a different position. If they are ambitious to raise their standard of living, children are a liability. Special food and clothing must be purchased and, in many countries, school fees must be paid. If there are no relatives nearby the whole burden of rearing children is thrown on the mother who has little freedom. Money spent on a child competes with furniture and even the possibility of a motor car. Thus at least amongst the more affluent and ambitious town dwellers family planning is more likely to appeal.

So far we have been dealing with countries with land to spare. Now we come to those that have little or none. If the farmer has a large family, two consequences may result, the farm may be kept intact or it may be divided amongst the children. If it is kept as a unit children that cannot be supported by the farm will have to migrate to the town. This may not however induce the farmer to limit his family.

If, on the other hand, the farm is small and is divided amongst the children, it will be broken up into tiny fragmented holdings that will not support a family. In these conditions, a farmer with his children's welfare in mind may deliberately limit the size of his family. Equal division of property amongst children was part of the Code Napoleon and there can be little doubt that the birth rate amongst peasant farmers in rural France declined in the nineteenth century for this reason.

With this one exception, we must therefore expect the increase in rural population to continue. In areas where there is land to spare such as South America, parts of tropical Africa and parts of South East Asia this may not produce any acute problem – at least not yet. In other areas where there is no land to spare, increased food supplies must come from higher yields on land already under cultivation.

As most of the farm land is in the hands of the small farmer, it is he who must learn to increase production. Is he likely to succeed? There are two opposing theories of the effect of population pressure on agricultural productivity. One theory propounded by W. Allan [1] assumes that if population exceeds a certain 'critical density', crop and livestock yields will decline. There is evidence to support this point of view. In much of tropical Africa, the farmer clears a piece of forest and grows crops for two or three years. Yield per hectare declines however as humus in the soil is exhausted and weeds increase. If the rainfall is high, plant nutrients are washed out and erosion may take place. Cultivation is therefore abandoned and the forest is allowed to regenerate. It may however take ten years or more for the fertility to recover. This system works reasonably well but if the population increases and land is scarce, the farmer is compelled to clear the land after a much shorter period before the soil fertility has recovered. Much the same is true when the number of grazing livestock is increased beyond the capacity of the pasture. The livestock may then eat the pasture down to the roots and destroy the plants.

The opposite theory is proposed by Ester Boserup [2] who believes that population pressure forces farmers to adopt more intensive forms of agriculture. Over the long period, this is certainly true. Less than 1,000 years ago, Europe was farmed with shifting cultivation and supported only a small population. As numbers grew, more intensive methods were eventually devised and most of the land is now cropped continuously. The same is true of China and some other parts of Asia where highly intensive forms of cultivation have been evolved and the land carries a very large population.

It would be foolish, however, to assume that intensive systems will automatically appear to feed a steadily growing population in any part of the world. In the instances quoted, the population increase was very slow, often far less than 1 per cent and this allowed ample time − often many centuries − to devise more intensive systems. One must also add that there are many areas with severe physical limitations to intensification such as drought, or cold, that are likely to make intensification impossible or prohibitively expensive. Even apart from such limitations, there are substantial differences in the inherent fertility of agricultural land. The Ganges basin in India is very fertile and has ample water below the surface that can be used for irrigation. The land can thus carry a huge population. Most African soils are less fertile and it is doubtful if many of them could ever carry as many people.

Unfortunately if the population is likely to double every twenty-five or thirty years, it may not be possible to discover and adopt productive new systems in time. If so, land will be overcropped and overgrazed as Allan has suggested.

It is sometimes assumed that even if the system does not change, more labour on the land will help to increase yields. In fact, once there is enough labour to plant, weed and harvest the crop at the proper season, the marginal productivity of extra workers soon falls to zero. Indeed it becomes negative because they consume food that would otherwise be available for sale.

Increases in output and in population are essentially a matter of balance. A successful example is Japan. In the last 100 years, population has grown by less than 1¼ per cent a year. This was sufficient to supply the workers needed for industry. The rural population remained almost static and as there was very little extra land to be reclaimed, the farm size remained at about one hectare. There was however sufficient time to adopt more intensive cultivation and in spite of a huge increase in population Japan is still largely self sufficient in rice, the staple food. Although the farms are small, thefarmers now enjoy a surprisingly high standard of living.

Unbalanced growth, on the other hand, can go badly wrong. When potatoes were introduced into Ireland in the eighteenth century, they produced a large increase in food. Unfortunately, there was a population explosion and the rural population grew as fast as potato growing spread. In the 1840s, the outbreak of a new disease, blight, (Phytophthora infestans), caused the potatoes to rot and there was widespread starvation. Millions fled to Scotland, England and the United States and the population is believed to have fallen from eight to three million. This is an example worth study by those who believe that a population can never outgrow its food supply.

To return to the present day, the problem is to increase production. This means more output per farmer and more output sent to market. It also means as the stock of land becomes used up, more output per hectare. This is the task that confronts the family farmer who is in charge of most of our agricultural land. Can he meet this challenge? The official answer is that we must rely on the scientist to breed better varieties, to combat pests and diseases and so forth. We must then rely on the extension services to carry the results to the farmer. Sometimes the system works with a fair degree of success. At other times we must confess that the results are often disappointing. Farmers are reluctant to cooperate and are branded by the extension officer as stubborn and ignorant. In some cases this is true, but in other cases it is not the farmer but the advice that is at fault. He will not apply fertiliser because he doubts whether the increased yield will pay the cost. He will not sow a cash crop early enough because he is giving first priority to the food crops on which his family depends. He refuses to grow a new crop altogether because he is not convinced that it will pay better than the crop it displaces. In many cases the misunderstanding is because the extension officer looks for technical perfection — the farmer is more interested in the economics of production and in spite of his lack of education, his judgement is often surprisingly shrewd. This is where the agricultural economist should come into the picture. Unfortunately he is often of little help to the adviser. Whereas the extension officer has research stations and experimental farms to back him up, the agricultural economist usually has very little authentic data on which he can rely. Many excellent economic studies have been made but they are usually on too small a scale and they lack continuity. Thus although one might have data to cover one group of villages, the economist would hesitate to apply the results fifty miles away where conditions might be quite different. As a result, the agricultural economist plays only a very minor role in advisory work.

It may be of interest to note that the same problem arose in developed countries and efforts were made to overcome them. Let me quote the United Kingdom because I know more of the details there. The extension services there were rudimentary until the outbreak of war in 1939. There was a threat of starvation and the extension services were built up rapidly to encourage food production. For this reason accurate information was necessary on farmers' costs and returns so that prices could be manipulated to encourage maximum production of the foods most urgently required. To do this a national economic survey was rapidly set up. The government chose to use university economists to do the field work because they were already conducting surveys as part of their research. The government could however have organised the work themselves.

These farm income surveys covered the whole country and have continued ever since. Indeed, from the beginning they were an integral part of the process of formulating agricultural policy. More recently, a similar system has been adopted throughout the EEC and data from all the nine member countries are now assembled in Brussels. The data from such surveys are equally useful as an aid to the extension services. As soon as the war was over, attention in Britain was turned from maximising production to increasing efficiency and for the first time, the agricultural economics departments were brought into the advisory field. Since then, they have collaborated closely with the extension services providing them with efficiency standards, planning handbooks and the like.

It seems to me that the time has come to apply the same methods in developing countries, but so far as I am aware, they have not been backed up by continuous national surveys based on random samples. It is true that extension officers try to do small surveys to collect information but in most cases the data would not stand up to any statistical test of representativeness. As a result, the budgets they prepare to persuade farmers to adopt certain improvements are often unrealistic and hopelessly optimistic. Any farmer misled by such advice will be doubly suspicious next time – and not without justification.

Three years ago, I took some sabbatical leave and was invited by FAO to lead a team to Ghana to help to organise a planning department in their Ministry of Agriculture. It seemed to me essential to planning to have a national farm income survey. After some experiments we mounted one, and carried it through. We were told that farmers would refuse to cooperate. In fact, we had very few refusals. Not surprisingly the farmers did wonder why we were asking them questions about money. We answered them quite frankly as follows:

'The government in Accra has to make decisions – the prices you are to get, the seed and fertiliser you may need. They cannot do this sitting in an office in Accra, so we have come to find out how farmers are getting on. We cannot visit all the farms so we have chosen a few and you are one. We are relying on you to tell us about your farm.' This seemed to work, especially as we were prepared to listen to their grievances.

The survey was carried out on a random sample of 1,300 farms. We also decided to prepare a farm classification based on the crops and livestock that the farm produced. One problem was that most fields contained a mixture of three or four crops. We did however devise a system to deal with this.

We now have trading accounts giving details of receipts, payments and produce used for each type of farm by size and region. This information is of immense value in formulating policy. If, for example, the government wished to encourage farmers to grow more maize, we could estimate whether maize at the price offered would compete with existing crops on the farms concerned. We could also estimate the number of maize specialists to whom the price is of vital importance and the number of mixed farms growing some maize who could be persuaded to grow more if the price was high enough to tempt them to change their cropping.

Information of this kind is equally useful to extension officers in planning new campaigns. They can prepare realistic budgets based on what really happens on farms. Presented in this form, advice can be far more palatable to the farmer.

Budgets showing the effect on farm income of the project concerned are of course normally included in projects for the World Bank. A ministry of finance should insist on similar estimates for schemes submitted for internal financing. In the absence of accurate data on which to base cost benefit exercises, there is a strong temptation for a director of agriculture to spend lavishly on a scheme that will produce something spectacular, such as a dam that will impress the ministry concerned and appear in the newspapers.

Of even more importance, farm income surveys should be used to monitor projects already in operation. Using results from the farm incomes survey as a yardstick, he can assess the increases in productivity shown by government schemes such as state farms, irrigation schemes and resettlement programmes. He can set the increase in output against the capital expended to see whether a worthwhile return is being shown.

It is worth noting that an agricultural economist in government service could easily make himself unpopular if he criticises projects being conducted by other sections of his ministry. Such comment should not of course be in public. It is thus desirable that the agricultural economist in public service should be able to report in confidence to his minister or permanent secretary in charge of the ministry.

An even more severe test would be to set the cost of the extension services in an area against the increase in production in the area.

There is another service that the agricultural economist could make to farm improvement — detailed studies of the family farm as an economic unit. It is a far more rational organisation than many economists realise. Indeed after centuries of trial and error, one would expect that the systems in operation were well chosen given the inputs and constraints with which the farmer had to operate. This is not to say that technology could not effect improvements. But before we ask the farmer to do something new we must be quite sure that when the new technique is fitted into his farm routine, it will really give him a worthwhile return. There have been dozens of ingenious farming schemes that looked plausible on paper but which failed in practice. The usual reason is that the farmer was expected to adopt a difficult and expensive technique that saddled him with debt payments that swallowed up most of the gain. To quote a simple example, farmers are still urged to give up crop mixtures and grow single crops in neat rows. So far as we could find, crop mixtures nearly always had a higher output per hectare than single crops. Mixtures are not of course suitable for tractor cultivation but these farmers cannot afford tractors and have enough labour to cultivate by hand.

At first sight mechanisation seems to have no place on small farms. Tractors save man hours but if the rural population is increasing, labour is not a scarce resource. There are however seasonal peak demands and if work is delayed, the yield suffers. A tractor that hastens land preparation and the sowing of crops at the beginning of the wet season can increase output her hectare. If the small farmer cannot afford a tractor, who is to supply it? One solution is the ministry of agriculture. A disadvantage is that if the tractor is used only for part of the year the service may lose money. Another alternative is that somewhat larger farmers with twenty hectares or more can buy a tractor and can do work on contract for their smaller neighbours.

One fact that quickly emerges from a study of individual farm records is that some farmers are much more successful than others. The best consistently make five or even ten times as much cash profit as others with the same resources. Successful farmers are well worth study because the reason is not always apparent. It may be something obvious such as the use of good seed or fertiliser but usually this is only a small part of the story.

It is also worth recalling that farmers can be innovators. The introduction of cocoa farming into Ghana eighty years ago is a well known example but there are many others. Once an innovation of this kind is accomplished, the scientists can help it on by improving varieties, finding the right fertilisers and pesticides to use. The extension officer can however perform a service by recognising and publicising new ideas that do not necessarily come out of a textbook.

One must admit, however, that one of the greatest handicaps to progress is the public image of the family farmer as a poor and ignorant peasant. He is often despised — not least by his own children whose ambition is to get away from farming as soon as possible. This is unfortunate because it means a drain of the most able children from this important industry. One way to change the image is to encourage larger commercial farms. Let me make it clear that I am not thinking of large plantations but of a much more modest size. If, for example, the typical small arable family farm is one to four hectares, the size I have in mind might be around five to twenty hectares. These are genuine commercial farms employing labour and with an appreciable amount of capital.

We have studied such farms particularly in Uganda [3] and Ghana. It might be thought that the best apprenticeship for such an undertaking would be a life time of farm work. We found that although many of these commercial farmers had been born on a small farm, they had often also worked elsewhere. A man might for example start with a market stall, then buy a truck to transport produce, then build up a trading business. As he accumulated capital he had a hankering to return to his own village. He then acquired land and planted trees. As the trees came into bearing he moved on to the farm and as he prospered he built himself a fine house. He was then a man of substance. Some large farmers were former civil servants, teachers or army officers. They knew less about farming but possessed capital or knew how to borrow it. Many of them started new enterprises such as dairy farming in Uganda where their education helped them to master the quite difficult technique of producing milk for market in a hot climate. Others bought tractors and after cultivating their own land, did work on contract for neighbours. Some were failures and lost their money, but others were very successful. One notable point was that although a knowledge of farming was an advantage, a knowledge of how to handle capital and labour was even more important. I should add that most of these larger farms were on newly cleared land — they were not formed by displacing small farmers.

A small class of more affluent commercial farmers can be an asset. They can become leaders in the community, helping to organise cooperatives and dealing on fairly equal terms with traders. They can ask the extension services far more sophisticated questions and expect a practical answer. Above all, their presence shows that farming can be an outlet for an intelligent boy with ambition.

To sum up, what should be our objective in improving family farms? Is it output per acre or output per man? We have a choice. If land is scarce and population increase is out of hand, all that may be possible is to settle as many families as possible on the minimum area in the hope that they will somehow scratch a bare living. We then finish with a countryside that is a rural slum of poverty stricken people. This is a gospel of despair and we must try to avoid it. A better objective is higher output per man for this is the way to ensure a rising standard of living. And there should be scope in farming for the man with talent. It is of interest that in Kenya even where land is scarce, resettlement schemes make provision for a small proportion of larger units for men with capital and business ability.

We should however end on a note of optimism. In Sweden less than 100 years ago, there were farmers in the forest still practising shifting cultivation, cutting down trees, burning them, growing crops for a year or two, then moving on. They lived in rough wooden houses with a standard of living very little different from farms in the forest zone of West Africa now. Now they are amongst the most prosperous family farmers in the world with incomes of $10,000 or more. Apart from some iron ore and timber, Sweden has very few natural resources not enjoyed by most developing countries. They did however limit their population to eight million.

There can be little doubt about the importance of the topic with which we are dealing today. The problems posed are difficult but if we ignore them, they will not go away. We still have some time in hand and these problems can be solved. The agricultural economist can play an important role if he can make his voice heard — not merely as a prophet of doom but by showing how practical solutions can be found.

Notes

[1] W. Allan, *The African Husbandman*, Oliver and Boyd, London, 1965.
[2] Ester Boserup, *The Conditions of Agricultural Growth*, George Allan and Unwin Ltd., London, 1965.
[3] Audrey I. Richards, Ford Sturrock and Jean M. Fortt, *Subsistence to commercial farming in present-day Buganda*, Cambridge University Press, 1973.

Discussion on paper by Sturrock

Nihal Amerasinghe

The need to increase agricultural production in the face of an ever expanding population is a perplexing problem confronting all third world countries. The problem of increasing agricultural production in developing countries could be conveniently grouped into two categories based on the availability of suitable agricultural lands, viz. overpopulated developing countries that are fortunate enough to have sufficient agricultural land and the less fortunate with little or no land for further expansion. A common feature is the wide variation in the farm types that are found with different resource endowments and potential. The general consensus was that Allan's 'critical density' theory regarding the influence of population on agricultural production, was untenable, particularly in the light of Asia's experience. In fact, the evidence seemed to favour Boserup's contention that population pressures on the land force farmers to adopt more intensive techniques of agricultural production.

The level of productivity prevailing on peasant farms in the less developed countries leaves much to be desired. In this regard the role of both formal and informal education seem to be fundamental. At the present time the agricultural extension services, particularly farmer training programmes, could be considerably improved. It is not only important to ensure that farmer education is realistically planned and implemented but that the other essential inputs are also available in time and in the form required. The need to provide sufficient incentives to motivate farmers to increase agricultural production cannot be overemphasised. The neglect of appropriate markets besides other conventional production incentives have often thwarted development efforts. In other words a piecemeal approach to agricultural development will not suffice. An integrated programme of action is necessary to ensure sustained agricultural production. The BIMAS programme in Indonesia is a good example of such an effort where an increase of over 50 per cent in rice production was registered during the five year period 1970–75.

In the provision of inputs it is imperative to note that marginal benefits will not provide necessary stimuli to bring about change and development. Farmers have to contend with many hazards and their traditional behavioural patterns are understandable in view of the subsistence goals of farm production. Therefore, it is imperative that incentives to production are substantial. The gap between technical knowhow and what prevails under actual farm conditions could be attributed to this fact.

There is no gainsaying that the agricultural sector of developing countries will have to support the vastly expanding populations for many years to come due to the lack of the necessary resources for the development of industrial and manufacturing sectors. Clearly, the approach to agricultural productivity cannot be via the productivity of land alone due to the population pressures of most developing countries. The solution to the food problem is not mass production *per se* but production for and by the masses. If increasing the efficiency of land was the only goal of production, the social problem of unemployment would be exacerbated. Redistribution of population into other sectors does not seem to be possible at the present time due to the large numbers involved and the slow rate of growth of these sectors. For instance in Indonesia, of the total population of 130 million people, 70 per cent is concentrated in Java. Although the density of the population is extremely high, it is impracticable to suggest a policy of redistribution due to the restricted opportunities of doing so. Likewise in India where more than 120 million farmers and 70 million operational holdings are involved reorganisation of farms and farming systems would seem unthinkable due to the logistical problems involved.

Group approaches to farming seem to offer some respite to the problems of increasing land productivity without deepening the problem of rural unemployment, particularly in areas where there is an unfavourable man/land ratio. In fact, group farming approaches are now being pursued with vigour in a number of developing countries. Beside the attraction of this approach in offering some solution to the problem of growing unemployment, it also provides a convenient organisational approach for introducing scientific methods of farming.

The resource endowment situations of farmers seem fundamental in determining their success or failure. In planning programmes of intensification this aspect should be carefully examined and the potentials for development explored on this basis. Another aspect which needs further examination is a study of the factors which motivate peasant farmers and their behavioural patterns, if we are to quicken the process of agricultural development by providing the appropriate stimuli.

SPECIAL SESSION IV

Policies and Programmes for Agricultural Development: The Role of Economic-Social Science Analysis and of Research Agencies in Seeking Solutions

Policies and programmes for agricultural development: the role of economic-social science analysis and of research agencies in seeking solutions

A.R. Teixera Filho

The rapid increase in world population makes it vitally urgent to increase food production. The governments of developed and developing countries must be willing to take action not only in the face of hunger, but concentrate on long range aspects of the food problem. World food supplies are, and probably will be, distributed in accordance with purchasing power or effective demand and not according to nutritional requirements. A permanent solution to the problem includes population control and major efforts to plan agricultural research directed toward a long term solution of the agricultural production and food supply problem, particularly in those climatic zones where very little research has been historically undertaken.

Agricultural research policy

An agricultural research policy must be based on the fact that the objectives of agricultural research are not academic or speculative. The objective when possible must be strictly practical and oriented towards the improvements of agricultural production and the living standard of the agricultural producer. A complete national research programme should take into consideration the nature of future innovations and technology; and proceed to evaluate the impact on, and the response of, the economic, social, and political sectors to these potential changes. The nature and the objectives of research programmes should be determined by the stage of development of the economy:—

Initial development stage Estimate present and future economic importance of various commodities and then divide research in proportion to the increase of economic importance of each of them.

Intermediate development stage Allocate research resources according to income elasticities for different agricultural products and various other aspects of products such as quality, quantity, services, convenience, etc.

Advanced countries Quantify potential growth targets of various crops based on visualised new technologies and divide research resources according to estimated marginal value of the new technology in relation to the existing level.

In general one can say there is no single method or technique on which decision making could or should be based. The need for informed judgement must be accepted and that further exploration of methodologies is necessary.

Economic and institutional analysis in agriculture research

All problem-oriented research programmes must have an economics component directed specifically at the economic issues associated with the major technological problems to be attacked. First, economic analysis should evaluate the economic and social factors at the micro-level of generated technologies. These include: (a) design of physical/biological experiment to permit efficient economic analysis; (b) production function analysis of experimental and related data; (c) determination of optimal systems of farming; and (d) product and input price and marketing research.

In addition to micro-economic considerations, economists in association with other social scientists must consider aggregate macro-economic issues. Four of the most significant of these issues are: (a) internal and external supply and demand studies for food and other agricultural commodities given priority in research programmes; (b) internal and external supply and demand studies for inputs or factors of production; (c) regional disparities and other potential problems associated with implementation of new technologies; and (d) relative price structure of major agricultural inputs in relation to food and other agricultural products.

Other studies should evaluate the impacts of the research findings in terms of their effects on growth, equity and risk bearing potentialities of the new techniques created or to be created. In addition, in relation to the food shortage problem, a new approach has to be developed in evaluation of cost and real value of various food crops in terms of nutrients.

Theoretical considerations in agricultural research

The progress of agricultural research can best be understood with the help of theory and with examination of past experiences.

1. The Theory of Induced Innovation — According to this theory, factor endowments provide the motivating power for technical change in agriculture.
2. Social Interest Groups as Determinants of Research Policy — According to this theory, technical change is a cumulative process in which socio-economic and political-bureaucratic structures interact to define the demand for and the supply of new technologies. The United States and Japan, starting from entirely different factor endowment situations, had their agricultural research induced toward saving the scarce resources, land in Japan and labour in the United States.

In both theories a few elements play key roles. The first emphasises the natural supply and demand forces influencing the factor and product prices as the signals of scarcities. The second places emphasis on the socio-economic political structure. Both of them recognise the role of available scientific knowledge and of the body of trained personnel to sense the market orientation or to follow the commands of the governing structure. The power of the society plays an important role in the second model.

Formulating agricultural and food research programmes

A new organisational structure is proposed based on the concept of a 'mission-oriented systems approach'. The objectives would be:

(a) to develop conceptual definitions and methods for structuring agricultural research efforts toward improvement of food supply systems;
(b) to develop concepts and frameworks for establishing short and long range dynamic research and development (R and D) programmes, maximising the tangible benefits resulting from R and D.

Research planning is identified with the future consequences of present decisions. To increase the likelihood that useful information will, in fact, result from research activities, the research must be planned and a complete set of methodology has to be developed.

Research planning should begin with suitable identification and analysis of the system or systems of existing and potential production technology. The second stage should be an information analysis that reveals the existence and adequacy of available information on the system under study. Once all information available and needed has been established the research strategy should take into consideration the interrelationships between technical and economic change. The fourth step in agricultural research planning is to formulate a research programme whose goals cover the information needs of economically justified research.

Agricultural research in the United States

The value of agricultural research and technology development has been demonstrated in the United States and other developed countries. According to USDA published indices of agricultural productivity, the ratio of outputs to inputs per acre in 1972 as compared to the mid-1930s has risen by forty-five per cent. The production per man hour has more than doubled. The number of people supplied by each farmer has risen from fifteen to fifty-two. During this same time, the acreage harvested per consumer has been reduced by nearly one half. The rate of return on additional investment in agricultural research and extension has been forty-five to fifty per cent per year over the past forty years. This has kept food prices low. Americans spend only about sixteen per cent of their income on food.

A considerable amount of the success was due to a continuous and large amount of effort directed to agricultural and related research that created the largest and most efficient agricultural production machine in the world.

Agricultural research in tropical regions

The low level of real research investment in the major developing country climatic zones, especially in the tropical and desert zones, partly explains the relatively poor agricultural performance of these regions. The relatively small amount of agricultural research effort undertaken and performed in tropical conditions till now did not show great food and other agricultural production possibilities.

Lately, many research institutes, national as well as international, are seen and recognised as promising contributors to boosting food production. The effect of increase in research investment was dramatised by the Green Revolution. It was realised that the unused available resources of land are not located where the imbalance in the rates of growth of population and food is more intense. This places additional burden on the need to increase yields of the available and already utilised resources.

The following are the first three of a list of ten recommendations of agricultural research priorities made by the United States Board of Agricultural & Renewable Resources:

1. Expand research on photosynthesis so as to increase crop productivity.

2. Strengthen research on biological nitrogen fixation to establish coordinated programmes for developing field demonstrations.

3. Develop techniques for genetic manipulation beyond those of conventional plant breeding, including *in vitro* techniques for asexual approaches and broadcrosses between crop species.

Tropical areas with abundant intensive solar radiation and continuous growing seasons with large amount of water supply present much higher potential for these kinds of experiments and the resulting technology than do temperate zones with limited growing seasons. Temperate zones are often deficient in solar radiation, growth and activities of soil bacteria are practically stopped for nearly half or a larger part of the year.

In addition, a large number of tropical plants until now very little exploited in terms of possible food production, present the greatest challenge for genetic architects to introduce desirable characteristics like increasing protein content of some tree crops.

Brazil and its commitment to agricultural R and D

The research and the rapidly growing literature on economic and agricultural development in Brazil shows that it holds untapped and underutilised agricultural resources that in due time could become one of the important breadbaskets to help feed the hungry world.

The development of agricultural research in Brazil has gone through four periods. The first period ran from the late nineteenth century up to the mid-1940s, when plantation agriculture was at its peak. The second period went from the mid-1950s to the mid-1960s; economic expansion of the industrial base was a clear prerogative in the allocation of resources. The third period began in the early 1960s and continued until the creation of the Empresa Brasileira de Pesquisa Agropecuària — EMBRAPA (Portuguese acronym for Brazilian Agricultural Research Corporation) in 1972. Since the creation of EMBRAPA, the Brazilian Federal Government has decided to invest heavily in research on agricultural sciences. The budget for 1976 exceeded 100 million dollars.

Technical assistance and rural extension activities in Brazil have long been fragmented. Since the early 1970s the government started taking positive steps to strengthen the extension system. In mid-1974, the Brazilian Enterprise for Technical Assistance and Rural Extension (EMBRATER) was created as an autonomous corporation within the Ministry of Agriculture. EMBRATER regards itself as a catalyst for bringing about technical, economic and social change in the agricultural sector. At the national level it coordinates its work with agencies handling research, rural credit, commercialisation, etc. The National Commission of Agricultural Research and Technical Assistance (COMPATER) has been set up as the coordinating link between EMBRAPA and EMBRATER and will be responsible at the federal level for synchronising, reviewing and coordinating programmes of both agencies. The main point of interaction between research and extension is intended to be at the farm level, where technological packages are to be prepared as a result of discussions between researchers, farmers and extension staff.

The tendency is to dissociate research from university teaching, thus advisory services tend to make the research programme mission-oriented and responsive to the needs of farmers and consumers rather than follow the scientific interest of the academic community.

The social, economic and political structure of the poor countries may be such that the price signals of the market get distorted and do not communicate the right indications to research investment. Their social and economic environment often ensures that research institutes do not respond to the needs of farmers and consumers.

EMBRAPA is a public corporation, which means that it operates like a private corporation. Thus it can use all types of financial and human resources and can sell its services to all kinds of clients. EMBRAPA's principal product is technology and its primary client, the federal government. National priorities are established by the federal, and regional priorities by the state, governments in terms of products for export and domestic consumption. The major tool of execution for the whole programme is a centralised system of research planning that establishes a methodology which permits the setting of objectives and goals, the selection of the most appropriate measures for their attainment and the choice of ways and means to carry out the selected measures.

Brazil has accumulated a stock of knowledge that is useful to her agriculture. Extension people, farmers and researchers meet together on an informal basis, with the objective of organising available knowledge into technological packages for different classes of farmers. Training abroad and hiring foreign professionals are considered as being most applicable to the Brazilian situation. Out of some 1,200 professional research workers, more than 550 are doing full time graduate work. During the whole study period they are paid a full salary and educational allowance.

The role of the economist at EMBRAPA's Agricultural Research Centre embraces the following list of activities: establishing good working relationship with other research scientists; defining the existing production system; participating in development of technological packages; performing economic analysis of experimental data; making analysis of distributional effects of potential innovation; estimating labour requirement of new technology; quantifying of future technology; and assisting in planning of new research.

The importance of Brazilian model to other developing countries

The socio-economic structures in the rural areas of the developing countries will favour a centrally guided research system that is aggressive in visualising the directions its resource should be used. The idea of a centrally planned research organisation and programme has helped in Brazil to combine the scarce, highly trained scientists into strong and solid interdisciplinary research teams. When farmers do not communicate their needs to the research organisation, the central coordination should provide a lead to the research agencies in carrying out their task of furthering knowledge.

In Brazil, the association of the interdisciplinary teams with a systems approach to the farmers' problems has been adopted, and hopefully the time span from the understanding of the problem by researchers to the adoption of new technologies by farmers will be shortened.

The capacity for innovating in agricultural technology is essential for agricultural development. McDermott (1975) refers to research as a technological innovation process. The key is in the transfer and diffusion of agricultural technology from temperate to tropical ecosystems through problem oriented adaptive research. The capacity to transfer depends heavily on indigenous research capability. It is also important to specific countries that they know where potentially transferrable discoveries of technology and technical knowledge are being made.

The Brazilian model of a centralised agricultural research system is a potential partial solution to the food crisis through increased food production in the tropics using the new technology which it hopes to produce. Agricultural research-based activities taking into consideration geo-climatic diversity and furnishing the location-specific evidence must be the basis of innovation and new technological packages for all developing countries.

Unanswered questions and unsolved problems

The application of advances in agricultural technology, such as those associated with the Green Revolution, seem to increase in both absolute and relative terms the income disparities between poor and rich farmers in developing countries. The new challenge is to create labour-intensive, land and capital saving technology for small scale farmers in developing areas. Whether the modern technique of plant design through genetic architecture based on somatic or body cell reproduction can or cannot create this technology is an open question.

This paper offers an optimistic view on the solution of the food crisis as a production problem. However, it has some reservations:

1. a rural development strategy designed to improve the economic and social life of the rural poor is still an unsolved problem;

2. the role of the social scientist has not been clearly defined within the context of the food crisis and also constitutes an unanswered question.

Final remarks and policy recommendations

Despite the great difficulty inherent in trying to predict the future, the author of this paper believes that current decisions concerning agricultural research, particularly in developing countries, will be instrumental in producing food in the future.

Two broad groups of research can be recognised:

1. research that serves the scientific community;

2. research that serves the public.

The latter kind of research must be mission-oriented or problem solving research. Over the years the agricultural research programme, which was strongly production-oriented, has made a significant contribution to farming efficiency in the United States and thereby, directly and indirectly to the whole world. This also helped in concentrating food production in temperate zone on a worldwide basis. In the long run, increased understanding of the biological principles underlying agricultural productivity will serve as a major contribution. In the short run, however, problem-oriented adaptive research can considerably increase agricultural and food production. Research should focus on ways of decreasing dependence upon chemically synthesised nitrogen fertiliser and on increasing the supply of biologically fixed nitrogen by forage and grain legumes and nitrogen-fixing associations of micro-organisms with grasses, shrubs trees, lichens and marine organisms and the design of new cropping systems.

As far as social science policy is concerned, the action-oriented research must shift its focus from the character and personality of the farmer to the socio-economic conditions that lead him to accept or reject change. Certainly we need to know far more than we do about the economic, social and political relations in agriculture and more about the relations between the rural farm and urban groups. These for most part are untouched territory. Research on resource development and public policy can also stand expansion.

The chief objective of agricultural research and development must be to increase welfare where human misery is greatest. Some parts of the tropics constitute such areas.

A sound agricultural policy, correctly articulated with the national development policy as a whole, is essential if the national goals are to: increase food output, improve nutrition and cope with the interaction between food supply and growth of population. Eventually the place where additional food can be produced and the place where food is needed will not be the same. The commercial demand for agricultural and food products will continue to be closely tied to world economic conditions. A food crisis in the world poverty belt will not create effective demand. This is because impoverished and malnourished people cannot get their foodstuffs in the market. Since the market cannot indicate actual need, the situation may require a new way of sensing how research should react in response to food scarcity. Centralised planning of food production research by each country and the coordination of their efforts on an international level may be the best solution to this world crisis. It is hoped that the Brazilian model described in this paper is a correct step in this direction.

Today's world food production system was built mainly by and for the people of temperate climates. The people who live in the tropical climates can use this experience to build one for themselves.

References

(1) Arnon, I. Organization and Administration of Agricultural Research, New York: Elsevier Publishing Company Ltd. 1968.
(2) Boyce, Janes K. and Evenson, R.E. National and International Agricultural Research and Extension Programs, New York: Agricultural Development Council Inc. 1975.
(3) Castro, José P.R. and Schuh, G.E. Um Modelo Econômico Para Determinar

Prioridades em la Investigacion Agrícola y una Prueba para la Economia Brasileira (original in English) in Metodos para la Investigacion Agrícola aplicad en America Latina — CIAT, CALI. 1975.
(4) De Janvry, Alain. The Organisation and Productivity of National Research Systems ADCRTN, Conference on Resource Allocation in National and International Agricultural Research, New York. 1975.
(5) Evenson, Robert E. Comparative Evidence on Return on Investment in National and International Research Institutions, Conference on Productivity in International Agricultural Research, Airlie House, Virginia. January 1975.
(6) Evenson, Robert E. Economic Aspects of the Organization of Agricultural Research (in) Walter L. Fishel's Resource Allocation in Agricultural Research, Minneapolis: University of Minesota Press. 1971.
(7) Evenson, Robert E. and Kislev, Yoav. Agricultural Research and Productivity, New Haven: Yale University Press. 1975.
(8) Hayami, Y. and Masakatsu, A. Efficiency and Equity in Public Research: Rice Breeding in Japan's Economic Development, American Journal of Agricultural Economics, Vol. 57, no. 1. February 1975.
(9) Hayami, Y. and Ruttan, V. Agricultural Development, an International Perspective, Baltimore: The Johns Hopkins Press. 1971.
(10) Heady, E.O. Agricultural Problems and Policies of Developed Countries, Oslo: Farmers Publishing Ltd. 1966.
(11) Hertford, R., Ardila, J., Roches, A., and Trujillo, C. Productivity of Agricultural Research in Colombia, New York, ADCRTN. 1975.
(12) Kislev, Y. and Rabneri, Uri. Animal Breeding, A Case Study of Applied Research, The Hebrew University, Rehovot, Israel (mimeographed).
(13) Lamborg, M., Ries, S.K., Tschirley, F.H., and Wittwer, S.H. Crop Productivity Research Imperatives — An International Conference Sponsored by Michigan State University, Agricultural Experimental Station and The Charles F. Kettering Foundation, East Lansing: Michigan — Kettering. 1975.
(14) McDermott, J.K. The Technology of Technological Innovation (mimeographed), Washington. 1975.
(15) Mesarovic, Mihajlo and Pestel, Eduard. Mankind at the Turning Point, The Second Report to the Club of Rome, Bergenfield: New American Library. 1974.
(16) Morss, Elliott R. *et al.* Strategies for Small Farmers Development, Boulter Westview Press. 1976.
(17) Moseman, A.H. Agricultural Sciences for Developing Nations, Washington American Association for Advancement of Science. 1964.
(18) Pastore, J. and Alves, Eliseu R.A. Reforming the Brazilian Agricultural Research System, Prepared for the Conference on Resource Allocation and Productivity in International Research, Airlie House, Virginia. January 1975 (mimeographed).
(19) Petterson, W. Economic Return to Public Investment in Agricultural

Research and Extension, mimeographed, St. Paul University of Minesota, Economic Development Center. 1975.
(20) .... and Fritzharris, J.C. Productivity of Agricultural Research in the United States, New York, ADCRTN. 1975.
(21) Population, Food and Agricultural Development Report of a Seminar Organised in collaboration with the Food and Agricultural Organization, the United Nations and the United Nations Fund for Population Activities, Rome. December 1975.
(22) Ruttan, V.W. and Hayami, Y. Strategies for Agricultural Development, Food Research Institute Studies, Vol. II, no. 2, 1972.
(23) Salmon, S.C. and Hanson, A.A. The Principles, Practices of Agricultural Research, London, Leondvd Hill. 1964.
(24) Schuh, G.E. Some Economic Consideration for Establishing Priorities in Agricultural Research (mimeographed). 1972.
(25) Scobie, Grant M., Posada, Rapel T. The Impact of High Yielding Rice Varieties in Latin America, with special emphasis on Colombia, A Preliminary Report, Cali Colombia, CIAT. 1976.
(26) Sisler, D.G. The World Food Situation: What is the US Role? Ithaca *in*, Cornell Agricultural Economics Staff Paper no. 75-7. 1975.
(27) Tybout Richard A. (ed.). Economics of Research and Development, Columbus, Ohio State University Press. 1965.
(28) Ulbricht, T.L.V. Summary Report of Meeting for the Study of the Relationships between Agricultural Research and its Socio-Economic Environment, Organization for Economic Co-operation and Development, Directorate of Agriculture, Paris. December 1975.
(29) UN Food and Agricultural Organization, Commodity Review and Outlook, 1974–1975 Rome. 1975.
(30) US Department of Agriculture − Beef Production, ARS, NRP, no. 20360, USDA, Program no. 22678 − Draft. January 1976.
(31) US Department of Agriculture ARS Management and Planning System, Program Structure, Concepts Guidelines, For Development ARS-NRP's Implementation, Washington. March 1976.
(32) US Department of Agriculture ERS/FAS, Outlook for US Agricultural Exports, Washington. May 1976.
(33) US Department of Agriculture − The Farm Index. June 1976.
(34) World Food and Nutrition Study, Enhancement of Food Production for the United States, a Report of the Board on Agriculture and Renewable Resources, Washington D.C. National Academy of Sciences. 1975.
(35) World Food Nutrition Study − Interim Report of the Steering Committee, Washington D.C., Washington D.C. National Academy of Sciences. 1975.

Discussion on paper by Teixera Filho

B.B. Qutraishi

In the opening of the discussion the basic message of the main paper was seen as a need for the community of scientists not to devote themselves exclusively to academic research but to pay increasing attention to practical and problem orientated research in developing countries. Mere spelling out of the activities required for the scientist in the farm sector was not enough. Rather, full attention needed to be paid to identifying the financial, technical, personnel and institutional constraints on the performance of agricultural scientists.

A further study area was suggested in addition to those in the main paper. This related to the behaviour of farm entrepreneurs and the situations which surround them. Without a continuous updating of the empirical evidence relating to the human factor, it would be difficult to develop the right type of technology at research stations and also to achieve the dissemination of knowledge about farm innovations. Hence a feedback system is needed that would lead towards the establishment of correct priorities in the research areas. Suitable attention to problems of different ecological areas were seen as best handled by rationalising the geographical dispersal of research institutions. The need for closer coordination among social and physical scientists on the one hand, and on the other, with both those and the extension agencies was stressed. Problems of storage and marketing and the updating of the technical capability of the rurally based human agents who supported farm production processes, also required close attention of policy makers.

The role of economic analysis was stressed in relation to the use of resources for production, consumption and investment for further production. Indian institutions for economic and social research greatly facilitated the planning for agricultural development. National sample surveys of consumer behaviour in both rural and urban areas and the national sample surveys of agricultural holdings carried out by the Indian Statistical Institute, and agro-economic research centres for the evaluation of agricultural development projects, etc., enabled the planning commission to carry out development programmes in India. Such economic analysis involves social value judgements about consumption and investment. A development project might generate large additional consumption by generating additional employment or it might generate more saving and investment by concentrating productive efforts in the hands of larger units of production. For an appropriate evaluation values would need to be assigned to consumption relative to investment.

Factors affecting agricultural production and its growth can broadly be classified into five categories: (1) technological, (2) environmental, (3) social, (4) institutional, and (5) economic. Within the setting of these factors it would be desirable to carry out an appropriate programme of economic research. The crux would be to identify inhibiting factors and promoting factors in relation to growth of production. Some such factors may be related to psychological incentives and disincentives connected with institutional arrangements. Appropriate socio-economic research might lead to the removal of major disincentives. Studies relating to land tenure and supply response to price are examples. Some factors may be related to the effect of environmental conditions on cost of production. Appropriate surveys could help appropriate allocation of productive resources over a region according to th principles of comparative advantage.

There was also need for studies of the demographic and social conditions of people connected with farming, providing an evaluation of the status of each person in the household economy and his net contribution to the household enterprise; this would help in formulation of household-specific programmes including family size limitations. Other factors which help or hinder production relate to organisational and infrastructural facilities. A careful assessment of structures of such facilities can open up new dimensions of productive enterprise. Economic analysis can also help in indicating appropriate technologies and the appropriate mode of their implementation.

This emphasis on the importance of economic analysis appeared to gain some of its force from a belief that the main paper was perhaps unduly concerned with technical agricultural research. The neglect of welfare problems in the paper caused particular concern. Policies and programmes for agricultural development were seen as requiring the motivation of the objective of maximising agricultural surplus in conformity with a reasonable level of living for the farming community.

There was some question of the relevance of research programmes to the decision maker. How can priorities in designing a research programme be established, for example? The speaker stressed in reply that a centrally guided research programme had to be based on the fact that the objectives of agricultural research were strictly operational. Priorities had to be guided by the state of development of a particular economy. Overall, the discussion demonstrated more areas of agreement than disagreement with the paper.